EUSTACE MULLINS

THE WORLD ORDER
OUR SECRET RULERS

A Study in the Hegemony of Parasitism

OMNIA VERITAS

EUSTACE CLARENCE MULLINS
(1923-2010)

THE WORLD ORDER
OUR SECRET RULERS

*A Study in the
Hegemony of Parasitism*

1985 & 1992

Published by
OMNIA VERITAS LTD

OMNIA VERITAS®

www.omnia-veritas.com

Contents

- **ACKNOWLEDGEMENTS** **11**
- **FOREWORD** **13**
- **PREFACE TO SECOND EDITION** **15**
- **CHAPTER ONE** **17**
  - THE "NEW" WORLD ORDER 17
- **CHAPTER TWO** **22**
  - THE ROTHSCHILDS 22
- **CHAPTER THREE** **83**
  - SOVIET RUSSIA 83
- **CHAPTER FOUR** **109**
  - FRANKLIN D. ROOSEVELT 109
- **CHAPTER FIVE** **121**
  - THE BUSINESS IN AMERICA 121
- **CHAPTER SIX** **152**
  - THE CIA 152
- **CHAPTER SEVEN** **199**
  - THE BECHTEL COMPLEX 199
- **CHAPTER EIGHT** **212**
  - THE FOUNDATIONS 212
  - APPENDIX I 293
- **CHAPTER NINE** **295**
  - THE RULE OF THE ORDER 295
- **OTHER TITLES** **323**

EUSTACE MULLINS

Dedicated to American patriots
and their passion for liberty

EUSTACE MULLINS

ACKNOWLEDGEMENTS

I wish to thank the staffs of the following institutions for their unfailing courtesy, cooperation and assistance in the preparation of this work:

THE LIBRARY OF CONGRESS, WASHINGTON, D.C.

NEWBERRY LIBRARY, CHICAGO, ILL.

NEW YORK CITY PUBLIC LIBRARY,

NEW YORK ALDERMAN LIBRARY,

UNIVERSITY OF VIRGINIA MCCORMICK LIBRARY,

WASHINGTON & LEE UNIVERSITY

Foreword

When he was proffered the cup of hemlock by his fellow-citizens, Socrates' last words were,

"Crito, I owe a cock to Asclepius; will you remember to pay the debt?"

A gentleman is responsible for his obligations, and this book is the repayment of the efforts of three great men who chose me as their protege — Ezra Pound, the dominant literary figure of our time; George Stimpson, the most respected journalist in Washington (the title has been vacant since his death); and H. L. Hunt, whose spectacular business success blinded the public to his brilliant philosophical achievements It was H.L. Hunt who invented the term "The Mistaken" for the self-corrupted members of the new class who now control our world — he might have added that they could also be described as "The Misshapen", because of their warped and perverted sense of values.

The present work is also an expression of another Greek attitude — gratitude for life. Michael Lekakis introduced this astounding Greek attribute to me some thirty years ago. I describe it as "astounding", because no one today thinks of being grateful for life. Who can conceive of "gratitude for life" in an existence of eternal and worldwide slavery imposed upon humanity by the minions of the World Order?

In *The Greek Way*, Edith Hamilton says,

"Tragedy was a Greek creation because in Greece thought was free."

We do not have tragedy today because of the thought control imposed by the World Order. Instead, we have "Newspeak" and "doublethink" in the world of *1984*. I was privileged to sit in on a number of conversations between Edith Hamilton and Ezra Pound, in which the conversation was uninhibited and far-reaching — freedom of thought in a federal institution in which one of the talkers was held as a political prisoner! Pound describes these talks in *The Cantos*,

> "And they want to know what we talked about? 'de litteris et de armis, praestanti busque ingeniis.'"

Nietzsche also discoursed on "tragic pleasure", which no longer exists, because the World Order, in its anxiety to maintain control of every aspect of our lives, has banned passion. As a poor substitute, it gives us drugs and degeneracy.

There are many facts in this book which you, the reader, will not wish to accept. I ask you to accept nothing, but to make your own investigations. You may find even more astonishing true facts than I have managed to glean in thirty-five years of intensive and in-depth research.

Finally, we have Edith Hamilton's rendering of Socrates' most notable admonition,

> "Agree with me if I seem to you to speak the truth; or, if not, withstand me might and main that I may not deceive you as well as myself in my desire, and like the bee leave my sting in you before I die. And now let us proceed."

Eustace Mullins,
November 1, 1984

PREFACE TO SECOND EDITION

My search for the names and addresses of the secret rulers of the world became a mediaeval quest to find the Holy Grail which would fling open the doors of freedom for the oppressed and betrayed peoples of the world, particularly those in my own country. These World Order minions fear exposure more than they fear armed force or a legal system which would punish them for their crimes against humanity. I discovered that the hidden manipulators of the World Order had maintained their power by a very simple technique, which I have likened to a masked ball. The bal masque enables the Gnostics, the Knowing Ones, to identify their friends and enemies because they alone know who is wearing what costume. It is a masquerade which depends entirely upon disguise, that is, on things which are not what they seem. H. T. Martineau wrote in 1833, in *Three Ages*, 1.1

> "A troop of gentlemen, whose country could not be divined from their complexions, since each wore a mask."

Persons whose country cannot be divined from their complexions - bandits wore a mask to prevent their victims from identifying them. The bandits of the World Order have succeeded in robbing the whole world through the technique of the bal masque, the disguise which enables them to carry on their Satanic work without being identified and prosecuted.

The bal masque is the ideal vehicle for this program, because the World Order gained its present power in Europe of the nineteenth century. It was a truism among the old European aristocracy that "Balls are given for those who are not invited". The guests attend because of duty or career, to spend an evening in the company of boring persons when they would much rather be elsewhere. The reward of being a guest at a bal masque is to be one of the Knowing Ones, those who know which masque hid the face of the King, which costume is that of the Grand Vizier. The other guests never knew whether they were talking to a mere courtier, or to a powerful personage. The masses, with their faces pressed against the windows of the ballroom, know none of the celebrants, and will never know. This is the technique of the World Order, to be masked in mystery, with its hierarchy protected by their anonymity and their masks, so that those who revolt will strike out against the wrong targets, insignificant officials who are expendable.

The World Order record is one of horror, as the ghosts of the massacred billions cry out for retribution. Its true nature is described by that master of the macabre, Edgar Allan Poe, in *The Masque of the Red Death*,

> "While the pestilence raged most furiously abroad, the Prince Prospero entertained his thousand friends at a masked ball of the most unusual magnificence. And now was acknowledged the presence of the Red Death. He had come like a thief in the night. And one by one dropped the revelers in the blood-bedewed halls of their revel, and died each in the despairing posture of his fall. And Darkness and Decay and the Red Death held illimitable dominion over all."

What Poe depicts is what is actually happening to the present world under the ministrations and conspiracies of the World Order - increasing pollution, disease and famine ending in worldwide desolation and the disappearance of our species. What is the alternative? We can survive by ripping the mask off of the face of the Red Death, and by sending him back to that hell from which he came. God made the earth for the living, and we are overdue in our attack on the Brotherhood of Death. We must not be inveigled into more contrived "wars" for the profit of the World Order, nor can we afford to continue to be misled by their control over the media, the educational process, and our governmental institutions.

Chapter One

The "New" World Order

In 1985, as a sequel to the history of the Federal Reserve System[1], this writer published *The World Order* as a compendium of additional information on this subject. It never occurred to me to call it "The New World Order" because my researches had traced its depredations back for some five thousand years. Perhaps in response to the exposes in this volume, the spokesman for the Brotherhood of Death went public with their claims for a "New World Order", which essentially was the Brave New World described by Aldous Huxley in his groundbreaking novel. Behind all demands for this new order were the same imperatives, as listed by Professor Stanley Hoffman, in *Primacy or World Order*,

> "What will have to take place is a gradual adaptation of the social, economic, and political system of the United States to the imperatives of world order."

As Professor Hoffmann points out, the United States is the primary target of the missiles of the New World Order because it still retains, however, perverted and distorted, the essential machinery for a republic which provides for the freedom of its citizens. The Order's present goals were originated by Lord Castlereagh at the Congress of Vienna in 1815, when he handed over Europe to the victorious Money Power, as exemplified by

---

[1] *The Secret of the Federal Reserve*, Omnia Veritas Ltd, www.omnia-veritas.com.

the presence of the House of Rothschild. This was "the balance of power", which was never a balance of power at all, but rather a worldwide system of control to be manipulated at the pleasure of the conspirators. Henry Kissinger has been busily reviving this program for renewed control, as he wrote in a think piece for *Newsweek*, January 28, 1991,

> "We now face 'a new balance of power'. Today, it translates into the notion of 'a new world order', which would emerge from a set of legal arrangements to be safeguarded by collective security."

When minions of the World Order such as Henry Kissinger call for "collective security", what they are really seeking is a protective order behind which they can safely carry out their depredations against all mankind. This was very reluctantly identified by President George Bush, after months of dodging questions about the "new world order" which he had publicly called for, when he finally stated it really was "a United Nations peacekeeping force". This took us back to the Second World War, which produced the United Nations. Walter Millis, in *Road to War, America 1914-17* further removed this program to the First World War, when he wrote,

> "The Colonel's (Edward Mandel House) sole justification for preparing such a bath of blood for his countrymen was his hope of establishing a new world order of peace and security as a result."

Note the call for "security"; once again, this is the cry of the international criminals for protection as they carry out their universal work of sabotage and destruction. House had first laid out the program for this "world order" in his book, *Philip Dru-Administrator*, in which Dru, (House himself) became the guiding force behind the government and directed it to the goals of world order. The same forces set up a Second World War, from which the United Nations emerged as the new guarantor of "collective security". Random House Dictionary tells us that the United Nations was created in Washington January 2, 1942, when twenty-six nations allied against the Axis, or "fascist" Powers. In *The American Language*, H.L. Mencken says that President Roosevelt coined the term, "United Nations" in conference with Prime Minister Winston Churchill at the White House in December of 1941, on the eve of the Pearl Harbor attack which manipulated us into World War II. The United Nations became an active entity at the Dumbarton Oaks conference in 1944, when Great Britain, the United States and Russia set it in motion as a financial dictator.

If the United Nations was created to fight "fascism", its mission ended in 1945, when Fascism was defeated by military force. Fascism derives its name from the bundle of rods which ancient Roman officials carried into court to punish offenders. Thus, fascism historically means law and order, the rule of law, and the intent to punish criminals. This, of course, is what the conspirators of the World Order wish to avoid at all costs. The Oxford English Dictionary defines Fascism as "one of a body of Italian nationalists which was organized in 1919 to oppose Communism in Italy." Other definitions state simply that the Fascists were organized "to fight Bolshevism". Thus the United Nations essentially was set up to battle against "anti-Communists" as exemplified by Germany, Italy and Japan. When this goal was successful in 1945, the United Nations no longer had a historic mission. Nevertheless, it continued to function, and the Rockefellers donated the most expensive parcel of real estate in Manhattan for its world headquarters. It was against this background that the Governor of New York, Nelson Aldrich Rockefeller, addressed a meeting at the Sheraton Park Hotel on July 26, 1968, in which he called for the creation of "a new world order".

Rockefeller ignored the fact that it was Adolf Hitler who had preempted this title as "My New Order" for Europe. The phrase was an attractive one to our politicians, as President Bush revealed when he addressed Congress on September 11, 1990, in a speech carried nationally on television, in which he called for "a new world ... A world quite different from the one we have known ... a new world order." He continued to reiterate this demand in subsequent addresses on television, declaring on January 29, 1991 in his annual State of the Union address,

> "It is a big idea - a new world order, where diverse nations are drawn together in common to achieve the universal

aspirations of mankind, peace and security, freedom, and the rule of law."

He repeated this toxin on February 1, 1991 in three separate addresses on the same day, in which he emphasized the new world order call. He modestly refrained from pointing out that it was not a new phrase, and that it had been adopted by Congress in 1782 for the Great Seal of the United States, the incomplete pyramid with its occult eye, and the phrase "Novus Ordo Seclorum" beneath it, identifying this nation as committed to "a new world order" or a new order for the ages which apparently depended upon pyramid power for its fulfillment. This symbol dated from 1776, when Adam Weishaupt, founder of the Illuminati sect, formulated a program remarkably similar to that of the world order conspirators today. Weishaupt called for:

1. Abolition of all monarchies and all ordered governments.

2. Abolition of private property and inheritances.

3. Abolition of patriotism and nationalism.

4. Abolition of family life and the institution of marriage, and the establishment of communal education for children.

5. Abolition of all religion.

It was hardly accidental that the Rothschilds, when they hired Karl Marx and the League of Just Men to formulate a program, received the Communist Manifesto of 1848, which contained the above formula. Weishaupt's activists had taken over the Freemason movement in 1782, which then became one of the vehicles for the enactment of this program. Its true origin in ancient Oriental despotism was revealed on the editorial page of the *Washington Post* January 5, 1992, when philosopher Nathan Gardels warned that "the ideal area for the new world order would be China, not the United States." Gardels points out that Marxism was a product of Western philosophy, i.e. Hegel, but that a world order would produce Oriental despotism. He supported his thesis with quotes from the Japanese Prime Minister, who complained that "abstract notions of human rights" should not interfere with foreign policy, and from Chinese leaders who denounced demands for independent liberty as "garbage".

President Bush modestly pointed out one of his aides, Gen. Brent Scowcroft, as the author of the magical phrase, "new world order". *People magazine*, November 25, 1991 said,

> "Scowcroft's influence first became evident last year, several weeks after Iraq's invasion of Kuwait, Again while fishing, he and Bush came up with the idea of "a new world order", an ambitious phrase meant to suggest a new United States foreign policy in the post-cold war era."

Who is Scowcroft? In Washington, he has been known for years as one of Henry Kissinger's ubiquitous lackeys, coming to prominence when he served Kissinger on the National Security Council. He then joined the firm of Kissinger Associates, of which he became president. Kissinger praises him in People's magazine, saying

> "He's very unobtrusive, but he's tenacious as hell in fighting for his point of view. He's not a yes-man."

This was an amazing claim from Kissinger, who had never once heard a "No" from Scowcroft during all the years that he served him. People magazine also mentioned Scowcroft's lack of attention to the business at hand.

> "Often teased for dozing during long, uneventful meetings, Scowcroft brushes off such twitting."

The media was horrified to learn that President Reagan occasionally dozed during long, boring official presentations, but finds it excusable that Scowcroft, who as the present head of their National Security Council, might be expected to keep his wits about him, is guilty of the same offense. The excessively friendly media attitude towards Scowcroft is also reflected in Parade magazine which enthused in the issue of December 15, 1991,

> "Brent Scowcroft, 66, is a highly regarded military strategist who has never been tarred by the brush of scandal."

Yes men rarely venture into scandalous situations.

Chapter Two

The Rothschilds

> *"Let me but issue and control a nation's money, and I care not who writes its laws."*
>
> Mayer Amschel Bauer (Rothschild)

In its issue of Dec. 19, 1983, *Forbes* Magazine noted that "Half of Germany's top ten banks are Frankfurt based."

The modern world's financial system, an updating of the Babylonian monetary system of taxes and money creation, was perfected in Frankfurt-on-Main, in the province of Hesse. Mayer Amschel Bauer (later Rothschild) discovered that although loans to farmers and small businesses could be profitable, the real profits lay in making loans to governments. Born in Frankfurt in 1743, Mayer Amschel married Gutta Schnapper. He served a three year apprenticeship in Hanover at the Bank of Oppenheim. During this period, he had occasion to be of service to Lt. Gen. Baron von Estorff. Von Estorff was the principal adviser to Landgrave Frederick II of Hesse, the wealthiest man in Europe. Frederick was worth from 70 to 100 million florins, much of it inherited from his father, Wilhelm the Eighth, brother of the King of Sweden. Baron von Estorff advised the Landgrave that Mayer Amschel showed an uncanny ability to increase money through his investments. The Landgrave immediately sent for him.

At this time, King George III was trying to put down the American Rebellion. His troops were being outfought by the hardy Americans, who were accustomed to wilderness battles. Mayer Amschel arranged for King George to hire 16,800 sturdy young Hessian soldiers from the Landgrave, a considerable addition to the Hesse's fortune. This advantageous relationship came to a halt with the sudden death in 1785 of the Landgrave, who was only twenty-five years old. However, Mayer Amschel attained absolute influence over his successor, Elector Wilhelm I, who, like Mayer Amschel, had also been born in 1743. It was said that they were like two shoes, so well did they go together. It was a pleasant change from Mayer Amschel's relationship with the former Landgrave, who had been a very difficult and demanding person. In fact, the Landgrave's sudden death had luckily placed Mayer Amschel in charge of the largest fortune in Europe.

As he prospered, Mayer Amschel placed a large red shield over his door of the house in the Judengasse, which he shared with the Schiff family. He took the name "Rothschild" from his sign. In 1812, when he died, he left one billion franks to his five sons. The eldest, Anselm, was placed in charge of the Frankfort bank. He had no children, and the bank was later closed. The second son, Salomon, was sent to Vienna, where he soon took over the banking monopoly formerly shared among five Jewish families, Arnstein, Eskeles, Geymuller, Stein and Sina. The third son, Nathan, founded the London branch, after he had profited in some Manchester dealings in textiles and dyestuffs which caused him to be widely feared and hated. Karl, the fourth son, went to Naples, where he became head of the occult group, the Alta Vendita. The youngest son, James, founded the French branch of the House of Rothschild in Paris.

Thus strategically located, the five sons began their lucrative operations in government finance. Today, their holdings are concentrated in the Five Arrows Fund of Curaçao, and the Five Arrows Corp. Toronto, Canada. The name is taken from the Rothschild sign of an eagle with five arrows clutched in its talons, signifying the five sons.

The first precept of success in making government loans lies in "creating a demand", that is, by taking part in the creation of financial panics, depressions, famines, wars and revolutions. The overwhelming success of the Rothschilds lay in their willingness to do what had to be done. As Frederic Morton writes in the Preface to *The Rothschilds*,

> "For the last one hundred and fifty years, the history of the House of Rothschild has been to an amazing degree the backstage history of Western Europe.... Because of their success in making loans not to individuals but to nations, they reaped huge profits. Someone once said that the wealth of Rothschild consists of the bankruptcy of nations."

In *The Empire of the City*, B.C. Knuth says,

> "The fact that the House of Rothschild made its money in the great crashes of history and the great wars of history, the very periods when others lost their money, is beyond question."

On July 8, 1937, the *New York Times* noted that Prof. Wilhelm, a German historian, had said,

> "The Rothschilds introduced the rule of money into European politics. The Rothschilds were the servants of money who undertook to reconstruct the world as an image of money and its functions. Money and the employment of wealth have become the law of European life; we no longer have nations, but economic provinces."

On June 4, 1879, the *New York Times* noted,

> "Baron Lionel N. de Rothschild, head of the world famous banking house of Messrs. Rothschild & Co. died at the age of 71. He was son of the late Baron N.M. Rothschild who founded the house in London in 1808 and died in 1836. His father came to the conclusion that in order to perpetuate the fame and power of the Rothschilds, which had already become worldwide, it was necessary that the family be kept together, and devoted to the common cause. In order to do this, he proposed that they should intermarry, and form no marital unions outside the family. A council of the heads of

the houses was called at Frankfurt in 1826, and the views of Baron Nathan were approved."

John Reeves, in his authorized biography, *The Rothschilds, the Financial Rulers of Nations*, noted that when the family met in London in 1857 for the marriage of Lionel's daughter Leonora to her cousin Alphonse, son of James Rothschild of Paris, Disraeli (Prime Minister of England) declared,

> "Under this roof are the heads of the family of Rothschild - a name famous in every capital of Europe and every division of the globe. If you like, we shall divide the United States into two parts, one for you, James, and one for you, Lionel. Napoleon will do exactly and all that I shall advise him."

This was the political origin of the American Civil War. The Rothschilds feared the rapidly growing and increasingly prosperous free American Republic, and they privately resolved that it would be less of a danger to their worldwide interests if it were broken up into two smaller and weaker nations.

In *The Rothschilds: the Financial Rulers of Nations*, John Reeves writes,

> "The first occasion in which Nathan assisted the English government was in 1819, when he undertook the loan of $60 million; from 1818-1832 Nathan issued eight other loans totaling $105,400,000; he subsequently issued eighteen Government loans totaling $700 million. To the Rothschilds, nothing could have occurred more propitiously than the outbreak of the American revolt and the French Revolution, as the two enabled them to lay the foundation of the immense wealth they have since acquired. The House of Rothschild was (and is) the ruling power in Europe, for all the political powers were willing to acknowledge the sway of the great financial Despot, and, like obedient vassals, pay their tribute without murmur... Its influence was so all-powerful that it was a saying, no war could be undertaken without the assistance of the Rothschilds. They rose to a position of such power in the political and commercial world that they became the Dictators of Europe. To the public the archives of the family, which could throw so much light upon history, are a profound secret, a sealed book kept well hidden."

On July 27, 1844, Mazzini said,

> "Rothschild could be King of France if he so desired."

The *Jewish Encyclopedia* noted (1909 edition),

> "In the year 1848 the Paris house (of Rothschild) was reckoned to be worth 600,000,000 francs as against 352,000,000 francs held by all the other Paris bankers."

Prof. Wemer Sombart wrote,

> "The principal loan floaters of the world, the Rothschilds, were later the first railway kings. The period of 1820 onwards became the 'Age of the Rothschilds' so that at the middle of the century it was a common dictum: There is only one power in Europe and that is Rothschild." (*Jews and Modern Capitalism*).

Hearst's *Chicago Evening American* commented, Dec. 3, 1923,

> "The Rothschilds can start or prevent wars. Their word could make or break empires."

Reeves notes, "The fall of Napoleon was the rise of Rothschild." Napoleon was later slowly poisoned to death with arsenic by a Rothschild agent. They had no need of another "return from exile"

The *New York Evening Post* noted July 22, 1924,

> "The Kaiser had to consult Rothschild to find out whether he could declare war. Another Rothschild carried out the whole burden of the conflict which overthrew Napoleon."

The Kaiser's Chancellor, Bethmann-Hollweg, who actually precipitated World War I, was a member of the Frankfort banking family, Bethmann, and a cousin of the Rothschilds.

After the fall of Napoleon, Salomon persuaded the ruler of Austria to issue patents of nobility to the five brothers. The Congress of Vienna was the emergence of the moth from its cocoon. The diktat of this Congress was a simple one — the aristocracies of Europe must submit to our will, or they are doomed. The death sentence upon the noble lines of Europe was pronounced by those who had the will to carry out their edict. It took another century to perfect the work, not because the killers were weak, but because they wished to proceed cautiously, without revealing their full strength. In combat, the decisive weapon is the one your opponent does not know about.

It was not necessary to pronounce a death sentence upon the ruling families of America, because there were none. During the 19th century, a few descendants of colonial entrepreneurs had amassed wealth, and could afford a life of leisure and travel. They remained slavishly dependent upon Continental arbiters in every matter requiring personal taste and judgment. Because they had no guiding philosophy, and no program, this American "upper class" never made it to the top of the stairs. They remained "below stairs" as servants of the London princes of the World Order. Their self-abasement not only manifested itself in an unusually high rate of suicide, but also in the slower forms of self-destruction, alcoholism, drug addiction, and homosexuality.

Homosexuality is not so much a type of sexual drive as it is the expression of deeper needs, the desire for self-degradation, or the seeking of a partner whom one can humiliate and degrade. It could hardly be unexpected that such a "ruling class" would eagerly hail the twentieth century crusade to enthrone Communism as the vehicle of the World Order.

In their quest for wealth, the Rothschilds did not overlook either the small farmer or the stockpiling and wholesaling of grain. They developed a "farm loan" system which has been the curse of the farmers for more than a century. R. F. Pettigrew noted in the *British Guardian*,

> "This system of banking (causing the ultimate ruin of all those who cultivate the soil) was the invention of Lord Overstone, with the assistance of the Rothschilds, bankers of Europe."

One of their greatest triumphs was the successful outcome of the Rothschilds' protracted war against the Russian Imperial Family. The family name of the Romanovs was derived from Roma Nova, New Rome. It embodied the ancient prophecy that Moscow was to become "the New Rome." The family originated with Prince Prus, brother of Emperor August of Rome, who founded Prussia. In 1614, Michael became the first Romanov Czar.

After the fall of Napoleon, the Rothschilds turned all their hatred against the Romanovs. In 1825, they poisoned Alexander I; in 1855, they poisoned Nicholas I. Other assassinations followed, culminating on the night of Nov. 6, 1917, when a dozen Red Guards drove a truck up to the Imperial Bank Building in Moscow. They loaded the Imperial jewel collection and $700 million gold, loot totalling more than a billion dollars. The new regime also confiscated the 150 million acres in Russia personally owned by the Czar.

Of equal importance were the enormous cash reserves which the Czar had invested abroad in European and American banks. The *New York Times* stated that the Czar had $5 million in Guaranty Trust, and $1 million in the National City Bank; other authorities stated it was $5 million in each bank. Between 1905 and 1910 the Czar had sent more than $400 million to be deposited in six leading New York banks, Chase, National City, Guaranty Trust, J.P. Morgan, Hanover, and Manufacturers Trust. These were the principal banks controlled by the House of Rothschild through their American agents, J.P. Morgan, and Kuhn, Loeb Co. These were also the six New York banks which bought the controlling stock in the Federal Reserve Bank of New York in 1914. They have held control of the stock ever since.

The Czar also had $115 million in four English banks. He had $35 million in the Bank of England, $25 million in Barings, $25 million in Barclays, and $30 million in Lloyd's Bank. In Paris, the Czar had $100 million in Banque de France, and $80 million in the Rothschild Bank of Paris. In Berlin, he had $132 million in the Mendelsohn Bank, which had long been bankers to Russia. None of these sums has ever been disbursed; at compound interest since 1916, they amount to more than $50 billion. Two claimants later appeared, a son, Alexis, and a daughter, Anastasia. Despite a great deal of proof substantiating their claims, Peter Kurth notes in *Anastasia* that

> "Lord Mountbatten put up the money for court battles against Anastasia. Although he was Empress Alexandra's

nephew, he was the guiding force behind Anastasia's opposition."

The Battenbergs, or Mountbattens, were also related to the Rothschild family. They did not wish to see the Czar's fortune reclaimed and removed from the Rothschild banks.

Kurth also notes

> "In a 1959 series on the history of the great British banks, for example, the Observer of London remarked of Baring Brothers, 'The Romanovs were among their most distinguished clients. It is affirmed that Barings still holds a deposit of more than forty million pounds that was left to them by the Romanovs. Anthony Sampson editor in chief, said no protests were made. This story is generally considered to be true."

In the early 19th century, the Rothschilds began to consolidate their profits from government loans into various business ventures, which have done very well. Fortuitous trading on the London Stock Exchange after Waterloo gave Nathaniel Mayer Rothschild a sizeable portion of the Consols which formed the bulk of the deposits of the Bank of England. Joseph Wechsberg notes in *The Merchant Bankers*,

> "There is the Sun Alliance life insurance company, most aristocratic of all insurance companies, founded by Nathan Rothschild in 1824; Brinco, the British New foundland corp., founded by the British and French Rothschilds in l952; the Anglo-American corp.; Bowater, Rio Tinto and others."

Not only does the Bank Rate of the Bank of England affect the interest rates in other nations; the price of gold also plays a crucial role in the monetary affairs of nations, even if they are no longer on the gold standard. The dominant role played by the House of Rothschild in the Bank of England is augmented by another peculiar duty of the firm, the daily fixing of the world price of gold. The *News Chronicle* of Dec. 12, 1938 describes this ritual:

> "The story of the gold-fixing has often been told. How every weekday at 11 a.m. the representatives of five firms of bullion brokers and one firm of refiners meet at the office of

Messrs. Rothschild (except on Saturday) and there fix the sterling price of gold. There is, however, a great deal of activity which lies behind his final act — this centralization of the demand for, and the supply of gold in one office and the fixing of the price of gold on that basis. A price of gold is first suggested, probably by the representative of Messrs. Rothschild, who also acts for the Bank of England and the Exchange Equalization Account."

The banking houses privileged to meet with the Rothschilds to set the world price of gold are known as "the Club of Five". In 1958, they were: N.M. Rothschild, Samuel Montagu, Mocatta and Goldsmid, Sharps Pixley, and Johnson Matthey.

In 1961, the London Accepting Houses operating by approval of the Governor of the Bank of England were: Barings: Brown, Shipley; Arbuthnot Latham; Wm. Brandt's & Sons; Erlangers; Antony Gibbs & Co.; Guinness Mahon Hawkins; S. Japhet; Kleinwort & Sons; Lazard Bros.; Samuel Montagu; Morgan Grenfell; N.M. Rothschild; M. Samuel, J. Henry Schroder; and S.G. Warburg; These chosen firms rule the financial establishment in "the City" of London.

In 1961, the leading business groups in England were listed by Wm. M. Clarke as:

1. Morgan Grenfell Ltd. (Lord Bicester) the Peabody J.P. Morgan firm;

2. Jardine Mathieson;

3. Rothschild-Samuel-Oppenheimer, comprising Rio Tinto, British South Africa Co. Shell Petroleum, Brinco (British Newfoundland Corp.);

4. Lazard Brothers - Shell, English Electric, Canadian Eagle Oil;

5. Lloyd's Bank;

6. Barclay's Bank;

7. Peninsular & Orient Lines;

8. Cunard;

9. Midland Group Eagle Star-Higginson (Cavendish-Bentinck);

10. Prudential;

11. Imperial Chemical Industries;

12. Bowater;

13. Courtauld's;

14. Unilever.

Although this list shows the Rothschild group as only one of fourteen, in fact they hold large positions or influence in the other groups of this list.

In 1982, the principal directorships held by the London Rothschilds were: Lord Rothschild - N.M. Rothschild & Sons, Arcan N.V. Curaçao, chmn Rothschilds Continuation, and Rothschild Inc. USA. Edmund Leopold de Rothschild - N.M. Rothschild & Sons, Alfred Dunhill Ltd., Rothschild Continuation, Rothschild Trust, Rothman's International, chmn Tokyo Pacific Holdings NV; Baron Eric Rothschild — N.M. Rothschild & Sons; Evelyn de Rothschild — chmn N.M. Rothschild & Sons, DeBeers Consolidated Mines Ltd. South Africa, Eagle Star Insurance Co., chmn The Economist Newspaper Ltd., IBM UK Ltd., La Banque Privee S.A., Manufacturers Hanover Ltd., Rothschild Continuation Ltd., chmn United Race Courses Ltd; Leopold de Rothschild - N.M. Rothschild& Sons, Alliance Assurance Co., Bank of England, The London Assurance, Rothschild Continuation Ltd; Rothschild Continuation Holdings AG Switzerland, Sun Alliance and London Assurance Co., Sun Insurance Office Ltd.

The British firms comprising the major basis of the Rothschild fortune are: Sun Alliance Assurance, Eagle Star, DeBeers, and Rio Tinto. Eagle Star's directors include Duncan Mackinnon, of Hambro Investment Trust; Earl Cadogan, whose mother was a Hambro; Sir Robert Clark, chmn Hill Samuel Co.; Marquess Linlithgow (Charles Hope) whose mother was a Milner — he married Judith Baring; Evelyn de Rothschild; and Sir Ian Stewart of Brown Shipley Co., who has been parliamentary private secretary to the Chancellor of the Exchequer since 1979.

DeBeers directors include Harry F. Oppenheimer, Sir Philip Oppenheimer, A.E. Oppenheimer, N.F. Oppenheimer, Baron Evelyn de Rothschild, and Sidney Spiro. Spiro is also a director of Rio Tinto, Hambros Bank, Barclays Bank, and Canadian Imperial Bank of Commerce. DeBeers interlocks with Anglo-American Corp. of South Africa, of which Harry F. Oppenheimer is chairman, and Anglo-American Gold Investment Co. of which Julian Ogilvie Thompson is chairman, and Harry F. Oppenheimer director.

DeBeers interlocks with Hambros Bank, whose chmn is Jocelyn Hambro; directors are R.N. Hambro, C.E. Hambro, Hon. H.W. Astor, Sir Ian Morrow, chmn UKO Int. and The Laird Group, International Harvester, Rolls Royce, and the Brush Group; J.M. Clay, director of the Bank of England; Mark Weinberg, and Sidney Spiro.

Rio Tinto's chmn is Sir Anthony Tuke; he is also chmn Barclay's Bank, and member Trilateral Commission. Directors are Lord Shackleton, Lord Privy Seal, chmn RTZ Dev. Corp.; Lord Charter is of Amisfield, grandson of Earl of Wemys, married to daughter of Viscount Margesson, private secretary to Queen Elizabeth, director of Claridge's Hotel, and Connaught Hotel; Sir David Orr, chmn Unilever; and Sidney Spiro, Hambros Bank. The firm now trades as RTZ Corp. described as

> "a Rothschild holding company on mining deals which in July 1989 bought British Petroleum worldwide mining rights for $3.7 billion, the biggest ever private deal between two British companies."

The principal Rothschild firm is Sun Alliance Assurance, which Nathan Mayer Rothschild founded in 1824, with Sir Alex Baring, Samuel Gurney, and Sir Moses Montefiore, with an initial capital of five million pounds. Chmn of Sun Alliance is Lord Aldington (Toby Low) who is also chmn Westland Aircraft, director of Citibank, Citicorp, and Ge Ltd; Lord Aberconway, dep chmn; H. VA. Lambert, chmn Barclay's Bank; Earl of Crawford (Robert A. Lindsay, whose mother was a Cavendish —

he is also chmn National Westminister Bank, former private secretary to the Secretary of Treasury. Minister of State for Defense, Minister of State for Foreign and Commercial Affairs; Lord Astor, whose mother was the daughter of Earl of Minto he is the former chairman of The *Times*; Sir Charles Ball, of Kleinwort Benson, also director of Chubb & Sons., Barclay's Bank, Cadbury Schweppe; Sir Alan Dalton, director Natl Westminster Bank; Duke of Devonshire (his mother was a Cecil, one of England's three ruling families since the Middle Ages; Sir Derek Holden-Brown, chmn Allied Breweries, director Hiram Walker; J.N.C. James, trustee Grosvenor Estates, which owns large sections of London; Henry Keswick, chmn Matheson & Co.; Lord Kindersley, exec, director of Lazard Bros., director of Marconi, English Electric, British Match, Swedish Match; Sir Peter Matthews, chmn Vickers; J.M. Ricchie, chmn British Enkalon, director of Vickers, Bowater Ltd.; Evelyn de Rothschild, chmn N.M. Rothschild & Sons.

The Rothschilds have had a large position in Vickers for many years. Chmn is Sir Peter Matthews, also director of Lloyd's Bank and Sun Alliance; directors are T. Neville; Baron Braybrooke; Earl of Warwick (the Salisburys, one of three ruling families in England); Sir Alastair Frame, chief exec. Rio Tinto Zinc, director of Plessey & Co. UK, and the Atomic Energy Authority. Chmn of Vickers in 1956 was Edward Knollys, son of the private secretary to King Edward VII forty years, & George V 5 years.

For more than a century, a widespread belief has been deliberately fostered in the United States that the Rothschilds were of little significance in the American financial scene. With this cover, they have been able to manipulate political and financial developments in this country to their own advantage. In 1837, the Rothschilds let their American representative, W.L. & M.S. Joseph, go bankrupt in the Crash, while they threw their cash reserves behind a newcomer, August Belmont, and their secret representative, George Peabody of London. Bermingham notes in *Our Crowd,*

> "In the Panic of 1837, Belmont was able to perform a service which he would repeat in subsequent panics, thanks

to the hugeness of the Rothschild reservoir of capital, to start out in America operating his own Federal Reserve System."

After 1837, August Belmont (Schonberg) was publicly advertised in the financial press as the American representative of the Rothschilds. When Belmont participated in a financial operation, everyone knew that the Rothschilds were involved. When Belmont took no part, and the transaction was handled by J.P. Morgan & Co., and or by Kuhn, Loeb Co., everyone "knew" that the Rothschilds were not involved.

George Peabody had established his business in England through his connection with Brown Bros, (now Brown Bros Harriman) and Brown, Shipley). He had become an unidentified agent for Lord Rothschild as early as 1835. Although there is no statue of George Peabody in the Wall Street area, there is one in London, just opposite the Bank of England. George Peabody became "the favorite American" of Queen Victoria. His old lunchbox occupies a prominent place in the London office of Morgan Stanley to this day. By 1861, George Peabody had become the largest trader of American securities in the world. To put pressure on the Lincoln government, he began unloading them and driving prices down. At the same time, J.P. Morgan, allied with Morris Ketchum, was depleting the American gold supply by shipping it to England. He ran the price from $126 ounce to $171 ounce, reaping a good profit, and putting more financial pressure on the Lincoln government. This was one of many financial operations directed by the Rothschilds for their own political and financial goals. As George Peabody had no son to take over his firm, he took on Junius Morgan as partner; Junius son John Pierpont Morgan, became known as "the most powerful banker in the world", although his principal role was to secretly carry out commissions for the House of Rothschild. Morgan was a direct descendant of Alexander Hamilton, who had chartered our first central bank, the Bank of the United States, at the behest of Rothschild interests.

The *New York Times*, Oct. 26, 1907, noted in connection with J.P. Morgan's actions during the Panic of 1907,

"In conversation with the *New York Times* correspondent, Lord Rothschild paid a high tribute to J.P. Morgan for his efforts in the present financial juncture in New York. He is worthy of his reputation as a great financier and a man of wonders. His latest action fills one with admiration and respect for him."

This is the only recorded instance when a Rothschild praised any banker outside of his own family.

On March 28, 1932, the *New York Times* noted,

> "London: N.M. Victor Rothschild, twenty-one-year-old nephew of Baron Rothschild, is going to the United States soon to take a post with J.P. Morgan & Co., it was learned tonight. It is usual for progressive British bankers to send their young men to western states temporarily, one of the most notable believers in the practice being the Anglo-American banking house of J. Henry Schroder & Co."

The Morgan-Rothschild connection explains the otherwise incomprehensible mystery of why J.P. Morgan, famed as "the most powerful banker in the world", left such a modest fortune at his death in 1913, a mere $11 million after his debts were secured. Although the present members of the Morgan family seem financially secure, none of them is counted among the "big rich".

In *Brandeis, A Free Man's Life*, Arpheus T. Mason notes,

> "Young Adolph Brandeis (Justice Brandeis' father) arrived in New York, travelled for a while in the East and then went on to the Midwest. Young Brandeis' pleasure and facility in travel were greatly enhanced by the companionship of a young friend of the Wehles then on a business trip to the United States to secure information about American investments for the House of Rothschild. Thanks to his companion's contacts and letters of introduction, Adolph saw places and met people not accessible to most foreigners."

Bermingham notes in *Our Crowd*,

> "In the autumn of 1874, Baron Rothschild summoned Isaac Seligman to his office — some $55 million of U.S. Bonds were to be offered by three houses, the House of Seligman, the House of Morgan, and the House of Rothschild."

This was the first time that the Seligmans had been asked to participate in an issue with the Rothschilds. They were more than grateful, and thus another ally of the Rothschilds began to operate in America.

A notable advantage of J.P. Morgan's work for the House of Rothschild was the carefully cultivated belief that Morgan, if not openly "anti-Semitic", avoided participating in operations with Jewish banking firms, and that his firm would not hire anyone of Jewish background. It was the same deception which Nathan Mayer Rothschild had hired Morgan's predecessor, George Peabody, to perform in London. It was a traditional belief on Wall Street that if you wished to deal with a "gentiles only" firm, you went to J.P. Morgan; if you wanted a Jewish firm, there were a number of houses available, but the most influential, by far, was Kuhn, Loeb Co. In either case, the customer was never made aware that he was dealing with an American representative of the House of Rothschild.

Jacob Schiff, who brought the Kuhn, Loeb firm to its preeminent role in American finance, was born in the Rothschild house at 148 Judengasse, Frankfort, which the Rothschilds shared with the Schiff family. In 1867, Abraham Kuhn and Solomon Loeb, two Cincinnati dry goods merchants, founded the banking house of Kuhn, Loeb. In 1875, Jacob Schiff arrived from Frankfurt to join the firm. He married Therese, Solomon's daughter. He also brought a large amount of Rothschild capital into the firm, enabling it to expand tenfold. In 1885, Loeb retired; Jacob Schiff ran the firm from 1885 to 1920, when he died.

At no time has the House of Rothschild ever indicated publicly that it had any interest in the firm of Kuhn, Loeb Co. George R. Conroy stated in *TRUTH magazine*, Boston, Dec. 16, 1912,

> "Mr. Schiff is head of the great private banking house of Kuhn, Loeb & Co., which represents the Rothschild interests on this side of the Atlantic. He has been described as a financial strategist and has been for years the financial minister of the great impersonal power known as Standard Oil. He was hand-in-glove with the Harrimans, the Goulds and the Rockefellers in all their railroad enterprises and has

become the dominant power in the railroad and financial world of America."

This is one more revelation of the hidden power of the Rothschild interests in America. Not only has it directed the Rockefeller enterprises from the time that National City Bank of Cleveland, a Rothschild bank, financed the early expansion of Rockefeller, South Improvement Co., which enabled him to crush his competitors through illegal railway rebates, but it has also been the power behind the scenes of the Harriman fortunes (now Brown Brothers Harriman). It explains the frequent appointments (never elections) of W. Averell Harriman, the dominant power in the Democratic Party, while his partner's son, George Bush, is the Republican president. It explains the secret writing of the Federal Reserve Act by Paul Warburg of Kuhn, Loeb & Co., and the even more secret deals which caused it to be enacted into law by Congress. It explains how the United States could fight World War I with Paul Warburg in charge of its banking system through the vice chairmanship of the Federal Reserve Board; Bernard Baruch as dictator of American industry as Chairman of the War Industries Board; and Eugene Meyer financing the war through his position as chairman of the War Finance Corporation (printing government bonds in duplicate); Kuhn, Loeb partner Sir William Wiseman with Col. House correlated British and American intelligence operations; Kuhn, Loeb partner Lewis L. Strauss was acting head of the U.S. Food Administration under Herbert Hoover. Meanwhile, Paul's brother, Max Warburg, headed the German espionage system; another brother was German commercial attaché in Stockholm, traditional listening post for warring nations, and Jacob Schiff had two brothers in Germany who were financing the German war effort. It was a classic case of a "managed conflict", with the Rothschilds manipulating both sides from behind the scenes. At the Versailles Peace Conference, Bernard Baruch was head of the Reparations Commission; Max Warburg, on behalf of Germany, accepted the reparations terms, while Paul Warburg, Thomas Lamont and other Wall Street bankers advised Wilson and the Dulles brothers on how "American" Interests should be handled at this all-important diplomatic conference.

The Rothschilds had decided upon the formula of a "managed conflict" for the First World War because of the difficulty they had encountered in defeating the Boers from 1899 to 1901. After illegally annexing the Transvaal in 1881, the British had been turned back with a sounding defeat at Majubaby by Paul Kruger. In 1889, because of the discovery of vast wealth in gold and diamonds in South Africa, the Rothschilds came back to loot the nation with 400,000 British soldiers pitted against 30,000 "irregulars", that is, farmers with rifles, whom the Boers could put into the field. The Boer War was started by Rothschild's agent, Lord Alfred Milner, against the wishes of a majority of the British people. His plans were aided by another Rothschild agent, Cecil Rhodes, who later left his entire fortune to the furtherance of the Rothschild program, through the Rhodes Trust, a by no means infrequent denouement among Rothschild agents, and the basis of the entire "foundation" empire today.

The British fought a "no prisoners", scorched earth war, destroying farms, and mercilessly shooting down Boers who tried to surrender. It was in this war that the institution of "concentration camps" was brought to the world, as the British rounded up and imprisoned in unsanitary, fever-ridden camps anyone thought to be sympathetic to the Boers, including many women and children, who died by the thousands. This genocidal policy would next be used by the Rothschild financed Bolsheviks in Russia, who adopted the Boer War concept to murder 66 million Russians between 1917 and 1967. There was never any popular reaction to either of these atrocities, because of the control of media which makes discussion of these calamities a taboo subject.

The career of Lord Alfred Milner (1854-1925) began when he was a protege of Sir Evelyn Baring, the first Earl of Cromer, partner of Baring Bros., bankers, who had been appointed Director General of Accounts in Egypt. Baring was then the financial advisor of the Khedive of Egypt. Since 1864, Milner had been active in the Colonial Society, founded in London in that year. In 1868, it was renamed the Royal Colonial Institute, and was heavily financed by Barclays Bank, and by the Barings, Sassoons and Jardine Mathieson, all of whom were active in founding the Hong Kong Shanghai Bank, and who were heavily interested in the Asiatic drug traffic. The staff economist of the Royal Colonial Society was Alfred Marshall, founder of the monetarist theory which Milton Friedman now peddles under the aegis of the Hoover Institution and other supposedly "rightwing" think-tanks. Marshall, through the Oxford Group, became the patron of Wesley Clair Mitchell, who then taught Burns and Friedman.

In 1884, Milner augmented the work of the Royal Colonial Society with an inner group, the Imperial Federation League; both groups now function as the Royal Empire Society. Vladimir Halperin, in *Lord Milner and the Empire*, writes,

> "It was through Milner and some of his friends that the Round Table Group came into being. The Round Table, it should be said, is an authority to this day on all Commonwealth interests."

He states that Milner raised a considerable sum for the work of the Round Table, including 30,000 pounds from Lord Astor, 10,000 pounds from Lord Rothschild, 10,000 pounds from the Duke of Bedford, and 10,000 pounds from Lord Iveagh. Milner launched a magazine called the *Empire Review*, later called the *Round Table quarterly*.

Halperin also notes another contribution of Milner,

> "He played an important part in the drafting of the famous Balfour Declaration in December of 1917. It is a fact, that, with Balfour, he was its co-author. As far back, as 1915, Milner had realized the need for a Jewish National Home, and had never ceased to be warmly in favor of its creation. Milner, like Lloyd George, Amery, and many others, saw that the Jewish National Home could also contribute to the security of the Empire in the Near East."

The Milner Round Table later became the Royal Institute of International Affairs-Council on Foreign Relations combine which exercises unopposed control for the World Order over foreign and monetary policy in both the United States and Great Britain. Milner trained a group of ambitious young men who became known as his "Kindergarten". It included John Buchan, future Gov. Gen. of Canada, Geoffrey Dawson, later editor of the *Times*, and prominent supporter of "appeasement" with the "Cliveden Set" (led by Lord Astor, who owned the *Times*); Philip Kerr, 11th Marquess, Lord Lothian, the youngest member of the Kindergarten; he served as private secretary to Lloyd George from 1916-20, and was given credit as largely responsible for the German provisions of the Treaty of Versailles. His Who's Who goes on to say that he played an important part in dealing with India, all dominions, and the United States. He was Ambassador to the United States 1935-40, and was a close friend of Waldorf and Lady Astor; George Joachim Goschen, a Liberal who was hailed as the greatest Chancellor of the Exchequer, head of the Cunliffe Goschen banking house with Lord Cunliffe, Governor of the Bank of England. Goschen was also chancellor of Oxford and the University of Edinburgh; his brother, Baron Sir Edward Goschen was Ambassador to Berlin when Bethmann-Hollweg told him that the Belgian Treaty was a mere "scrap of paper"; Leopold S. Amery, who had two sons, Leopold, who was executed as a traitor in 1945, and Julian, who married Prime Minister Harold MacMillan's daughter, and served as leftwing correspondent on the Spanish Front 1938-9, Churchill's personal representative to Chiang Kai-Shek, 1945, Round Table Conference on Malta, 1955, Council of Europe, 1955-56. The senior Leopold Amery is described as "a passionate advocate of British imperialism"; he was on the staff of the *Times*, and wrote a 7 vol. history of the South African War for the *Times*; served in the Cabinet from 1916-22, MP 1911-45, first Lord of Admiralty, 1922-24, Secretary of State for India, 1940-45, and arranged for India to have independence. He was a trustee of the Rhodes Trust.

The Milner-Rothschild relationship was described in Terence O'Brien's biography, *Milner*, p. 97,

> "Milner went to Paris on some business with Alphonse de Rothschild Business calls in the City included a formal visit to Rothschilds weekend with Lord Rothschild at Tring, and visit with Edward Cecil, Lord Salisbury at Hatfield while spending a weekend with Lord Rothschild at Tring a Press Lord gave him a sleepless night (no further explanation given) talks with Rothschild."

Milner attended a Zionist dinner given by Lord Rothschild, sitting next to Lawrence of Arabia, who interpreted for him in a talk with King Feisal. On p. 364, O'Brien notes,

> "Milner lost no time in recreating his links with the City. He went first to Rio Tinto which reelected him to its Board and before long Rothschild asked him to be its chairman."

Rio Tinto was one of the key firms in the Rothschild empire. Herbert Hoover was also appointed a director of Rio-Tinto; he would soon be asked to head the "Belgian Relief Commission" which prolonged World War I from 1916 to 1918.

The Milner role in starting the South African War is described in *British Supremacy in South Africa*. Chap. 1 is headed "Sir Alfred Milner's War", explained as follows:

> "On 19 March Chamberlain telegraphed to him, 'The principle object of His Majesty's Government in South Africa is peace. Nothing but a most flagrant offense would justify the use of force'."

p. 22,

> "Milner had come to believe that war with the Transvaal was both inevitable and desirable. Milner had at last convinced Chamberlain that British supremacy in South Africa would be jeopardized unless the power of the Transvaal was broken."

There is the evidence that Rothschild's Round Table minion, Milner, cold-bloodedly precipitated the Boer war for his master's gain.

John Hays Hammond, chief mining engineer for the House of Rothschild, also was sent to South Africa to precipitate the war. He formed the *Outlanders Reform Committee*, with Lionel Phillips, head of gold and diamond mining firm Eckstein-the Comer House; George Farrar of East Rand Property Mines; and Col. Frank Rhodes, brother of Cecil Rhodes. The Committee was financed by Abe Bailey, Solly Joel, Barney Barnato, and the Ecksteins, all of whom were big winners in the partition of the gold and diamond properties after the war. During this activity, Hammond was arrested by Paul Kruger, sentenced to death for promoting revolution, and was allowed to leave only after paying a $100,000 fine; he was then hired by the Guggenheims at $500,000 year salary, and in 1921 became chief lobbyist for the Council on Foreign Relations in Washington.

Like other enterprises with which the Rothschilds have been connected, the Bank of England has been a center of international intrigue and espionage since its founding in 1694. Although the Rothschilds did not become associated with the Bank until 1812, when Nathan Mayer Rothschild increased his fortune 6500 times by taking advantage of false rumors that somehow swept the London Stock Exchange, purporting that England had lost at Waterloo. The Bank of England originated in a revolution, when William III, Prince of Orange, drove King James II from the throne. Since the Bank of England Charter was granted by William in 1694, there has never been another revolt against the Crown. The royal family has been secure because the source of money, crucial to a revolution, has remained under control.

King Charles II had managed to retain a shaky position because of support from the Duke of Buckingham (George Villiers), and others whose first names formed the word "CABAL", introducing a new term for intrigue. His successor, James II, tried to placate the powerful lords of England, but even his longtime supporters, scenting a change of power, began secret negotiations with the Prince of Orange. Wilhelm I, Prince of Orange, had been married several times, to Anne of Saxony, Charlotte de Bourbon, and Princess de Coligny. Today, every ruling house of Europe, as well as those out of power, is a direct descendant of King William, including Queen Juliana of the Netherlands, Margaretha, Queen of Denmark, Olaf V of Norway, Gustaf of Sweden, Constantine of Greece, Prince Rainier of Monaco, and Jean, Grand Duke of Luxembourg, whose son married the daughter of C. Douglas Dillon.

Lord Shrewsbury (Charles Talbot) had been given places by both Charles II and James II; nevertheless, he played a leading role in the revolution. He took 12,000 pounds to Holland to support William in 1688, returned with him, and was made secretary of state. Sidney Godolphin, one of James II's last adherents, joined with the Duke of Sunderland and the Duchess of Portsmouth in correspondence with William prior to his invasion of England, and was appointed head of the treasury by William. Henry Compton, Earl of Northampton, and Bishop of London, had been removed by James II; he signed the invitation to William to come to England; he was reinstated in his seat in 1688; his son Francis became Lord Privy Seal. John Churchill, first Duke of Marlborough, had entered into negotiations with the Prince of Orange in Oct. 1687, and expressed his readiness to support him in Aug. 1688. To allay James II suspicions, Marlborough then signed a renewed oath of fidelity to him Nov. 10, 1688. On Nov. 24, 1688, he joined the forces of William of Orange.

Although William had married Mary, the daughter of James II, and had a legitimate claim to the throne of England, he could not take power as long as James II was on the throne. Therefore, he entered England with a force of 10,000 foot soldiers and 4000 horse, a small force with which to conquer a great kingdom. With him were Churchill, Bentinck, (the first Earl of Portland), Earl of Shrewsbury, and Lord Polwarth, whose descendant is a prominent member of the Anglo-American banking establishment. James II fled to the court of Louis XIV and was declared abdicated.

This event was subsequently celebrated in English history as the "Glorious Revolution". King James II had married a Catholic, Mary of Modena, in 1673, and launched a campaign to return England to the Roman hierarchy, after more than one hundred years of Protestant rule. His two daughters were being brought up as Protestant, but he then bore a son, who was baptized as a Catholic, ensuing a Catholic heir to the throne. It was this situation which precipitated the Glorious Revolution. In 1688, James had an army of 40,000, all of whose officers were Roman Catholic. The invader, William, had only 13,000 men. To compound his problems, his ships were blown off course, and missed their landing target, James was informed that his troops, most of whom were Protestant, would not obey their Catholic officers, and that they would not defend him. He then abdicated to France. A subsequent attempt to make a comeback in Ireland also met with defeat, which initiated the "Troubles" which have continued there to this day.

As King of England, William signed a Declaration of Rights on February 13, 1689, which ended the king's power to suspend Parliament or to dispense with its laws. England was now a constitutional monarchy, a form which has endured to the present day. This agreement placed the monarchy on an annual salary, which had to be voted on by Parliament. The purse strings were now firmly in the hands of the legislators. In 1694, William chartered the Bank of England. Since that time, there has never been a revolution, because no political force in England was able to raise money to finance such a challenge.

In 1701, Parliament enacted the Act of Settlement, which banned the Catholic Stuarts from ever making a claim to the throne. Future monarchs must be members of the Anglican Church, and could not be married to a Catholic. Under this unified government, England experienced a great flowering of culture, hence the name, the Glorious Revolution. With the establishment of the Bank of England, enormous fortunes were created, and great estates were built throughout the country. William was succeeded by Queen Anne, who produced seventeen children, none of whom survived. Her staff plied her with rich food, so that she became very fat and suffered poor health. When she died, there were numerous claimants to the throne. The successful claimant, the Elector of Hanover, from Germany, bolstered his claim by the research of the scholar, Gottfried Wilhelm Leibniz (1646-1716). Leibniz spent twenty years in the documentation of the Brunswick's family's claim, publishing his findings as Codex Juris Gentium Diplomaticus Hannoverae. Leibniz had been secretary of the Rosicrucian Society in Nuremberg in 1667. He loyally served the Brunswick family of Hanover as a genealogist and historian. He documented that Elizabeth, the Protestant daughter of King James I, had married Frederick the Fifth, Elector of Palatine. Their daughter, Sophie, married Ernest Augustus, the first Elector of Hanover. Although she died before Queen Anne, her son, now Elector of Hanover, was able to overcome the other claimants because of Leibniz' carefully documented reports. Leibniz not only brought the Hanovers to England, but also Freemasonry. His Rosicrucian connections, which he shared with his English counterpart, Francis Bacon, placed a Freemason on the throne of England. Taking the name of George I, Hanover spoke no English, and indignantly refused to learn the language of his new domain.

Marlborough, ancestor of Winston Churchill (whose former daughter in law, Pam Harriman, is the leading power in the Democratic Party) is described in *The Captain General*, by Ivor Brown,

> "The Commissioner of Public Accounts found that the Duke of Marlborough had accepted gifts amounting to some 60,000 pounds from Antonio Machado and Sir Solomon de Medina, contractors for bread and wagons for the army abroad, and 20% of all money allotted for payment of troops, some 175,000 pounds (later revised to 350,000 pounds)."

Marlborough claimed it had all been spent for intelligence, but witnesses testified he could not have spent more than 5000 pounds for this purpose in all of his campaigns. Donald Chandler's biography of Marlborough points out that

> "The bread contractors such as Solomon and Moses Medina, Mynheer Hecop, Solomon Abraham, Vanderkaa and Machado, were for the most part Spanish or Dutch Jews of varying reliability and venality."

Chandler says that they consistently gave short weight or added sand to their corn sacks. For a number of years, Medina, as chief army contractor, contributed an annual commission of 6000 pounds a year to Marlborough as his rake off on army contracts.

In addition to his English supporters, who were previously loyal to King James II, William brought with him from Amsterdam the group of avaricious financiers who were also the suppliers of his armies. One of his first official acts was the conferring of knighthood on Solomon de Medina. Machado and Pereira provisioned his armies in Spain and Holland; Medina supplied Marborough in Flanders; Joseph Cortissot supplied Lord Galway in Spain, and Abraham Prado supplied the British army during the Seven Year War.

The most important act of William's reign was his granting of the charter of the Bank of England in 1694, although most of his biographers omit this salient fact. The concept of a central bank which would have the power of note issue, or issuing money, had already taken hold in Europe. The Bank of Amsterdam was started in 1609; its members aided William in his conquest of England. The Bank of Hamburg was chartered in 1619; the Bank of Sweden began the practice of issuing notes in 1661. These banks were chartered by financiers whose ancestors had been bankers in Venice and Genoa. As the tide of world power shifted northward in Europe, so did the financiers. The Warburgs of Hamburg had begun as the Abraham del Banco family, the largest bankers in Venice.

An interesting technique is revealed by the Charter of the Bank of England — it was slipped through as part of a tonnage bill, which was later to become a recognized parliamentary technique. The Charter provides that

> "rates and duties upon tonnage of ships are made security to such persons as shall voluntarily advance the sum of 1,500,000 pounds towards carrying on the war against France."

Other European banks, such as the Banks of Genoa, Venice and Amsterdam, were primarily banks of deposit, but the Bank of England began the practice of coining its own credit into money, the beginning of the monetarist movement. The Bank of England soon created a "new class" of moneyed interests in the City, as opposed to the power of the old barons, whose fortunes derived from their landholdings. Of the five hundred original stockholders, four hundred and fifty lived in London. This was the dawn of the preeminence of the "City", now the world's leading financial center. For this reason, the Rothschilds identified their key American banks with the code word "City".

Early descriptions of the shareholders of the Bank of England identify them as "a Society of about 1300 persons". They included the King and Queen of England, who received shares to the value of 10,000 pounds each; Marlborough, who invested 10,000 pounds - he also invested large sums from his "commissions" in the East India Co. in 1697, and later became

Governor of the Hudson Bay Company, which paid a 75% dividend; Lord Shrewsbury, who invested 10,000 pounds; Godolphin, who invested 7000 pounds — he predicted that the Bank of England would not only finance trade, but would carry the burden of her wars, which was proven true in the next three hundred years. Virginia Cowles writes, in *The Great Marlborough*,

> "England emerged from the war as the dominant force, because the Bank of England's credit system enabled her to bear the burden of war without undue strain."

Other charter subscribers were William Bentinck, later the first Earl of Portland; he had been a page in William of Orange's household, accompanied William to England in 1670 on his initial visit, handled the delicate negotiations of his marriage with Mary in 1677, and prepared the details of William's invasion of England. He was given the title of Earl of Portland, and became the most trusted agent of Williams foreign policy. In 1984, we find the 9th Duke, Cavendish Bentinck, is chmn of Bayers UK Ltd, and Nuclear Chemie Mittchorpe GMBH, Germany; he also had a distinguished career in foreign service, joining the Foreign Office in 1922; he represented England at the successive Paris, Hague and Locarno conferences, was chmn Joint Intelligence for the Chiefs of Staff 1939-45, and Ambassador to Poland during the critical years of 1945-47, when that country was turned over to the Soviet Union, with England's surreptitious support.

Other charter subscribers to the Bank of England were the Duke of Devonshire (William Cavendish) who built Chatsworth; he also had signed the invitation to William to assume the throne of England; he was High Steward at Anne's Coronation in 1702, and was said to lead a profligate private life - (the present duke sold seven drawings in July 1984 for $9.2 million) the 11th Duke married Deborah Freeman Mitford daughter of Baron Redesdale - his present brother-in-law, Baron Redesdale, is vice president of Chase Manhattan Bank; the Duke of Leeds, Sir Thomas Osborne, who also signed the invitation to William - he was lord high treasurer and had arranged the marriage of Mary - he was later impeached for receiving a large bribe to procure the charter of the East India Co. in 1691 - because of his favored position at court the proceedings were never concluded, and he left one of the largest fortunes in England; Earl of Pembroke, (Thomas Herbert), who became the first lord of the admiralty, and later lord privy seal; Earl of Carnarvon, who is also Earl of Powis and Earl of Bradford; Lord Edward Russell, created Earl of Orford 1697; he had joined the service of William in 1683, was appointed treasurer of the Navy 1689, first lord of admiralty 1696-17, and lord justice 1697-1714 (Sir Robert Walpole, the famed British leader, was created Earl of Orford in the second creation); William Paterson, usually credited with being the founder of the bank of England - he was forced out within a year; Sir Theodore Janssen, who invested 10,000 pounds; Dr. Hugh Chamberlen; John Asgill, an eccentric writer and pamphleteer; Dr. Nicholas Barbon, son of Praisegod Barebones, who started the first insurance company in Great Britain: John Holland, a reputed Englishman who also started the Bank of Scotland in 1695; Michael Godfrey, who died at Namur, Belgium on his way to Antwerp to establish a branch of the Bank of England - he was the first deputy governor of the Bank of England, and nephew of Sir Edward Godfrey, who was murdered by Titus Oakes in 1678; Sir John Houblon and twenty members of his family were also early stockholders; Sir John became lord of the admiralty, and Lord Mayor of London; his brother James was deputy governor of the Bank of England; Salomon de Medina, later knighted by William III; Sir William Scawen; Sir Gilbert Heathcote, director of Bank of England 1699-1701, and from 1723-25; he was Sheriff and later Lord Mayor of London, founded the New East India Co. in 1693; his parsimony was ridiculed by Alexander Pope in his quatrains; Sir Charles Montague, first Earl of Halifax, and Chancellor of the Exchequer - the present Earl is a director of Hambros Bank; Marquess Normandy, John Sheffield, also held the title of Duke of Buckingham - he is buried in Westminster Abbey; Thomas Howard, Earl of Arundel, comptroller of the royal household; Charles Chaplin; and the philosopher, John Locke.

In his *The Bank of England, A History*, Sir John Clapham notes that by 1721, a number of Spanish and Portuguese Jews had been buying stock in the Bank of England — Medina, two Da Costas, Fonseca, Henriquez, Mendez, Nunes, Roderiquez,

Salvador Teixera de Mattos, Jacob and Theodore Jacobs, Moses and Jacob Abrabanel, Francis Pereira. Clapham notes that since 1751 there has been very little trading in Bank of England stock; it has been very closely held for more than two centuries.

The Bank of England has played a prominent role in American history - without it, the United States would not exist. The American colonists considered themselves loyal Englishmen to a man, but when they began to enjoy unequalled prosperity by printing and circulating their own Colonial scrip, the stockholders of the Bank of England went to George III and informed him that their monopoly of interest-bearing notes in the colonies was at stake. He banned the scrip, with the result that there was an immediate depression in the commercial life of the Americas. This was the cause of the Rebellion; as Benjamin Franklin pointed out, the little tax on tea, amounting to about a dollar a year per American family, could have been borne, but the colonists could not survive the banning of their own money.

The Bank of England and the Rothschilds continued to play a dominant role in the commercial life of the United States, causing panics and depressions for the Rothschilds whenever their officials were instructed to do so. When the Second Bank of the United States expired in 1836, and President Jackson refused to renew it, creating great prosperity in the United States when government funds were deposited in other banks, the Rothschilds punished the upstarts by causing the Panic of 1837. As Henry Clews writes, *Twenty-Eight Years on Wall Street*, p. 157,

> "The Panic of 1837 was aggravated by the Bank of England when it in one day threw out all the paper connected with the United States."

By refusing to credit American notes and stocks, the Bank of England created financial panic among the holders of that paper. The panic enabled Rothschild's agents, Peabody and Belmont, to reap a fortune in buying up depreciated stocks during the panic.

The Bank of England has played a prominent role in wars, revolutions, and espionage, as well as business panics. When Napoleon escaped from Elba in 1815, the London gold market jumped overnight from 4 lb. 6d to 5 lb.7. The leading buyer was

Nathan Mayer Rothschild, who was under orders from the British Treasury to dispatch gold to the Duke of Wellington, grouping to stop Napoleon. After Waterloo, the price of gold dropped.

During the twentieth century, the most important name at the Bank of England was Lord Montague Norman. His grandfather, George Warde Norman, had been governor of the Bank of England from 1821-1872, longer than any other man; his other grandfather, Lord Collet, was Governor of the Bank of England from 1887-89, and managing partner of Brown Shipley Co. in London for twenty-five years. In 1894, Montague Norman was sent to New York to work in the offices of Brown Bros.; he was befriended by the W.A. Delano family, and lived with the Markoe family, partners of Brown Bros. In 1907, Norman was elected to the Court of the Bank of England. In 1912, he had a severe nervous breakdown, and was treated by Jung in Switzerland. He became deputy governor of the Bank of England in 1916, and later served until 1944 as Governor. *The Wall Street Journal* wrote of him in 1927,

> "Mr. M. Collet Norman, the Governor of the Bank of England, is now head and shoulders above all other British bankers. No other British banker has ever been as independent and supreme in the world of British finance as Mr. Norman is today. He has just been elected Governor for the eighth year in succession. Before the war, no Governor was allowed to hold office for more than two years; but Mr. Norman has broken all precedents. He runs his Bank and his Treasury as well. He appears to have no associations except his employees. He gives no interviews. He leaves the British financial world wholly in the thick as to his plans and ideas."

The idea that one individual ran the Bank of England to suit himself, with no influences, is too ridiculous to be considered. What about the Rothschilds? What about the other shareholders? Carroll Quigley, in *Tragedy and Hope* notes that

> "M. Norman said, I hold the hegemony of the currency. - He is called the currency dictator of Europe."

Lionel Fraser of J. Henry Schroder Wagg notes in his autobiography, *All to the Good*, that he was in charge of Lord Norman's personal investments. He also notes of the firm of

Helbert Wagg, former jewelers from Halberstadt and now a London banking house (later J. Henry Schroder Wagg),

> "The firm was official brokers on Stock Exchange to the great and all powerful House of Rothschild."

Both Wagg and Schroder had been in business in London for 159 years when they merged in 1960. Another writer notes that Lord Norman frequently consulted with J.P. Morgan before making his Bank of England decisions. Gordon Richardson, chairman of J. Henry Schroder from 1962-72, then became Governor of the Bank of England from 1972-83, when he was succeeded by Robert Leigh-Pemberton, chmn of the National Westminister Bank, also director of Equitable — he married into the Cecil-Burghley family.

The present directors of the Bank of England are: G. W. McMahon, deputy governor since 1964, economic analyst Treasury 1953-57, adviser British Embassy Washington 1957-60; Sir Adrian Cadbury, chmn Cadbury Schweppes, dir. IBM UK; Leopold de Rothschild, N.M. Rothschild & Sons etc; George V. Blunden, exec. dir. Bank of England since 1947, served with IMF 1955-58; A.D. Lochnis, dir. J. Henry Schroder Wagg; G. A. Drain , member Trilateral Commission, treasurer European Movement, Franco-British Council, British North American Committee, lawyer for many union and health associations; Sir Jasper Hollom, has been on the board since 1936; D.G. Scholey, chmn S.G. Warburg Co., Orion Insurance, Union Discount of London, Mercury Securities, which now owns S.G. Warburg Co. Irwin Holdings; J.M. Clay, dep. chmn Hambros Bank, chmn Johnson and Firth Brown Ltd; Hambros *Life* Assurance; Sir David Steel, chmn British Petroleum, dir. Kuwait Oil Co., The Wellcome Trust, trustee The Economist (whose chmn is Evelyn de Rothschild); Lord Nelson of Stafford, chmn GE Ltd. chmn Royal Worcester Co., Natl Bank of Australasia, International Nickel, British Aircraft, English Electric, Marconi Ltd. chmn World Power Conference, Worshipful Co. of Goldsmiths, Middle Eastern Assn; Lord Weir, chmn The Weir Group, chmn Great Northern Investment Trust; E.A.J. George, exec, dir Bank of England, dir. Gilt-Edged Division Bank of England, IMF 1972-72, Bank for International

Settlements 1966-69; Sir Hector Laing, chmn United Biscuit, Allied Lyons, Royal Insurance; Sir Alastair Pilkington, chmn Pilkington Bros. Glass, dir. British Petroleum, British Railways Board.

The Bank of England also dominates the Bank of Scotland, whose chmn is Robert Bruce, Lord Balfour; his title Balfour of Burleigh was created in 1607; he is manager of English Electric and Viking Oil; he married the daughter of magnate E.S. Manasseh. Directors of Bank of Scotland include Lord Clydesmuir, also dir. Barclays Bank, and Rt. Hon. Lord Polwarth, director of Halliburtons, which interlocks with the Rothschild First City Bank of Houston and Citibank, Imperial Chemical Industries, Canadian Pacific, and Brown and Root Wimpey Highland Fabricators, which interlocks with George Wimpey PLC, largest construction firm in the British Empire, whose 44 companies have revenues of 1.2 billion pounds per year. Lord Polwarth's daughter married Baron Moran, High Commissioner of Canada, who previously served as Ambassador to Hungary and to Chad; Baron Moran's daughter married Baron Mountevans, manager of Consolidated Goldfields.

Directors of George Wimpey PLC included S.S. Jardine; Viscount Hood, who is chmn Petrofina UK, and director J.Henry Schroder Wagg, and Union Miniere; and Sir Joseph Latham, chmn Ariel International, director Deutsches Kreditbank.

Wimpey Co. interlocks with Schroder Ltd, parent of J.Henry Schroder Wagg. The Earl of Airlie (David Ogilvy) is chmn of Schroder; he married Virginia Ryan, grand-daughter of Otto Kahn and Thomas Fortune Ryan; The Earl is also director of Royal Bank of Scotland; directors of Schroder include Lord Franks, director of the Rockefeller Foundation, the Rhodes Trust, and Kennedy Center; he is a former Ambassador to the United States; G.W. Mallinkrodt; Sir E.G. Woodruffe of Unlever; and Daniel Janssen of the Bank of England.

One of the great Rothschild hoaxes was the "disarmament movement" of the early 1930s. The idea was not to disarm, but to persuade the nations to junk what arms they had so they could later be sold new ones. "The merchants of death", as they were popularly known in those days, were never more than errand boys for their true masters, "the bankers of death", or, as they were also known, "the Brotherhood of Death". In 1897, Vickers, in which Rothschilds had the largest holding, bought Naval Construction and Armament Co., and Maxim Nordenfeldt Guns & Ammunition Co. The new Vickers-Maxim Co. was able to test its products in the Spanish-American War, which was set off by J&W Seligman Co. to obtain the white gold, (sugar), of Cuba; the Boer War of 1899-1901, to seize the gold and diamond fields of the Witwatersrand, and the Russo-Japanese War of 1905, designed to weaken the Czar and make the Communist Revolution inevitable. These three wars provided the excuse for tooling up for the mass production of World Wars I & II. In 1897, an international power trust was formed, consisting of DuPont, Nobel, Koln, and Rottweiler, which divided the world into four distinct sales territories.

The chmn of Vickers, Sir Herbert Lawrence, was director of Sun Assurance Office Ltd; Sun Life Assurance, and chmn the London committee of the Ottoman Bank; directors included Sir Otto Niemeyer, director of the Bank of England, and the Anglo International Bank; S. Loewe, the German arms magnate, Loewe & Co.; Sir Vincent Caillard President of the Ottoman Debt Council, financial expert on the Near East; and Sir Basil Zaharoff, the "mystery man of Europe".

The highwater mark of "the merchants of death" hoax was reached in the Nye Committee Hearings of 1934, copies of which are invariably missing in government libraries. Alger Hiss was investigator and counsel for the Committee. Typical was Chairman Nye's questioning of Mr. Carse of the Electric Boat Co. (a subsidiary of Vickers):

> **Chmn NYE**: In 1917, Mr. Carse, you drafted a letter to help Zaharoff avoid paying income tax on your commissions to him of $766,852. There is Exhibit 24, a letter dated Sept. 21, 1917, addressed to Mr. H.C. Sheridan, Washington, D.C. Who is Mr. Sheridan, Mr. Carse?
>
> **CARSE**: He owns the Hotel Washington. At that time he was the agent of Vickers Ltd. in this country, and he was also a

representative of Zaharoff. Mr. Sheridan handled Mr. Zaharoff's income tax with White and Case.

CHMN: Did you know that this was false, that this omission of a million dollars referred to was actually Sir Basil Zaharoff's income?

CARSE: No, I did not know anything about Zaharoff's income.

CHMN: But you have told us that a letter by Zaharoff six weeks earlier that 82,000 francs he received was his own personal income.

CARSE: I do not know what Zaharoff did in his business. He did not tell me.

CHMN: Did Zaharoff succeed in escaping the payment of income tax to the United States?

CARSE: I believe there was some settlement made. Sheridan handled it. Zaharoff was never a stockholder insofar as I ever knew. The men who handle very large stock do not put the stock in their own names.

CHMN: Zaharoff wrote to you 19 May, 1925, I desire no thanks for what I have done, because I am bound to attend to the interest of my firm of Vickers and the Electric Boat Co. in both of which I am a stockholder.

CARSE: I know he told me that, but I was never able to trace anything.

Sen. Clark then pursued questioning on how the armaments firms and oil companies promoted wars:

CLARK: So this whole occasion of arming Peru, and of the revolution in Bolivia on the basis of arming against Chile was based on erroneous rumor?

MR. SPEZAR: That is my impression.

CLARK: You wanted to interest the large oil companies in financing an armament program for South America.

CARSE: I was willing to present any proposition the government might approve with regard to any oil companies which might be interested."

The Nye Committee frequently came back to Zaharoff's activities, referring to him as "a kind of superspy in high social and influential circles". For many years he exercised great influence on Prime Minister Lloyd George of England. Zaharoff, who began his career as a brothel tout and underworld tough, arranged for Lloyd George to have an affair with Zaharoff's wife. Arthur Maundy Gregory, an associate of Lloyd George, was also a Zaharoff agent. Maundy Gregory for many years regularly peddled peerages in London clubs; knighthoods, not hereditary, were 10,000-12,000 lbs.; baronetcies went for as high as 40,000 lb., of which he paid Lloyd George a standard 5000 lb. each. Maundy Gregory was also closely associated with Sir Basil Thompson in British counter-espionage. Zaharoff, who was born in 1851 in Constantinople, married one Emily Ann Burrows of Knightsbridge. Maundy Gregory then introduced Emily Ann to the insatiable Lloyd George. From that time on, he was at Zaharoff's mercy. Although Zaharoff was closely associated with Lloyd George throughout World War I until 1922, when their association effectively ended Lloyd George's political career, the name Zaharoff appears nowhere in Lloyd George's extensive Memoirs. Lloyd George's political career came to an end after Zaharoff persuaded him to help the Greeks against Turkey in 1920, a disastrous adventure which brought about Lloyd George's downfall from political power. George Donald McCormick, in *The Mask of Merlin*, the definitive work on Lloyd George, states,

> "Zaharoff kept him (Lloyd George) closely informed on the Balkans. During the war, Zaharoff was sent on various secret missions by Lloyd George. The Big Three, Wilson, Lloyd George and Clemenceau, met in Zaharoff's home in Paris. On one occasion, Zaharoff went to German (in 1917) on Lloyd George's personal instructions, disguised in the uniform of a Bulgarian Army doctor. Clemenceau later said, 'The information which Zaharoff secured in Germany for Lloyd George was the most important piece of intelligence of the whole war.'"

Zaharoff was awarded the Order of British Empire in 1918 for this mission. McCormick also notes,

"Zaharoff had interests in Briey furnaces of the Comité des Forges. Throughout the war no action was taken against Briey or nearby Thionville, a German area vital to the German army. Orders to bombard Briey were cancelled on orders of Zaharoff. M. Barthe protested this event in a speech to the French Parliament January 24, 1919."

McCormick found that Zaharoff had made some interesting confessions to close associates. He boasted to Rosita *Forbes*,

"I made wars so that I could sell arms to both sides." He offered astute political advice to Sir Robert Lord Boothby, "Begin on the left in politics, and then, if necessary, work over to the right. Remember it is sometimes necessary to kick off the ladder those who have helped you to climb it."

In addition to his Vickers and Electric Boat stock, Zaharoff had large holdings in other armaments manufacturers, Krupp and Skoda. The Skoda Works of Czechoslovakia were controlled by the powerful Schneider family of Schneider-Creusot, headed by Eugene Schneider, whose grand-daughter married the present Duke of Bedford. The Nye Committee found that Vickers interlocked with Brown Boveri of Switzerland, Fokker, Banque Ottomane, Mitsui, Schneider, and ten other armaments firms around the world. Vickers set up a torpedo manufacturing firm, Societe Françaises des Torpilles Whitehead, with the former Whitehead Co., whose owner, James B. Whitehead, then became English Ambassador to France. Frau Margareta von Bismarck was a director of Société Françaises, as was Count Edgar Hoyos of Fiume.

At its peak in the 1930s, the Vickers network included Harvey Steel, Chas. Cammell & co. shipbuilding, John Brown & Co., Krupp and Dillinger of Germany, Terni Co. of Italy, Bethehem Steel and Electric Boat in the U.S., Schneider, Chatillon Steel, Nobel Dynamite Trust, and Chilworth Gunpowder Co. The trustee for the debentures of the armaments firms was Royal Exchange Assurance Co. of London, of which E. Roland Harriman of Brown Bros Harriman was a director.

As First Lord of the Admiralty, Winston Churchill obligingly changed the fuel of the entire English fleet from coal to oil, as a favor to the Samuel family which owned Royal Dutch Shell.

The most revealing works on the armaments dealers, the Nye Committee Hearings, and *Merchants of Death* are now fifty years old. On p. 167 of *Merchants* we find that

> "The Société Minière de Penarroya controls the most important lead mines of the world, accounting for one-eighth of the world's production. Since 1833 the French bankers, the Rothschilds, have controlled these mines, but in 1909 the Rothschild Bank entered into an alliance with the Metallgeschaft of Frankfurt, the company in which both the Kaiser and Krupp were heavily interested. This company remained under German and French control for about two years of the war. At the outbreak of hostilities, 10,000 tons of lead were shipped from these mines to Germany, via Switzerland. When shipments to France were resumed, the price was raised to such an extent that it more than doubled the price which the English paid for their lead. Free trade between Germany and France in important chemicals, for powder, etc. continued; the Swiss supplied both sides with electric power. All along their frontier great powerhouses sprang into being, facing Germany from Italy, producing iron, bauxite, chemicals and power. Zeiss products were exported to Britain throughout the war."

Dr. Ellis Powell told an audience at Queens Hall, London, March 4, 1917;

> "At the beginning of the war many thousands of German reservists were allowed to return to Germany although our Fleet could have stopped them. German individuals, firms and companies went on trading merrily in British names, collecting their debts, and indirectly, no doubt, financing German militarism. At the very moment when Germans were destroying our property by Zeppelin bombs we were actually paying them money instead of taking their holdings as part compensation for damage done. In January 1915 came the vicious decision by Lord Reading (Rufus Isaacs) and the Appeal Court, according to which the Kaiser and Little William Co. was a good British company, capable of suing

the King's own subjects in the King's own courts. ...The uninterrupted activity in this country of the Frankfort Metal Octopus is not an accident... Let me analyze one lurid case, which has stirred public indignation and anger to its depths. I mean the impudent survival of the German banks. We have now been at war nearly three years. Yet their doors are still open. They sent large quantities of bullion to Germany after the war started."

There was a remarkable amount of goodwill and free trade continuing during World War I among the warring nations. Of course the Americans did not wish to be left out of the great outpouring of goodwill in which forty million people were killed. It was not enough that the Americans were financing the war through their Federal Reserve System and the personal income tax, which, as Cordell Hull so aptly put it in his *Memoirs*, "had been passed in the nick of time" before the outbreak of the war; nor was it enough that the Americans were feeding the "Belgians", actually the Germans, through the Belgian Relief Commission, so that the war could be prolonged until the United States became a belligerent. Concerned Americans dedicated themselves to the proposition that American boys should be killed in the trenches with the British, the French, the Germans and other nationalities.

The warmongers set up three principal organizations to force the United States into World War I — the Council on National Defense, the Navy League, and the League to Enforce Peace. The Council on National Defense was authorized by act of Congress August, 1916, although there was no nation on earth known to be contemplating any attack on the United States. Pancho Villa had led a small group of bandits against Columbus, N.M., but this raid was hardly an occasion for national mobilization. It was a retaliatory strike because of the actions of New York bankers in Mexico — the Warburgs held the bonds of the National Railways of Mexico; George F. Peabody and Eugene Meyer and Cleveland H. Dodge owned the copper mines of Mexico; Seligman & Co. owned Electric Power and Light of Mexico. The Mexican Revolution was an uprising against President Porfirio Diaz, who had collaborated profitably with the Warburgs and Rockefellers for years. Percy N. Furber, president of the Oil Fields of Mexico Ltd. told C.W. Barron,

> "The Mexican Revolution was really caused by H.Clay Pierce, who owned 35% of Pierce-Waters Oil Co.; Standard Oil owned the other 65%. He wanted to get my property. He demanded of Diaz that he should take off the taxes on oil imports so that Standard Oil could bring in products from the U.S. Diaz refused."

Furber said that he put up the money for Francisco Madero to oust Diaz. Madero was then murdered by Victoriano Huerta, the pawn of Lord Cowdray, head of British oil interests in Mexico. In the resulting chaos, Villa and Zapata came to the fore, resulting in the Columbus raid.

The Council on National Defense was chaired by Daniel Willard, pres. B&O RR; other members were Bernard Baruch, Julius Rosenwald, Samuel Gompers, Walter S. Gifford, pres. of A T & T, also director Commission on Industrial Preparedness; Hollis Godfrey, pres. of Drexel Institute, married to a Lawrence of Boston; and Howard Coffin, pres. of Hudson Motor Car Co. Coffin's secretary, Grosvenor Clarkson, ran the Council. Godfrey claims in Who's Who that the Council was actually created by himself, Howard Coffin and Elihu Root.

The principals of the Navy League were J.P. Morgan of U.S. Steel, Charles Schwab of Bethlehem Steel, Col. R.M. Thompson of International Nickel, and B.F. Tracy, attorney for the Carnegie Steel Co. The principals of the League to Enforce Peace were Elihu Root, J.P. Morgan's lawyer; Lincoln Filene; Oscar Straus; John Hays Hammond, who had been sentenced to death for revolutionary activity in South Africa; Isaac Seligman; Perry Belmont, the official representative of the Rothschilds, and Jacob Schiff of Kuhn, Loeb & Co. The watchword of these millionaire bankers was "preparedness", and Asst. Sec of the Navy Franklin Delano Roosevelt was already letting large Navy contracts in 1916, a year before we got into the war.

Col. House wrote to President Wilson from London on May 29, 1914,

> "Whenever England consents, France and Russia will close in on Germany and Austria."

While preparing for war, Woodrow Wilson campaigned in 1916 on the slogan, "He kept us out of war". H.C. Peterson notes in *Propaganda for War*, Univ. Oklahoma Press, 1939,

> "To a large extent, the 9 million people who voted for Wilson did so because of the phrase, 'He kept us out of war.'"

Col. House later told Viereck that Wilson had concluded an agreement with the British in 1916, long before his campaign, to involve us in the war. Roosevelt repeated the process in 1939.

When we went into World War I, Wilson appointed his campaign fundraiser, Bernard Baruch, head of the War Industries Board. Baruch was later investigated by the Graham Committee. He testified,

> "I probably had more power than perhaps any other man did in the war; doubtless that is true."

He said of his prewar actions,

> "I asked for an interview with the President. I explained to him as earnestly as I could that I was deeply concerned about the necessity of the mobilisation of the industries of the country. The President listened very attentively and graciously, as he always does, and the next thing I heard, some months afterward, my attention was brought to this Council of National Defense."

MR. GRAHAM: Did the President express any opinion about the advisability of adopting the scheme you proposed?

BARUCH: I think I did most of the talking.

GRAHAM: Did you impress him with your belief that we were going to get into the war?

BARUCH: I probably did.

GRAHAM: That was your opinion at the time?

BARUCH: Yes. I thought we were going to get into the war. I thought a war was coming long before it did.

MR. JEFFRIES: Then the system you did adopt did not give the Lukens Steel & Iron Co. the amount of profit that the low-producing companies did?

BARUCH: No, but we took 80% away from the others.

MR. JEFFRIES: The law did that, didn't it?

BARUCH: The government did that.

GRAHAM: What did you mean by the use of the word 'we'?

BARUCH: The government did that Excuse me, but I meant we, the Congress.

GRAHAM: You meant that the Congress passed a law covering that.

BARUCH: Yes, sir.

GRAHAM: Did you have anything to do with that?

BARUCH: Not a thing.

GRAHAM: Then I would not use the word 'we' if I were you.

Although Baruch played a crucial role in funding Wilson's campaign, in 1916, he had not ignored Wilson's almost successful opponent, Charles Evans Hughes. Carter Field points out, in his biography of Baruch,

> "My personal view is that Baruch would have been tremendously important in the Hughes election, if Hughes had been elected in the close election of 1916, both in the conduct of the war and in the making of the peace."

Field continues,

> "Under this curious cloak of anonymity, Baruch exercised a very unusual type of political power in those early Wilson days. He was cultivated by most of the Wilson lights, who speedily found out that he could do more for them than they could do by directly appealing to Wilson. Naturally, there was no publicity for all this."

Field also says,

"For one thing, Wilson not only loved Baruch, he ADMIRED him. Mrs. Wilson makes this specific statement in her Memoirs."

Wilson's relations with others were not always marked by such deep affection. David Lawrence, in his biography of Wilson, *The True Story of Woodrow Wilson*, notes that in June, 1907, former President Grover Cleveland, a trustee of Princeton, publicly denounced Wilson's plans to alter the character of the school, making a "bitter attack". Cleveland had come to live in Princeton after he left the White House, and was deeply attached to the university. He died in the summer of 1908. That fall, when Wilson, as president of the school, made his annual opening speech, he made no mention of Cleveland's death, nor did he ever schedule a memorial exercise, as was the custom when a trustee passed away.

The Baruch-War Industries Board is particularly important to the present work, not only because of the dictatorial power exercised by Baruch during the war years, but because the WIB members have continued to govern the United States. From WIB and the American Commission to Negotiate the Peace came the Brookings Institution, which set national priorities for fifty years, NRA and the entire Roosevelt administration, and World War II. Working with Baruch at the WIB was his asst. chairman, Clarence Dillon of Dillon, Read; Robert S. Brookings, chmn Price Fixing Committee of WIB, later founded the Brookings Institution; Felix Frankfurter, chmn of the War Policies Labor Board; Herbert Hoover and T.F. Whitmarsh of the U.S. Food Administration; H.B. Swope, publicity agent for Baruch; Harrison Williams; Albert Ritchie, later Gov. of Maryland; Gen. Goethals; and Rear Adm. F.F. Fletcher. Goethals was replaced by Gen. Pierce, who was then replaced by Gen. Hugh Johnson, who became Baruch's right-hand man for many years. Field tells us that

"Gen. Hugh Johnson stayed on Baruch's payroll for two months after he became head of NRA (during the New Deal)"

Field quotes Woodrow Wilson as having Baruch at the WIB,

"Let the manufacturer see the club behind your door."

Baruch told the Graham Committee,

> "We fixed prices with the aid of potential Federal compulsion."

Left out in the Baruch-Wilson mutual esteem society was William Jennings Bryan, longtime head of the Democratic Party. Bryan not only opposed our entry into World War II — he dared to criticize the family which had organized the war, the Rothschilds. Because he dared to mention the Rothschilds, Bryan was promptly denounced as "anti-Semitic". He responded, "Our opponents have sometimes tried to make it appear that we were attacking a race when we denounced the financial policy of the Rothschilds. But we are not; we are as much opposed to the financial policy of J.P. Morgan as we are to the financial policy of the Rothschilds."

Because of the secret planning needed to launch a major war, control of the communications media was essential. Kent Cooper, president of the Associated Press, notes in *Life*, Nov. 13, 1944, "Freedom of Information",

> "Before and during the First World War, the great German news agency Wolff was owned by the European banking house of Rothschild, which had its central headquarters in Berlin. A leading member of the firm was also Kaiser Wilhem's personal banker (Max Warburg). What actually happened in Imperial Germany was that the Kaiser used Wolff to bind and excite his people to such a degree that they were eager for World War I. Twenty years later under Hitler the pattern was repeated and enormously magnified by DNB, Wolffs successors."

Cooper later noted in his autobiography, *Barriers Down*,

> "international bankers under the House of Rothschild acquired an interest in the three leading European agencies. (Havas, France; Reuters, England; Wolff, Germany)."

On April 28, 1915, Baron Herbert de Reuter, Chief of the Reuters Agency, shot himself. The cause was the crash of the Reuters Bank, which had been organized by Baron Julius de Reuter, founder of Reuter's, to handle foreign remittances without their being subjected to any accounting. He was succeeded by Sir Roderick Jones, who says in his autobiography,

> "Shortly after I succeeded Baron Herbert de Reuter in 1915, it so happened that I received an invitation from Mr. Alfred Rothschild, then head of the British House of Rothschild, to lunch with him in historic New Court, in the City."

Jones prudently refrains from telling us what was discussed at this meeting.

Only one member of Congress voted against the U.S. declaration of war against Germany in World War I, Jeanette Rankin. She was also the only member of Congress to vote against our entry into World War II. Opponents of Wilson's action were often beaten and imprisoned. Eugene Debs was sentenced to a long prison term. Congressman Charles Lindbergh ran for Governor of Minnesota on a platform opposing our participation in the war. The *New York Times* regularly ran scathing denunciations of his campaign. On June 9, 1918, it noted,

> "Rep. Clarence H. Miller denounced Lindbergh and the Non Partisan League as seditious. 'According to Mr. Lindbergh the Liberty Loan is an instrument devised by the money sharks. It seems inexcusable that any person allowed to be at large in the United States could entertain or express such a view of this.'"

Harrison Salisbury of the *New York Times* states,

> "I have searched out the records and they show that mobs trailed Charles K. Lindbergh Sr. during his 1918 campaign for the Republican nomination for the Minnesota governorship. He was arrested on charges of conspiracy along with the Non Partisan Leaguers; a rally at Madison, Minn, was broken up with firehoses; he was hanged in effigy in Red Wing, dragged from the speaker's platform, threatened with lynching, and he escaped from town amid a volley of shots."

Salisbury neglects to mention that a squad of Federal agents from the Bureau of Investigation, led by J. Edgar Hoover on his first important action, attacked Lindbergh and his family, dragged out all the copies of Lindbergh's Your Country at War, and burned them on the lawn; when young Charles rushed forward to stomp out the fire, Hoover knocked him down.

In the summer of 1917, Woodrow Wilson named Col. House to head the American War Mission to the Inter-Allied War Conference, the first such American mission to a European council. With House were his son-in-law, Gordon Auchincloss, and Paul Cravath, Kuhn Loeb's lawyer. Auchincloss was directorof Chase Natl. Bank, Solvay, Sofina, and Cross Sc Blackwell.

Meanwhile, Walter Lippman and another group were busily working on the plans for the League of Nations. Lippmann had founded the American branch of the Fabian Society in 1905 as the Intercollegiate Socialist Society, which later became the Students for a Democratic Society after a period when it was known as the League for Industrial Democracy; James T. Shotwell and other internationalists worked with Lippmann on this organization.

Although the war was going well for those who had promoted it, hostilities were ended somewhat abruptly by the unforeseen intervention of an aide to the Czar of Russia, Maj. Gen. Count Cherep Spiridovich, who says,

> "I had a long discussion with Gen. McDonough Chief of the War Intelligence Dept. in London; I submitted on Sept. 1, 1918 a report advising him peace with Bulgaria would provoke an uprising in Slavic Austria, panic in Germany and surrender of her armies; my advice was accepted; two weeks later peace was signed with Bulgaria, two weeks later Austria was out of the war, two weeks later Germany surrendered."

L.L. Strauss of Kuhn, Loeb Co. states he was one of four American delegates who conferred with the Germans at Brussels in March 1919 on the final armistice. On Nov. 11, 1918, the *New York Times* headlined,

> "REDS GRIP ON GERMANY: Konigsberg, Frankfurt-on-Main, Strasburg now controlled by Spartacist Soviets".

On Nov. 12, 1918, the *New York Times* stated,

> "The revolution in Germany is today, to all intents and purposes, an accomplished fact."

On the same day, the *New York Times* headlined,

> "Splendor Reigns Again; Jewels Ablaze"

The occasion was a gala evening at the Metropolitan Opera, with Caruso and Homer singing Samson and Delilah. Attending were the Otto Kahns with the French Consul-General; the George F. Bakers and his sister Mrs. Goadby Loew; Cornelius Vanderbilt and his daughters; the Whitney s, the J.P. Morgans, and the E.T. Stotesburys; the Fricks; Mrs. Bernard Baruch; her husband was in Europe on important business; Mrs. Adolf Ladenburg. These celebrants were also the principal investors in American International Corporation, which was financing the Bolshevik Revolution in Russia.

The American Commission to Negotiate Peace predictably included Walter Lippmann, the Dulles brothers, the Warburg brothers (Paul from the U. S., Max from Germany) L.L. Strauss, Thomas W. Lamont, as well as House, Wilson and Wilson's Secretary of State, Robert Lansing, the Dulles' uncle. Their genial host was Baron Edmond de Rothschild. Representing France at the Peace Conference was Finance Minister Klotz, who, according to Nowell-Baker, had for years been usefully employed by the Rothschilds to distribute bribes to the press. The Reparations Commission was established Jan. 25, 1919, with Bernard Baruch from the U.S., Klotz from France, and Lord Cunliffe, Governor of the Bank of England, representing England. Carter Field notes,

> "Nearly every afternoon Baruch had a pleasant session at the Crillon with three or four of his old cronies from the War Industries Board."

Wilson returned to the United States July 8, 1919, laden with one million dollars worth of jewelry, gifts from appreciative Europeans as a reward for his promise to get the U.S. into the League of Nations. Not a single member of Congress had been with him at the Paris Peace Conference. His associates were the

Fabians of America, Dr. James T. Shotwell, Eugene Delano, and Jacob Schiff. Herbert Hoover immediately joined Col. House as the most vociferous advocate of our joining the League of Nations.

Baruch later testified before the Graham Committee;

"I was economic advisor with the peace commission.

GRAHAM: Did you frequently advise the President while there?

BARUCH: Whenever he asked my advice I gave it. I had something to do with the reparations clauses. I was the American Commissioner in charge of what they called the Economic Section. I was a member of the Supreme Economic Council in charge of raw materials.

GRAHAM: Did you sit in the council with the gentlemen who were negotiating the treaty?

BARUCH: Yes, sir, some of the time.

GRAHAM: All except the meetings that were participated in by the Big Five.

BARUCH: And frequently those also."

The Reparations Commission ordered the Germans to issue four issues of bonds, all to be delivered to the Reparations Commission as follows:

1. 20 billion gold marks, 5 billion paper marks by May 1, 1921 for the army of occupation.

2. War cost of Belgium - 4 billion gold marks due May 1, 1926.

3. 40 billion gold marks at 20% interest from 1921-26, to be retired in 1951.

4. a 30-year provisional fund of general reparations. (Treaty of Versailles, Financial Clauses 248-63).

The bankers immediately began to treat these gigantic sums as sources of capital, to be monetarised by loans and other negotiable instruments. Lloyd George told the *N.Y. Journal American*, June 24, 1924;

> "The international bankers dictated the Dawes reparations settlement. The Protocol which was signed between the Allies and Associated Powers and Germany is the triumph of the international financier. Agreement would never have been reached without the brusque and brutal intervention of the international bankers. They swept statesmen, politicians and journalists to one side, and issued their orders with the imperiousness of absolute monarchs, who knew that there was no appeal from their ruthless decrees. The settlement is the joint ukase of King Dollar and King Sterling. Dawes report was theirs. They inspired and fashion edit. The Dawes Report was fashioned by the Money Kings. The orders of German financiers to their political representatives were just as peremptory as those of allied bankers to their political representatives."

Although the reparations clauses achieved the desired result of forcing the Germans to fight a Second World War, the primary result was the formation of a "front" world government, the League of Nations, while in the background the conspirators established their real governing body, the World Order, through the Royal Institute of International Affairs, and its American subsidiary, the Council on Foreign Relations.

In 1895, Cecil Rhodes, South African agent of the Rothschilds, established a secret society whose avowed purposes was as follows:

> "In the end Great Britain is to establish a power so overwhelming that wars must cease and the Millennium be realized."

To achieve this goal, he left $150 million to the Rhodes Trust. The Rothschild already had a group with similar aims, the Round Table, set up by Lord Alfred Milner, into which J.P. Morgan had been recruited in 1899.

The Council on Foreign Relations Handbook of 1936 states,

> "On May 30, 1919, several leading members of the delegations to the Paris Peace Conference met at the Hotel

Majestic in Paris to discuss setting up an international group which would advise their respective governments on international affairs. The U.S. was represented by Gen. Tasker H. Bliss (Chief of Staff, U.S. Army), Col. Edward M. House, Whitney H. Shepardson, Dr. James T. Shotwell, and Prof. Archibald Coolidge. Great Britain was unofficially represented by Lord Robert Cecil, Lionel Curtis, Lord Eustace Percy, and Harold Temperley. It was decided at this meeting to call the proposed organization the Institute of International Affairs. At a meeting on June 5, 1919, the planners decided it would be best to have separate organizations cooperating with each other. Consequently, they organized the Council on Foreign Relations, with headquarters in New York, and a sister organization, the Royal Institute of International Affairs, in London, also known as the Chatham House Study Group, to advise the British Government. A subsidiary organization, the Institute of Pacific Relations, was set up to deal exclusively with Far Eastern Affairs. Other organizations were setup in Paris and Hamburg, the Hamburg branch being called the Institut fur Auswartige Politik, and the Paris branch being known as Centre d'Études de Politique Étrangère, at 13 Rue de Four, Paris VI."

The Hamburg branch was established, of course, because of the Warburg family bank there.

Having dominated the Paris Peace Conference, Baron Edmond de Rothschild saw the establishment of the World Order through these groups as the crowning achievement of his life. The "founders" of the RIIA were, one and all, Rothschild men; honorary chairman of the CFR was Elihu Root, lawyer for Morgan and Kuhn, Loeb Co.; Alexander Hemphill, a Morgan banker, and Otto Kahn of Kuhn, Loeb Co.

The founders of the RIIA were Rothschild's principal South African agents; Sir Otto Beit, trustee of Rhodes Estate and director of British South Africa Co.; Percy Alport Molteno, son of the first Premier of Cape Colony; Sir Abe Bailey, owner of the Transvaal Mines, who worked closely with Sir Alfred Milner in starting the Boer War; John W. Wheeler-Bennett, who became Gen. Eisenhower's political adviser at SHAEF London 1944-45;

Sir Julien Cahn; and Lionel Curtis, colonial secretary of the Transvaal, who gave his address as the Round Table, 175 Piccadilly Rd., London. He was later appointed Beit lecturer on the colonial history of South Africa.

Other founders of RIIA included four members of the Astor family — Viscount Astor, Hon. F.D.L. Astor, M.L. Astor, and H.J.J. Astor, the latter being chmn of The *Times* and director of Hambros Bank. The first President of RIIA was Lt. Col. R.W. Leonard, president of the Coniagas Mines. The Lord Patron was Her Majesty the Queen. All Prime Ministers and Viceroys of the Colonies since 1923 have been Honorary Presidents of RIIA. Stephen King Hall, in his definitive work, *Chatham House*, says,

> "The Prince of Wales graciously accepted the office of Visitor. This appointment secured that the Institute could never be perverted to party or propaganda purposes."

The 1934 list of members of RIIA included Sir Austin Chamberlain, Prime Minister, Chancellor of the Exchequer, Lord Privy Seal, and Secretary of State for Foreign Affairs; Harold MacMillan, who married the daughter of the Duke of Devonshire and later became Prime Minister, and Lord Eustace Percy, Duke of Northumberland. The 1942 membership list includes Sir Roderick Jones, head of Reuters; G.M. Gatheren-Hardy; Sir Andrew McFadyen, chmn North British Borneo Co. and United Rubber Estates - he served with the British Treasury 1910-1917, represented the Treasury at the Paris Peace Conference 1919-20, was Gen. Secretary of the Reparations Commission, 1922-25; Commissioner of Controlled Revenues Berlin 1924-30, later with S.G. Warburg Co.; Col. Vickers; and Lord Brand, managing director Lazard Bros., who married Lady Astor's sister, Phyllis Langhorne, was dep. chmn British Mission in Washington 1917-18, financial adviser to Lord Robert Cecil, chmn Supreme Economic Council at the Paris Peace Conference; George Gibson, dir. Bank of England; John Hambro of Hambros Bank; Lord Derby (Edward Villiers), Lord of Treasury, Secretary of State for War, 1916-1918, who had a 69,000 acre estate in Lancashire, and Lord Cromer (Baring).

During its early years, RIIA was principally funded by the Rothschilds through donations funneled through Sir Abe Bailey and Sir Alfred Beit, with about $100,000 year; since then, it has been funded with many millions of dollars by the Rockefeller Foundation and the Carnegie Corporation.

In 1936 the RIIA $400,000 budget was also funded by the following corporate subscribers: N.M. Rothschild & Sons; British South Africa Co.; Bank of England; Reuters News Agency; Prudential Assurance Co.; Sun Insurance Office Ltd; and Vickers-Armstrong Ltd.; all of which were known as Rothschild enterprises. Other subscribers were J.Henry Schroder Co., Lazard Freres, Morgan Grenfell, Erlangers Ltd., and E.D. Sassoon Co.

A number of popular books now in circulation claim that the Council on Foreign Relations is the secret government of the United States. Nothing could be more incorrect. The members of the Council on Foreign Relations have never originated a single item of policy for the U.S. Government. They merely transmit orders to our government officials from the RIIA and the House of Rothschild in London. It is true that the CFR comprises a ruling elite in the United States, but they are mere colonial governors absolutely responsible to their overseers in the World Order. However, every prominent American mentioned in the present book is a member of the CFR, and therefore it is not necessary to note it each time a name is mentioned. Not only do they transmit orders to the White House, the Cabinet, the Federal Reserve Board of Governors, and other government institutions, but they also maintain absolute control of the foundations, whose duty it is to formulate policy or organize it in acceptable form to be transmitted to the government. Shoup's *Imperial Brain Trust*, 1969, notes that the CFR includes 22 trustees of Brookings Institution, 29 at Rand, 14 at Hudson, 33 at Middle East Institute, 14 of 19 trustees of the Rockefeller Foundation, 10 of 17 at Carnegie, 7 of 16 at Ford Foundation, 6 of 11 at Rockefeller Bros. Fund. This proves that the CFR runs these major foundations. In the academic world, CFR members number 58 on the faculty at Princeton, 69 at the University of Chicago, and 30 at Harvard. Of the banks which are the principal owners of Federal Reserve Bank stock, directors of Chase include 7 CFR members, 8 at J.P.

Morgan, 7 at 1st Natl. City (now Citibank), 6 at Chemical Bank, and 6 at Brown Bros. Harriman.

The 1968 list of CFR members included John J. McCloy, chmn of the board; Frank Altschul, secretary and vice-pres.; David Rockefeller vice-pres.; and directors Robert V. Roosa, Douglas Dillon, and Allen Dulles. McCloy also served as chmn Ford Foundation 1953-65, director of the Rockefeller Foundation, and personal lawyer to the Rockefeller family interests. His career is typical of a leading official of the World Order. While a student at Harvard, he became a protege of Felix Frankfurter. He joined the firm of Cravath, Swaine & Moore, lawyers for Kuhn, Loeb Co. where he remained from 1925-40. In 1940 Frankfurter recommended him to Henry Stimson as Asst. Sec, of War, where he remained from 1941-45. He wrote and issued the infamous political views of servicemen

> "unless there is a specific finding that the individual involved has a loyalty to the Communist Party which overrides his loyalty to the U.S."

Senator McCarthy termed this directive "treasonable".

McCloy succeeded Eugene Meyer as president of the World Bank from 1947-49, was appointed High Commissioner of Germany where he served from 1949-52, was chmn of the board Chase Natl Bank from 1953-61, and Rockefeller's attorney since then. He is a director of Union Pacific, Westinghouse, ATT, Dreyfus, Squibb, & Mercedes Benz. He married Ellen Zinsser, who is not otherwise identified in McCloy's 1947 Current Biography; in the 1961 issue, she is identified as the niece of Hans Zinsser, a bacteriologist. This is odd, because she is also the daughter of John Zinsser, partner of J.P. Morgan Co., and chmn of the board of Sharp & Dohme chemicals. It is an interesting footnote to history that the son-in-law of a J.P. Morgan partner should be appointed U.S. High Commissioner of a vanquished Germany.

The *New York Times* noted on Aug. 6, 1965,

> "JJ. McCloy Proposes Foundation Pattern for European Giving."

He stated at Salzburg,

> "I wish that there could be erected in Europe a complex of foundations whose representatives could exchange thoughts with those of American foundations and thus form a sort of informal approach to some of the great problems of the day."

"Informal" is the code word, of the World Order. It means "issuing from world headquarters". McCloy did not state the obvious, that five men control all of the major U.S. foundations, and that he wished they could have the same system in Europe.

The RIIA has worked closely with the London School of Economics, which was set up as a training school for the World Order bureaucrats. The school was established in 1920 with financial aid from the Rothschilds and Sir Julius Wernher. Sir Ernest Cassel later gave the school 472,000 pounds. Prof. J.H. Morgan wrote in *Quarterly Review*, Jan. 1939,

> "When I once asked Lord Haldane why he persuaded his friend Sir Ernest Cassel, grandfather of Lady Mountbatten, to settle by his will large sums on the London School of Economics, he replied, 'Our object is to make this institution a place to raise and train the bureaucracy of the future Socialist State.'"

Sir William Beveridge, author of Great Britain's ruinous Cradle to the Grave political program, was director of the London School of Economics from 1920-1937.

The British Empire has prospered on piracy, slavery and the drug traffic. Drakes Pirates became the Merchants Adventurers Co. (Sebastian Cabot) which later became the Chartered Co. of East India. It was reorganized in 1700. It originally paid the Hong of Canton silver for tea, but discovered they would accept opium instead. This fortuitous arrangement encountered resistance from some Chinese leaders, causing England to prosecute ten Opium Wars against China, from the Opium War of 1840-43 to the Manchurian Conquest of 1931.

In 1715 the British East India Co. opened its first Far East office in Canton. Crown Policy deliberately fostered opium addiction among the natives to facilitate British political control.

The British Empire was then threatened with bankruptcy if it lost the American colonies. In order to defeat the rebels, the profits of the opium trade with China were sent to the Elector of Hesse via Mayer Amschel Rothschild to hire 16,800 Hessian troops. Thus the drug traffic and the Rothschilds played a pivotal role in American history, although it has been ignored or deleted from the history books.

David Ricardo, father of the quantity theory of money and the "rent", or loot theory, was on the Court of Proprietors of the East India Co. He had John Stuart Mill appointed as Chief Examiner. The colonial minister of England during the Opium Wars was Edward Bulwer Lytton, who wrote the Treaty of Nanking in 1842, bringing England $21 million in silver and control over the free port of Hong Kong. Britain then allied with the Hong Society, the Triads and Assassins, to rule the Chinese to the present time. Bulwer Lytton's son was Viceroy of India during the 1880s at the height of the opium trade, and sponsored Rudyard Kipling's writings about the British Raj in India. The profiteers from the drug trade included William, Earl of Shelburne, who organized Britain's first Intelligence Service, whose agents were drawn from Britain's leading families. Its chairman was George Baring, and it employed Adam Smith, Jeremy Bentham, and Thomas Malthus. The Geneva headquarters was run by the Mallet Prevost family, whose descendants include Allen Dulles of the CIA.

Basil Lubbock's work, *The Opium Clippers*, 1933, lists the principal owners of British vessels engaged in the opium trade, with color illustrations of their flags. Most of them were ex-slavers. No. 1 was Hon. East India Co. (known to the Chinese as Hon John Co.); 2. Jardine Matheison; 3. Dent & Co.; 4. Pybus Bros.; 5. Russel & Co.; 6. Cama Bros.; 7. Duchess of Atholl; 8. Earl of Bale arras; 9. George IV; 10. Prince Regent; 11. Marquis of Camden; 12. Lady Melville.

On Feb. 1, 1927, the *New York Times* noted the passing of Sir Robert Jardine,

> "the son and heir of the late Sir Robert Jardine, and succeeded his father as the head of Jardine Mathieson & Co.

Hong Kong which for a long time held almost a monopoly in the importation of Indian opium into China."

Sir Robert had inherited $20 million and 20,000 acres in Scotland. Dr. William Jardine had settled in Canton in 1819.

The present Duke of Atholl owns 202,000 acres at Blair Castle, and is the only person in England authorized by the Crown to maintain a private army. Lady Melville's ancestor, George, the first Earl, welcomed William of Orange to the throne in 1688 and was appointed Lord Privy Seal.

In Paris, Banque Rothschild directors include Elie de Rothschild, director of New Court Securities, Banque Leumi de Israel, Five Arrows Fund N.V. Curaçao; Alain de Rothschild, Five Arrows Fund Curaçao, Banque Lambert de Bruxelles; Guy de Rothschild - Rio Tinto Zinc, New Court Securities, NY.; Sir James Goldsmith; Hubert Faure, Ambassador to Colombia, pres. Schneider Madrid and ten Otis companies; Bernard de Villemejane, pres. Imetal, director Copperweld. Sir James Goldsmith is also chmn Generale Occidentale which owns Grand Union and Colonial food stores in the U.S., Cavenham USA and Banque Occidentale; its directors include David de Rothschild (son of Guy), who is also director of Compagnie du Nord and Societe de Nickel.

Through the Belgian branch of the Rothschild family, we can trace the influence of the Rothschilds in Africa during the past century. Baron Leon Lambert financed King Leopold's Belgian empire; the Congo Syndicate included Baron Empain (la compagnie d'Orient) F. Philippson & Co., and Banque Outremer. This syndicate was allied with Banque de Paris, the Anglo-Italian Group, and the Peking Syndicate. The Congo empire came into being in 1885 after Leopold had financed Stanley's explorations. It included an area the size of Poland, and produced fabulous returns from Congo rubber, ivory and slaves. Later the Union Miniere acquired vast copper mines, the Compagnie de Katanga. One of their most ruthless agents was Emile Francqui, who later became Hoover's partner in China and in the Belgian Relief Commission; his name survives at Congo's Port Francqui. The Congo interests are now controlled by the Lamberts through Societe Generale de Banque, which merged the Societe Generale de Belgique, the oldest bank in Brussels, founded in 1822, and Banque d'Anvers, founded 1827; its secretary is Baron Fauconval, a director of the Rockefeller Foundation. Societe Generale acquired Union Miniere in Dec. 1981; in 1972 it had acquired Compagnie Outremer, formerly Banque Outremer, and in Dec. 1964, had acquired 25% of SOFINA, Societe Financier de Transport & Enterprises Industrielles, the largest holding company in Europe. These firms are controlled by the Rothschild bank, Banque Bruxelles Lambert, founded in 1840 by Baron Lambert. The present Baron is director of Societe Generale de Banque, and president of Compagnie Generale d'Enterprises Electrique which owns fifty power companies.

Banque Lambert de Bruxelles is also the Lambert of the Wall Street firm of Drexel Burnham Lambert, owning 19% of it. As the Belgian branch of the House of Rothschild, the Lamberts tremendous influence on American financial markets when they pioneered in the widespread use of high interest paying, high risk bonds, called "junk bonds", to take over and buy out may of the Fortune 500 companies in the United States. Insider trading became an increasing scandal, as many billions of dollars were made in quick profits by Drexel Burnham Lambert employees such as Michael Milken, who earned $500 million a year in his trading of junk bonds. He is now serving a prison term. These operations created the climate for a major recession which now plagues the nation.

Gerard Eskenazi is director of Compagnie Generale; he is also managing director of Electrorail. A., a holding company for Schneider S.A., European Trading and African Corp., and Canadian Investment Trust. The president of Electrorail is Baron Empain. Eskenazi is also director of Compagnie International des Wagons Lits (Thomas Cook travel agency). Baron Edouard Empain and his son Baron Francois Empain are also directors of Compagnie Generale.

Another Belgian holding company, Delhaizes Frere et Cie Leon, established 1867, now owns Food Giant and Food Town Stores in the U.S., renamed Food Lion.

Through Banque Bruxelles and its interlocking companies, the Rothschilds effectively control Belgium. They also interlock with the Thurn und Taxis interests in Germany. Prince Johannes Erbprinz Thurn und Taxis is said to be the richest man in Europe, controlling Bayerische Vereinsbank, fourth largest bank in Germany, which has four subsidiaries in Frankfurt, including Bankhaus Gebruder Bethmann. Bethmann-Hollweg of this family had been Chancellor under Kaiser Wilhelm, and had set off World War I. He was a cousin of the Rothschilds. Bayerische Vereinsbank also owns controlling interest in Banque de Paris et des Payes, and Banque de l'Europeene Paris. Thurn und Taxis is a direct descendant of William of Orange, who chartered the Bank of England; his mother, the Princess of Braganza of the former ruling house of Portugal, has three direct family connections with the present House of Windsor; Prince Thurn und Taxis also has four connections with the House of Windsor.

The Thurn und Taxis family has enjoyed eight hundred years of prominence in Europe. Originally Tasso of Bergamo, they later emigrated to Brussels. They supervised the postal service and intelligence of the Most Serene Republic of Venice, and later fulfilled the same post in the Hapsburg Empire. The present Prince has huge estates in Brazil; he is the financial adviser of the Rolling Stones; and his palace of St. Emmerans is larger than Buckingham Palace; it costs 2.5 million DM a year to maintain. The Regensburg branch of the family was allied with the Fuggers and the Wessers. They now finance the Pan European Union which is headed by the Hapsburg heir, Archduke Otto, and the Mont Pelerin Society, a subsidiary of Pan Europe.

The House of Hesse, which played such a crucial role in the founding of the Rothschild fortune, and in the founding of America, seldom appears in the news. On Nov. 17, 1937, six members of the family were killed in the crash of a Sabena airliner at the fog-shrouded Ostend airport. The head of the family, Grand Duke Ernst Ludwig (who had tried to end World War I by a desperate mission into Russia to confer with the Czar) had died on Oct. 9, causing the postponing of Prince Ludwig's marriage to Margaret Campbell Geddes in London for seven weeks. Grand Duke George, the new head of the family, his wife

Princess Cecilia of Greece and Denmark, two sons and the Dowager Duchess, as well as the newly born son of Princess Cecilia, were all killed. The child's unexpected arrival apparently caused the tragedy, as the pilot tried to land at Ostend, an unscheduled stop. Prince Ludwig, social attache at the German Embassy in London, went ahead with the wedding on the following day; his best man was his cousin Prince Louis Mountbatten. Two princes of Hesse had married two daughters of Queen Victoria; Beatrice had married Prince Henry of Battenberg; grandfather of the present husband of Queen Elizabeth.

Prince Ludwig's father-in-law, Sir Auckland Campbell Geddes, also had a Rothschild connection; he was chmn of Rio Tinto. He served as Minister of National Service, 1917-19, British Ambassador to the U.S., 1920-24. His brother, Sir Eric Geddes, was a member of the Imperial War Cabinet and First Lord of the Admiralty 1917-18, Minister of National Transport 1919-21, and later chmn Imperial Airways and Dunlop Rubber. His son, Sir Anthony Geddes, married into the Matthey family, became director of the Bank of England, dep chmn Midland Bank, director Shell Transport & Trading, and is now chmn Dunlop Holdings. Sir Auckland's son, the 2nd Baron, was with Shell Oil 1931-46, British Merchant Shipping Mission in Washington, 1942-44, Minister of War Transport, 1944-45, and is now director of Peninsular & Orient Steamship Lines.

On June 7, 1946, the *New York Times* headlined a front page story from Frankfort-on-Main; the army was seeking $1,500,000 in stolen jewels, later revised to $3 million value. The jewels, belonging to the House of Hesse, had been hidden in their cellar of their castle in 1944. They belonged to Princess Margaretha, sister of Kaiser Wilhelm. A party of U.S. Army officers had held a party at the Hesse castle to celebrate the anniversary of D-Day. During the party, they discovered 1600 bottles of wine buried in the cellar; beneath the wine they found the jewels. Ten of the celebrants drank the wine and divided up the jewels. Maj. Gen. J.M. Bevans, who was reprimanded, later returned his part of the loot. Wac. Captain Kathleen Durant and her husband, Col. J. Durant were tried after two quarts of diamonds were dug up in the backyard of their Falls Church home. Maj. David Watson also was sentenced; he had been previously awarded the Bronze Medal personally by Gen. Eisenhower for his supply work, and also received the Russian Medal for Battle Merit from Marshal Zhukov.

The House of Hesse is also known for the Curse of Hesse, their introduction of the family disease of haemophilia into many of the ruling houses of Europe, particularly the Spanish Royal Family and the Romanov family in Russia.

Old Mayer Amschel's heritage has survived intact, according to the *Washington Post*, Dec. 20, 1984, which notes that Frankfurt-am-Main is the financial capital of Germany, headquarters of the five dominant German banks, with 175 foreign banks established there. It also is headquarters for the Central Bank, and the country's largest stock exchange. Like Manhattan, it is also a center of vice and corruption, with sex shops, drugs, and frequent riots because of the presence of 11,000 American occupation troops.

Penetration of the United States is shown by a full-page ad in the *Wall Street Journal* Dec. 21, 1984, a solicitation to purchase all the outstanding shares of Scovill, Inc. by First City Properties, Inc. with the deal managed by Rothschild, Inc. One Rockefeller Plaza, New York. "First City" is the Rothschild code for banks originating under their influence from the "City of London" financial district. First City Properties, Beverly Hills, Calif, is headed by Samuel Belzberg, who also heads First City Financial Corp. Vancouver, First City Trust, Edmonton, and First City Development Ltd. He is a director of Dead Sea Canal Co. The Belzbergs started in Canada with a used furniture store (rag and bone men), and are now influential wheeler dealers on the American stock market.

Rothschilds Inc., established at the Rockefeller address, is successor to Banque Rothschild of Paris. Its co-chairmen are Guy de Rothschild and Evelyn de Rothschild. Directors are Lord Rothschild, head of N.M. Rothschilds & Sons, London; David de Rothschild, Nathaniel de Rothschild, Eric de Rothschild; Thomas L. Piper III, sr. vp Dillon Read and manager of the Rothschild's

New Court Securities; its managing director is Wilbur L. Ross Jr., who is also director of Peabody International, and N.M. Rothschild's & Sons International. Other directors of Rothschild International include John Loudon, former chairman of Shell Oil, director of Ford Motor Co., the Ford Foundation, Orion Bank and chairman of Atlantic Institute. He is a Grand Officer of the Order of Orange-Nassau, a group formed to commemorate the chartering of the Bank of England by William of Orange in 1694. Another director of Rothschild Inc. is G. Peter Fleck, born in Amsterdam, chairman New Court Securities, formerly with Erlangers, and the Banque de Pays de L'Europe Central of Paris, cited by Higham as a key bank during Nazi occupation of France. Fleck is also officer of the Order of Orange-Nassau.

Banque de Pays de l'Europe of Paris, (Paribas) was recently bought by Merrill Lynch. Paribas bought 50% of Dillon Read Ltd. in a consortium with Bruxelles Lambert (the Belgian Rothschilds), the Power Group and the Laurentian group of Canada, the Tata Group of India, Elders IXL holding company of Australia, Swiss Bank Can trade, and two British groups, Investors in Industry, a Bank of England group with nine English and Scottish banks, and the British postal pension fund.

Power Corp. of Canada directors included G. Eskenazi, of Belgian Rothschild firms, and William Simon, former Secretary of the Treasury of the U.S. The "Canadian connection", the Belzbergs and Bronfmans, demonstrates the growing power of the Rothschilds in billion dollar mergers and takeovers of U.S. industry, including DuPont. These mergers recall the same kind of activity taking place in 1929, just before the stock market debacle, and represent the battening down of the hatches before the storm.

Power Corp. interlocks with the leading newspaper chain of Canada, the Hollinger Group, which recently bought the most important newspaper in Israel, the *Jerusalem Post*, the national newspaper of record, which became the leading hawk for Gen. Ariel Sharon's aggressive acts, and which now advocates a new and stronger alliance between Mossad, Israeli Intelligence, and the KGB, supposedly to combat "anti-Semitism" and to discourage Germany's industrial productivity. Hollinger's also bought an important English paper, the *London Daily Intelligencer*. At the 6th annual banquet of the Hollinger Group, held in London, William F. Buckley, editor of the *National Review*, the leading neoconservative and CIA mouthpiece, effusively praised the chairman of Hollinger's, Conrad B lack, drivelling about his "encyclopaedic knowledge, his absolute sense of orientation, and his modest manners." Former Prime Minister Margaret Thatcher delivered the principal address, after which Blackroseto mention "the great debt I among so many owe her."

Other directors of Hollinger's are Henry Kissinger, of whom more later; liquor tycoon Peter Bronfman, chairman of Brascan Ltd., a Canadian enterprise of the Rothschilds which began in May 1945 as the British Newfoundland Corp. It was rechartered by William Stephenson, the famed assassin and spymaster known as "Intrepid", who renamed it British American Canadian Co; he then changed the name to World Commerce Corp. operating out of Panama, until it received its present name of Brascan. Also on the board of Brascan is Edgar Bronfman, president of the World Jewish Congress, and chairman of Seagrams liquor in New York. Also serving on the board of Hollinger Group is Lord Carrington, former Foreign Minister of Great Britain, a cousin of the Rothschilds who co-founded Kissinger Associates with Henry Kissinger, later was chairman of NATO in Brussels, and is now a director of Christie's, the art auction house.

Conrad Black was the protege of Edward Plunket Taylor, wartime spymaster with William Stephenson. Hollinger owns eighty newspapers and one hundred and fifteen weeklies in Canada, United States, Israel and England. The Rothschilds urged Black to purchase the *Jerusalem Post*, which was financed through the Gee Corp. of Vancouver, a financial cover for Li Ka-Shing, vice chairman of the Hong Kong Shanghai Bank, which has historically been known as the drug barons' bank. Black then added Evelyn de Rothschild, of N.M. Rothschild's & Sons, London, to the board, with Henry Jardine and Sir James Goldsmith, another relative of the Rothschilds. The Hollinger Group originally was created by Churchill during World War II through Edward P. Taylor; it merged with a firm called Argus, which controlled Canadian Breweries, the world's largest brewer, the operation was part of Churchill's using war funds to set up vast corporate conglomerates as the War Supplies Corp., a "nonprofit company". It later made one billion dollars profit during World War II. Also serving on the board of Hollinger Group in financier Frederick S. Eaton, Allan Gotlieb, former Canadian Ambassador to the United States until his wife's imbroglio with a secretary; and Paul Reichmann, of the billion dollar real estate holding firm, Olympia and York.

In addition to Hollinger Group, the largest owner of newspapers in Canada and the United States is Thomson International. Lord Kenneth Thompson was recently listed by Fortune as having a fortune of six billion dollars. These two chains control the thought process of most Canadians and Americans.

CHAPTER THREE

SOVIET RUSSIA

> "*The religion of Marxism is the falsification of knowledge whence comes this fierce hatred of intellectuals for the least barbaric societies of human history, and this rage to destroy the only civilizations to date that have emphatically conferred a dominant rule on intelligence?*"
>
> Jean François Revel, *The Flight from Truth; the Reign of Deceit in the Age of Information*

Soviet Russia was allowed to emerge from the destruction of World War II as one of the victors, solely because she was needed as the next "evil empire" against which the civilized West could launch a new Crusade. Because Russia was bankrupt, had lost 40 million of her population in the war, plus another 66 million murdered by the Bolshevik since 1917, and was unable to feed herself, once again the World Order was obliged to step in with enormous subsidies of food and material from the U.S., in order to maintain an "enemy power". The Belgian Relief Commission of 1916 became the Marshall Plan of 1948. Once again, the loads of supplies were shipped into Europe, ostensibly for our Allies, but destined to maintain the Soviet bloc.

Although Jacob Schiffs personal agent, George Kennan, had regularly toured Russia during the latter part of the nineteenth century, bringing in money and arms for the Communist revolutionaries (his grandson said that Schiff had spent $20 million to bring about the Bolshevik Revolution) more concerted aid was called for to support an entire regime. Kennan also aided Schiff in financing the Japanese in the Russo-Japanese War of 1905; the Japanese decorated Kennan with the Gold War Medal and the Order of the Sacred Treasure. In 1915, the American International Corporation was formed in New York. Its principal goal was the coordination of aid, particularly financial assistance, to the Bolsheviks which had previously been provided by Schiff and other bankers on an informal basis. The new firm was funded by J.P. Morgan, the Rockefellers, and the National City Bank. Chairman of the Board was Frank Vanderlip, former president of National City, and member of the Jekyll Island group which wrote the Federal Reserve Act in 1910; directors were Pierre DuPont, Otto Kahn of Kuhn, Loeb Co., George Herbert Walker, grandfather of President George H. Bush, William Woodward, director of the Federal Reserve Bank of New York; Robert S. Lovett, right-hand man of the Harriman-Kuhn, Loeb Union Pacific Railroad; Percy Rockefeller, John D. Ryan, J.A. Stillman, son of James Stillman principal organizer of the National City Bank; A.H. Wiggin, and Beekman Winthrop. The 1928 list of AIC directors included Percy Rockefeller, Pierre DuPont, Elisha Walker of Kuhn, Loeb Co., and Frank Altschul of Lazard Freres. In their program of aiding the Communists, AIC worked closely with Guaranty Trust of New York (now Morgan Guaranty Trust). Guaranty Trust's directors in 1903 included George F. Baker, founder of the First National Bank; August Belmont, representative of the Rothschilds; E.H. Harriman, founder of Union Pacific Railroad; former vice president of the U.S., Levi Morton, who was a director of U.S. Steel and the Union Pacific; Henry H. Rogers, partner of John D. Rockefeller in Standard Oil, also a director of Union Pacific; H. McK. Twombly, who married the daughter of William Vanderbilt, and was now the director of fifty banks and industries; Frederick W. Vanderbilt, and Harry Payne Whitney.

No one would seriously believe that bankers of this magnitude would finance an "anti-capitalist" revolution for the Communists, yet this is exactly what happened. These same men financed Woodrow Wilson's political campaigns, and it was these same men to whom Wilson referred in his opening address to the Paris Peace Conference, when he said,

> "There is moreover a voice calling for these definitions of principles and purposes which is, it seems to me, more thrilling and more compelling than any of the moving voices with which the troubled air of the world is filled. It is the voice of the Russian people. There are men in the United States of the finest temper who are in sympathy with Bolshevism because it appears to them to offer that regime of opportunity to the individual which they desire to bring about." (*The Great Conspiracy Against Russia*, Seghers and Kahn.)

The men of "the finest temper", to whom Wilson referred, the Morgans and the Rockefellers, did not really desire opportunity for the individual; what they desired was the lifelong imposition of slavery under the World Order, and this is the goal which they continue to strive to achieve, on a worldwide basis.

These Americans "of the finest temper" chose Lenin to do their work because he had outlined the plan they wanted in *The Threatening Catastrophe* in September, 1917.

> "1. Nationalisation of the banks. Ownership of capital which is manipulated by the banks is not lost or changed when the banks are nationalised and fused into one state bank, so that it is possible to reach a stage where the state knows whither and how, from where and at what time millions and billions are flowing.
>
> 2. Only control over bank operations providing they are merged into one state bank will allow, simultaneously with other measures which can easily be put into effect the actual levying of income tax without concealment of property and income. The state for the first time would be in a position to survey all the monetary operations, then to control them, then to regulate economic life.
>
> FINALLY, to obtain millions and billions for large state operations, without paying the capitalist gentlemen sky-high commissions for their services. It would facilitate the nationalisation of syndicates, abolition of commercial secrets, the nationalisation of the insurance business, facilitate the control of and the compulsory organization of

labor into unions, and the regulation of consumption. The nationalisation of banks would make circulation of checks compulsory by law for all the rich, and introduce the confiscation of property for concealing incomes. The five points of the desired program then, are nationalisation of the banks, nationalisation of the syndicates, the abolition of commercial secrets, and the compulsory organization of the population into consumer associations."

It was the publication of this program which catapulted Lenin into the leadership of Russia via the Bolshevik Revolution. In 1917, Frank Vanderlip publicly referred to Lenin as "the modern version of George Washington."

The Lenin program is not only the program of Soviet Russia — it is the program of Roosevelt's New Deal, Truman's Socialism, the postwar Labor Government in England, and the guiding principle of subsequent American Administrations. The Labor Government of England proved Lenin's dictum that the ownership of capital is not affected by the nationalisation of the banks, when they nationalised the Bank of England. The Lenin program is the entire program of the U.S. Internal Revenue Service, "the actual levying of income tax without concealment of property or income", "the confiscation property for concealing incomes". The Lenin program is the program of the big rich precisely because it abolishes private property, and puts it under the control of the state. The state is controlled by the big rich, the World Order.

The definitive authority of the Lenin program captured the attention of the financiers. Here was the opportunity to subdue and control all future competition with the power of a totalitarian state, to stifle future development, and to hold the entire population of the world in thrall to their greed. This program took Lenin back to Moscow to seize the government by force and to rule by terrorism. In *Germany and the Russian Revolution*, we find Telegram No. 952 D 2615, State Sec, to min in Copenhagen:

> "Your embassy is authorized to pay one million roubles to Helphand. The corresponding sum should be drawn from the Legation assets. Minister Copenhagen 23 Jan. 1916 — Dr. Helphand; The sum of a million roubles already reached

Petrograd, and devoted to the purposes for which it was intended."

On May 8, 1916, Berlin requested 130,000 M. for Russian propaganda. Under Secretary State to the Minister in Bern, telegram No. 348;

> "It was considered advantageous to Germany to bring out the members of Lenin's party, the Bolsheviks, who are about forty in number. The special train will be under military escort."

Vernadsky says, in his *Life of Lenin*,

> "In the autumn of 1915, the German Russian Social Democrat Parvus Helphand (Israel Lazarevitch) who had formerly been active in the Revolution of 1905, announced the paper published by him in Berlin, 'The Bell', his mission to 'serve as an intellectual link between the armed Germans and the revolutionary Russian proletariat... During the war Helphand was engaged in furnishing supplies to the Germany army in huge quantities, and so considerable amounts of money passed through his hands... A railway car in which were Lenin, Martov, and other exiles was attached to the train leaving for Germany from Switzerland on April 8, 1917. On April 13, Lenin embarked on the steamer sailing from Sassnotz to Sweden. So the trip through Germany took at least four days."

The Leninists quickly exhausted the funds advanced by the Germans when they reached Russia, and once again the Bolshevik bid for absolute power seemed in doubt. To whom should Lenin turn but his powerful friend in the White House? Wilson promptly sent Elihu Root, Kuhn Loeb lawyer and former Secretary of State, to Russia with $20 million from his Special War Fund, to be given to the Bolsheviks. This was revealed in Congressional Hearings on Russian Bonds, HJ 87 14.U5, which shows the financial statement of Woodrow Wilson's expenditure of the $100 million voted him by Congress as a Special War Fund. The statement, showing the expenditure of $20 million in Russia by Root's Special War Mission to Russia, is also recorded in the Congressional Record, Sept. 2, 1919, as given by Wilson's secretary, Joseph Tumulty.

Not to be outdone in generosity, J.P. Morgan & Co. also rushed financial assistance to the beleaguered Lenin terrorists. Col. Raymond Robins headed a Red Cross Mission to Russia. Henry P. Davison, J.P. Morgan's right-hand man (also a member of the Jekyll Island team which secretly wrote the Federal Reserve Act in 1910), had raised $370 million in cash for the Red Cross during World War I, of which several millions were brought to the Russians by Robins team. Aiding him in this charitable work were Frank Vanderlip, chairman of American International Corp., and William Boyce Thompson, another director of the Federal Reserve Bank of New York. Major Harold H. Swift, head of the meat packing family, accompanied Robins on this mission of mercy, or should we say business? Swift used the occasion to garner a $10 million meat order for his brother-in-law, Edward Morris, of Morris Co. On Jan. 22, 1920, the Soviets ordered another $50 million of meat from Morris Co.

Wall Street lawyer Thomas D. Thacher was also a key man of the Robins mission of mercy. The involvement of the J.P. Morgan firm with the Bolshevik Revolution is revealed in Harold Nicholson's biography of Dwight Morrow (Morrow was the father-in-law of Charles Lindbergh Jr.) as follows,

> "His (Morrow's) interest in Russia dated from March 1917 when Thomas D. Thacher, his law partner, had been a member of the American Red Cross Mission during the revolution. It was strengthened by his friendship with Alex Gumberg, who had come to New York as representative of the All-Russian Textile Syndicate. 'I have felt, he wrote in May 1927, that the time would come when something would have to be done for Russia.' He was himself active in furthering official relations between Soviet emissaries and the State Dept., and he provided M. Litvinoff with a warm letter of recommendation to Sir Arthur Salter in Geneva. Nor was this all. When in Paris he gave a dinner party at Foyot's to which he invited M. Rakovsky and other Soviet representatives."

Morrow's actions might be understandable by a professor of economics at Polytechnic U., but they are incredible from a partner of the world's most prominent banking firm. Alex Gumberg was no mewling social worker but a hardcore propagandist, who returned to the U.S. in 1918 as Trotsky's literary agent, and promptly placed two Trotsky manuscripts with publishers. Gumberg also became consultant to Chase National Bank, and Simpson Thacher and Bartlett. He had been business manager of the Soviet paper Novy Mir during the first months of revolution in Russia; when Raymond Robins' Red Cross Mission arrived in Russia, Gumberg served as interpreter and advisor to the Mission, working closely with Thacher. The present senior partner of Simpson Thacher and Bartlett is Cyrus Vance, who served as Carter's Secretary of State, and is now a director of the Rockefeller Foundation.

The international financiers, advised by Gumberg, now launched a worldwide propaganda campaign to sell the Bolsheviks as idealists, selfless humanitarians, and the modern disciples of Christ, who wished only to spread brotherhood and universal love throughout the world. The tune rang strangely against the backdrop of the machine guns steadily chattering in Russia as the "disciples of love" massacred millions of women and children, but none of their devout admirers in the United States heard this as a sour note.

From the outset, the "humanitarians" showed an excessive concern for the material wealth which they had seized from its rightful owners. The *New York Times* noted on Jan. 30, 1918, a despatch from Petrograd,

> "The people's commissaries have decreed a State Monopoly, of gold. Churches, museums and other public institutions are required to place their gold articles at the disposal of the State. Gold articles belonging to private persons must be handed over to the State. Informants will receive one-third of the value of the articles."

Lenin said,

> "The Soviet Union must carefully save its gold. When living with the wolves, howl like the wolves."

One of the first orders issued by the new regime was,

> "The banking business is declared a state monopoly." Signed: Lenin, Krylenko, Podvolsky, Gorbunov.

Marx's philosophy of history claims that the world operates solely through the economic organization of society, based on the production and exchange of goods. However, this is the world view of the parasite, who is concerned only with obtaining his sustenance from the host. The materialist reduction of life to the obtaining of food at someone else's expense eliminates first, man's spiritual life, second, all ideas, because the materialist idea explicitly excludes all other ideas, and third, the long term view, the concept of investing over a period of time for a return which will not be available for years or perhaps never. The parasitic view is limited to the next meal, or to creating a situation in which he cannot be dislodged before obtaining his next meal. This Marxist short term view has become the standard doctrine in American graduate schools of business, particularly Harvard, which was financed by George F. Baker and J.P. Morgan. The result is that American industry, limited by the short term view, has steadily declined for twenty-five years. The high interest rates imposed by the international bankers also force industry to concentrate on short term gains merely to pay interest on their loans.

Marx said,

> "The first function of gold is to give the commercial world a material by which to express value, that is, to express the value of all other goods, as homynous variables, that are qualitatively identical and quantitatively comparable." Karl Marx Soc. v. 23, p.104.

Marx's economic views were entirely compatible with the views of the banking establishment in the City of London and particularly the House of Rothschild. It is no accident that Karl Marx is buried, not in Moscow, but in London, nor is it an accident that the triumph and bloodbath of the Bolsheviks in Russia gave the Rothschilds and their associates one billion dollars in cash which the luckless Czar had deposited in their European and New York banks. Few people know that Marx had close relations with the British aristocracy, through his marriage to Jenny von Westphalen. She was related to the Scottish Dukes of Argyll, who had long been revolutionaries; and the Campbells, who set up the baptist splinter group, the Campbellites.

Jenny von Westphalen's ancestor, Anna Campbell, Countess of Balcarras and Argyll, was governess to the Prince of Orange from 1657-59, the future King William who later granted the charter of the Bank of England; Archibald Campbell, first Duke of Argyll, accompanied William on his voyage to England in 1688 to seize the throne. The present Earl of Balcarras is related to Viscount Cowdray, Weetman John Churchill Pearson, whose mother was the daughter of Lord Spencer Churchill; his sister married the Duke of Atholl, and he married the daughter of the Earl of Bradford. The Argyll-Balcarras family is represented by the Lindsay and Campbell families; the present Earl of Crawford, Robert A. Lindsay is the 29th Earl, and also the 12th Earl of Balcarras. He is also chairman of National Westminster Bank, director of Rothschild's Sun Alliance Assurance. His mother was a Cavendish. He was formerly private secretary to the Secretary of State, and later served as Minister of State for Defense and Minister of State for Foreign and Commercial Affairs.

Despite a later reputation for "anti-Communism", Herbert Hoover was not only the most tireless proponent of the League of Nations in partnership with Col. House; he also was the first American to step in with large scale assistance to prevent a massive uprising against the faltering Bolshevik regime. Hoover saved the Bolsheviks by organizing a massive program to rush food to the beleaguered Communists. Hoover enlisted one of his old colleagues from the World War Relief Agency, Maj. Gen. William N. Haskell, who had been head of American Relief Mission to Romania, and later directed all relief in the Caucasus and Russia.

On Sept. 23, 1921, Haskall embarked on his new mission of mercy, to feed the Bolsheviks so that they would have the strength to continue their mass murders of the landowners and businessmen. Haskell continued this relief work until 1923, when it was determined that the Bolshevik regime was no longer in danger. For this effort, Herbert Hoover won massive opposition in his later political career as an "anti-Communist". Things indeed are not always what they seem under the rule of the World Order. The Hoover effort had provided seven hundred tons of food and other supplies at a cost of $78 million. $20 million was appropriated by Congress for the program; $40 million came from public charities; $8 million worth of medical supplies was donated by the U.S. Army; and the Russians themselves paid $8 million from their gold supplies from the late Czar). After Gen. Haskell's departure, Stalin arrested anyone who had worked with them on this program. He could not afford to allow anyone to mention the help that his regime had received from a capitalist country. On Nov. 28, 1917, his associate, Col. House had cabled Wilson a few days after the Bolsheviks seized power, urging the extreme importance of suppressing all American newspaper criticism of the Bolsheviks; "It is exceedingly important that such criticism be suppressed." The telegram was placed in a confidential file, and only came to light six years later.

In *The Unknown War with Russia*, Robert J. Maddox noted in 1977,

> "Wilson greeted the March Revolution in Russia as a major step toward achieving the kind of postwar world he envisioned. He made sure the U.S. was the first to recognize the Provisional Government."

Maddox points out that Wilson insisted that No. 6 of his famous fourteen points at Versailles was that "Russia should continue under institutions of her own choosing", thus guaranteeing the future of the Bolshevik regime. His closest political aide, Col. House, sent his own secretary, Kenneth Durant, to Russia to become a secretary in the Soviet Bureau in 1920!

William Laurence Sanders, chairman of Ingersoll Rand, and deputy chairman of the Federal Reserve Bank of New York, wrote to Wilson, Oct. 17, 1918,

> "I am in sympathy with the Soviet form of government as the best suited for the Russian people."

George Foster Peabody, also deputy chairman of the Federal Reserve Bank of New York since 1914, and noted "philanthropist" who organized the General Education Board for the Rockefellers, stated that he supported the Bolshevik form of state monopoly. Thus we had three of the most prominent officials of the Federal Reserve Bank of New York on record as supporting Bolshevism, Sanders, Peabody and William Boyce Thompson. Thompson then announced he was giving one million dollars to promote Bolshevik propaganda in the United States! Because the Federal Reserve Bank of New York was controlled by five New York banks who owned 53% of its stock, and because these Five banks were directly controlled by N.M. Rothschild & Sons of London, we can only conclude that these three men were merely stating the preferences of their employer. William Boyce Thompson led one of the strangest migrations in history, when fifteen prominent Wall Street attorneys and financiers journeyed to Russia to save the tottering Bolshevik regime. J.P. Morgan cabled Thompson one million dollars for this mission from the National City Bank branch in Petrograd, which, significantly, was the only bank never molested by the Bolshevik government. The *Washington Post*, Feb. 2, 1918, stated,

> "William Boyce Thompson, who was in Petrograd until November, has made a personal contribution of one million dollars to the Bolsheviks for the purpose of spreading their doctrine in Germany and Austria."

The Thompson mission included Henry P. Davison, head of the American Red Cross, and one of the Jekyll Island conspirators in 1910 who secretly drafted the Federal Reserve Act; Thomas Thatcher; and Harold Swift, all of whom were founders of the Council on Foreign Relations. The National City Bank had already loaned Russia $50 million, and Guaranty Trust, whose directors were the leading financiers in New York, now became the financial correspondent for Soviet interests in America. In January 1922, Secretary of Commerce Herbert Hoover introduced on behalf of Guaranty Trust a resolution permitting relations with "the new State Bank at Moscow". Secretary of State Charles Evans Hughes strongly opposed this resolution, but Hoover succeeded in getting it approved. A German banker, Max May, now vice pres. of Guaranty Trust, became head of the foreign dept. of the Ruskombank in 1923, the first Soviet international bank. Who's Who states that Max May came to the U.S. 1883, naturalized 1888, vice pres. Guaranty Trust 1904-18, director and member of board Russian Commercial Bank 1922-25. J.P. Morgan and Guaranty Trust acted as the fiscal agents of the Soviet Government in the U.S.; the first shipments of "Soviet" gold, which was actually the Czar's gold, were deposited in Guaranty Trust.

In a typical move to disguise their operations, Otto Kahn and several officials of Guaranty Trust then founded an "anti-Communist" group, United Americans, which circulated virulent anti-Communist and anti-Jewish propaganda. Like most such organizations, it was designed to discredit and render impotent anyone opposed to Communism who became involved in its work.

On Feb. 1, 1919, Edward L. Doheny, the oil tycoon, told C.W. Barron, founder of the *Wall Street Journal*,

> "Pres. Eliot of Harvard is teaching Bolshevism. The worst Bolsheviks in the U.S. are not only college professors of whom President Wilson is one, but capitalists and the wives of capitalists. Frank C. Vanderlip is a Bolshevik. Socialism is the poison that destroys democracy. Socialism holds out the hope that a man can quit work and be better off. Bolshevism is the true fruit of Socialism."

The world headquarters of the Bolshevik movement was now at 120 Broadway on Wall Street. The Equitable Life Bldg. at 120 Broadway had been built by a corporation organized by Gen. T. Coleman DuPont. During the early 1920s, 120 Broadway not only housed Equitable Life, but also the Federal Reserve Bank of New York, whose directors were enthusiastically supporting the Bolsheviks; the American International Corporation, which had been organized to aid the Soviet Union; Weinberg and Posner, which received a $3 million order for machinery from the Soviet Union in 1919, and whose vice president was Ludwig Martens, first Soviet Ambassador to the U.S.; John McGregor Grant, whose operations were financed by Olaf Aschberg of Nya Banken, Stockholm, who had transmitted large sums furnished by the Warburgs for the Bolshevik Revolution; the London agent of Nya Banken was the British Bank of North Commerce, whose chairman was Earl Grey, a close associate of Cecil Rhodes — Grant had been blacklisted by the U.S. Government for his support of Germany during World War I; and on the top floor of 120 Broadway was the exclusive Bankers Club. These were the organizers of the World Order. Their instrument of power was gold. The Great Soviet Encyclopedia noted,

> "Under socialist economic conditions, gold is also a universal equivalent, used as a measure of value and a scale of prices. The gold content of the Soviet ruble was established at 0.987412 grams as per Jan. 1, 1961. In the world socialist market gold is used as the universal money."

Many Americans are puzzled by the relentless devotion of the Rockefeller Foundation to financing Communist organizations in many parts of the world. This dedication to Communism can be traced back to a crucial moment in the Bolsheviks' march to power. In 1917, Mackenzie King had established a lifelong relationship with John D. Rockefeller, Jr. whom he met in June, 1914. They had been born in the same year, 1874, and seemed to agree on everything. Soon, King was working closely with Frederick T. Gates and Ivy Lee to further the Rockefeller "philanthropies", which seemed to view Communism as the ideal vehicle to bring about world brotherhood. King wrote to this friend Violet Markham, "John D. Rockefeller Jr., the truest follower of Christ, has one purpose — to serve his fellow man." King resolved that his one purpose was to serve Rockefeller; he testified for him at the trial investigating the Colorado Iron and Fuel Co. massacre before the Walsh Committee (the Rockefellers later tried to have Walsh framed and expelled from the Senate, but failed due to the obstinacy of Burton J. Wheeler; J. Edgar Hoover played a crucial role in setting up the frame).

The Rockefellers helped Mackenzie King obtain government contracts for the Canadian Army during World War I, which set King up for later blackmail (the "Panama" hold over the vassals). King sold hundreds of tons of rotten meat to be sent to the Canadian Army in Europe; boots of "leather", which were mostly pasteboard and which disintegrated immediately in the water soaked trenches; rifles that jammed when they were fired; and collar type life preservers (previously condemned) which broke the soldiers' necks when they jumped into the water.

While Leon Trotsky was in New York in 1917, he received word to return to Russia at once to help bring off the Bolshevik seizure of power. The Rockefellers gave him $10,000 in cash for his journey, procured a special passport for him from President Woodrow Wilson, and sent Lincoln Steffens to safeguard him on the journey. When Trotsky's ship stopped in Halifax, the Canadian Secret Service, warned that he was on board, arrested him on April 3, 1917 and interned him in Nova Scotia. The patriotic agents knew that Trotsky was on his way to Russia to take Russia out of the war against Germany, which would free many German divisions to attack the Canadian troops on the Western Front. Prime Minister Lloyd George indignantly cabled demands from London that Trotsky be released, but the secret service ignored him. By means never explained, Mackenzie King then stepped into the breach and obtained Trotsky's freedom. Trotsky continued on his way to Russia, and became Lenin's chief deputy in the extermination of Russian citizens; he also organized the Red Army with the able help of Wall Street lawyer Thomas D. Thacher. The agents who had arrested Trotsky were dismissed from the service; their careers were ended. As a reward for his intervention, the Rockefellers appointed Mackenzie King head of the Rockefeller Foundation dept. of Industrial Research at a salary of $30,000 a year (the average wage in the U.S. at that time was $500 year). Frank P. Walsh testified before a U.S. Commission that the Rockefeller Foundation was a cloak for the Rockefeller plan to lead organized labor into slavery.

King also became a director of the Carnegie Corporation. A Lady Laurier left him a large mansion in Ottawa, and in 1921 a group of well wishers, led by Peter Larkin, refurbished and staffed it for him at a cost of $255,000. King then appointed Larkin High Commissioner of Canada in London. In 1940, the Canadian Parliament voted King, then Prime Minister of Canada "absolute and dictatorial powers for the duration". On King's 74th birthday in 1948, John D. Rockefeller Jr. gave him $100,000. The Rockefeller Foundation then put up $300,000 to pay for the writing of King's Memoirs. In his final years, King, still on the take, was exposed as a principal in the $30 million Beauharnais Power Co. swindle during the building of the St. Lawrence Seaway. King had accepted $700,000 from Beauharnais for the Liberal Party, and among other enticements had received a trip to Bermuda.

The Rockefellers figured in many pro-Soviet deals during the 1920. Because of the struggle for power which developed between Stalin and Trotsky, the Rockefellers intervened in October, 1926, and backed Stalin, ousting Trotsky. Years later, they would again intervene when the Kremlin was racked by disagreements; David Rockefeller summarily fired Khrushchev. John D. Rockefeller instructed his press agent, Ivy Lee in 1925 to promote Communism in the U.S. and to sparkplug a public relations drive which culminated in 1933 with the U.S. government recognition of Soviet Russia. In 1927 Standard Oil of New Jersey built a refinery in Russia, after having been promised 50% of the Caucasus oil production. The Rockefeller firm, Vacuum Oil, signed an agreement with the Soviet Naptha Syndicate to sell Russian oil in Europe, and made a $75 million loan to Russia. John Moody had stated in 1911,

> "the Standard Oil Co. was really a bank of the most gigantic character — a bank within an industry lending vast sums of money to needy borrowers just as other great banks were doing... the company was known as the Standard Oil Bank. As Rockefeller was no banker, this meant that the Standard Oil was being directed by professional bankers."

The Standard Oil operation has always been directed by the most professional bankers in the world, the Rothschilds; consequently, the Rothschilds through their agents, Kuhn Loeb Co. have maintained close supervision of the "Rockefeller" fortune.

In 1935, Stalin expropriated many foreign investments in Russia, but the Standard Oil properties were not touched. The Five Year Plans (1928-32, 1933-37, and 1938-42) were all financed by the international banking houses. During the 1920s, the principal firms doing business with Russia were Vacuum Oil, International Harvester, Guaranty Trust and New York Life, all firms controlled by the Morgan-Rockefeller interests.

Arthur Upham Pope's biography of Litvinoff notes that in March, 1921, a trade agreement was signed with Great Britain providing that gold sent in payment for machines bought by Russia would not be confiscated towards old debts or claims. This insured that Czarist gold sent to England would not be seized by his cousins, the British Royal Family. On July 7, 1922, Litvinoff revealed that the Russian delegation at the Hague Conference was negotiating with an important group of financiers which included Otto H. Kahn of Kuhn Loeb Co. A week later, Kahn arrived at The Hague. He stated,

> "The conference with the Russians will bring useful results and will lead to a closer approach to unity of views and policies on the part of England, France and the U.S. in respect to the Russian situation."

When Otto Kahn's wife visited Russia in 1936, she was treated like visiting royalty.

In 1922, the Chase National Bank had established the American-Russian Chamber of Commerce to promote trade with and government recognition of Russia. Its chairman was Reeve Schley, a vice president of Chase; he was a director of many corporations including Howe Sound, Electric Boat, the Yale Corp., chairman of Sundstrand and Underwood; he had served as director of the U.S. Fuel Administration from 1917-1919. His son, Reeve Schley Jr. was a Captain in the O.S.S. under Gen. Donovan in World War II. Both Chase and Equitable Trust led in granting credits to the Soviet Union during the 1920s. In 1934, Roosevelt established the Export Import Bank finance increased trade with the Soviet Union. During World War II, Chase was AMTORG'S principal bank in handling the many billions of dollars of Lend Lease transactions for Russia. Roosevelt went all out in supporting the Soviets perhaps because all three of his personal assistants, Alger Hiss, Lauchlin Currie and Harry Dexter White, were identified as Soviet agents. Hiss' mentor was Dean Acheson, formerly of J.P. Morgan Co. Asst Secretary of State A. A. Berle Jr. testified before the House Un-American Activities Committee Aug. 30, 1948 that "Acheson was the head of the pro-Russian group in the State Department." Acheson later became senior partner of Covington and Burling, obtaining the position for the firm as Washington legal representative for nine Communist governments. On April 29, 1943, the Board of Economic Warfare granted a special license to Chematar Corp. of New York to fill an order from the Soviet Purchasing Commission for 200 lb. uranium oxide, 220 lb. uranium nitrate, and 25 lb. of uranium metal, commodities virtually unknown at that time, thus launching the Soviet atomic program.

On Jan. 29, 1944, Special Ambassador W. Averill Harriman in Moscow informed the State Dept. that "we" must turn over to the Russians the currency printing plates which had been engraved for the U.S. Treasury by *Forbes* Co. of Boston. The State Dept. delayed action on this request for several weeks. On March 22, Harry Dexter White met with Gromyko at the Soviet Embassy and assured him the plates would be delivered. Both Harriman and White made daily demands until the plates were turned over to the Soviet Union April 14, 1944. The Soviet Union then printed $300 million in currency which was redeemed by the American taxpayers.

After the "Cold War" began, the financiers continued their efforts to aid the Soviets. In 1967, the *New York Times* announced that a new consortium had been formed to promote trade with Russia, composed of Cyrus Eaton's Tower Corp., Rockefeller's International Basic Economy Corp., and N.M. Rothschild & Sons of London. Eaton had begun his career as a $2 a day factotum for John D. Rockefeller, who later financed his purchase of Canadian Gas & Electric Corp. Eaton stated that Rockefeller soon interested him in Russian affairs. In an interview with Mike Wallace, Eaton claimed that under Communism, the people of the Soviet Union were entirely contented.

> "They were happy. I was amazed at their happiness and dedication to the system."

Eaton was one of the first defenders of the Stalin-Hitler Pact in 1939.

The Rothschilds have rarely been identified with Communist causes, preferring to remain in the background. Only one member, N.M. Victor Rothschild, who served an apprenticeship with J.P. Morgan Co., had become involved with the Apostles Club at Cambridge, described by Michael Straight as composed mostly of Communists who were also homosexual. Its well known members were Guy Burgess and Donald Mac Lean, Anthony Blunt, Keeper of the Queen's Pictures, and the double, or triple agent Kim Philby. During World War II Victor Rothschild, who was with MI5, lent his London flat at No. 5 Bentinck St. to Burgess, while his mother, Mrs. Charles Rothschild, hired Burgess as her investment counselor. Blunt left the staff of the Warburg Institute to work with MI5; he introduced Victor Rothschild to his aunt, Teresa Mayor, who later became Lady Rothschild. Blunt has been recently described as having had an "affectionate" relationship with the Queen.

The Rockefeller family is sometimes called the first family of the Soviet Union. When Nelson Rockefeller was nominated for vice president in 1967, Pravda indignantly denounced his critics, saying that charges against Rockefeller were designed only to discredit him, and that the accusations came from ultra right wing organizations. Senator Frank Church, attending the 1971 Dartmouth Conference at Kiev, was amazed to find that

> "David Rockefeller was treated like we would treat royalty in this country. The Russian people appear to evince an adoration of Rockefeller that is puzzling. When David Rockefeller's plane lands in Russia, crowds line up to greet him at the airport, and line the streets of Moscow as his limousine passes, hailing him with cries of RAHK FAWLER".

George Gilder remarked that no one knows how to revere, blandish and exalt a Rockefeller half as well as the Marxists.

After World War II, Dean Acheson frantically lobbied for an additional $300 million loan to the Soviet Union. Ed Burling, who was Frederic A. Delano's brother-in-law, had founded the firm of Covington and Burling of which Acheson was partner, with Donald Hiss, brother of Alger. When Acheson's lobbying failed to develop the Russian aid, the Council on Foreign Relations drafted the Marshall Plan as an alternative measure. Their publication, "Foreign Affairs", then published the "containment plan" as written by "X" (George Kennan. The policy of containment, which has been the official foreign policy of the U.S. toward the Soviet Union since 1947, guarantees not only Soviet Russia's borders, but her continued enslavement of the "Captive nations" which she holds by military force. Henry Luce, who always provided a forum for the international propagandists, reprinted the entire text of the July, 1947 Foreign Affairs article in *Life* magazine, July 28, 1947. Its key sentence was

> "The main element of any U.S. policy towards the Soviet Union must be the long-term, patient but firm and vigilant containment of Russian expansive tendencies."

Luce's *Time* magazine dubbed Kennan "America's senior policy-maker". He later became a fellow of the Institute of Advanced Study of Princeton. Kennan was the nephew and namesake of the George Kennan who operated as a Marxist agent for Jacob Schiff in Russia for many years before the Bolshevik Revolution, and was finally expelled by the Czarist Government. Kennan's pen-name "X" was a favorite identification of Socialist operatives. In 1902, the Socialist "X" Club had been founded in New York by John Dewey, whose Socialist program has dominated American education during the twentieth century. The other founders of the "X" Club were James T. Shotwell, founder of the League of Nations, United Nations etc.; Morris Hillquit, Communist candidate for Mayor of New York, Charles Edward Russell, and Rufus Weeks, vice president and managing director of *New York Life*, which was controlled by J.P. Morgan.

When Nikolai Khrushchev, dictator of the Soviet Union, came to New York Sept. 17, 1959, he was invited to dinner at W. Averill Harriman's Home. Thirty people attended, who controlled aggregate wealth of $40 billion; they included Russian born David Sarnoff, head of RCA, Philip Mosely of the Council on Foreign Relations; Herbert H. Lehman of Lehman Bros.; Dean Rusk of the Rockefeller Foundation; George A. Woods, First Boston Corp.; Thomas K. Finletter of Coudert Bros., former Secretary of the Air Force; John K. Galbraith, economist; Frank Pace of General Dynamics.

In Sept. 1960, Kruschev was entertained at Hyde Park at a dinner given in his honor by Eleanor Roosevelt. Present at this select gathering was Victor Hammer, who had fenced the Romanov jewels in the U.S. He sold many Faberge items to Lillian Pratt, wife of the General Motors tycoon; the collection is now in the Virginia Museum in Richmond, Va.

In 1973, the U.S.-USSR Trade and Economic Council, consisting of leading U.S. heads of corporations, was formed to promote "trade" read (gifts) to the Soviet Union. In 1976, G.M. Miller of Textron was named head of the Council. Shortly afterwards, he was appointed chairman of the Federal Reserve Board of Governors by Carter. The Bolshevik Revolution, which was nurtured through its most trying days by three directors of the Federal Reserve Bank of New York, William Boyce Thompson, George Foster Peabody, and William Woodward, continues to be supported by the Federal Reserve System. The Federal Reserve System maintains close ties with the Gosbank, the Soviet Central Bank, which controls the Communist Party of the USSR. Gosbank employs 5000 economists, and is known as a "passive", rather than an "active" bank of issue, meaning that it follows orders from other sources, as does the Federal Reserve Board of Governors. The Gosbank-Federal Reserve System "cooperation" in Soviet financial latters is handled through the Bank for International Settlements in Switzerland.

In 1949, the present flood of "Eurodollars" originated as European deposits of Communist dollar hoards in the Soviet Eurobank of Paris, Banque Commerciale pour Europe du Nord. The financiers then realized they created anew and even more untraceable source of paper money which had no backing. Anthony Sampson writes that

> "The more cosmopolitan banks with foreign experts and directors, such as Warburgs, Montagus, Rothschilds and Kleinworts, had also discovered a huge new source of profits in the market for Eurodollars."

These profits now amount to some two trillion dollars, all of which are obligations of the American taxpayer. This Ponzi operation was made possible by the exclusive "Central Bankers Club", the Bank for International Settlements, which had been established by Hjalmar Schacht, financier of the Nazi movement, Emile Francqui, guiding genius of Hoover's Belgian Relief Commission, and John Foster Dulles, heir to the title "most dangerous man in America". It was set up in May 1930 by the Hague Treaty to handle German reparations payments, which, of course, were never paid. BIS now controls one tenth of the world's gold, which it rents out at a profit. Its assets have increased by an astronomical 1200% in the past twenty years. U.S. shares of BIS are held by Citibank.

The Wall Street Journal noted editorially on Mar. 10, 1986,

> "Hasn't it struck most Western policy makers as odd that the Soviet Union, with a total annual hard currency income of about $32 billion from all sources (including arms sales) can sustain a global empire?"

The Journal noted that the Soviet Union has been a major player in the interbank market for many years, and that six Soviet-owned banks in the West have been the major beneficiaries of this global flow of interbank funds.

> "The largest Soviet-owned banks in the West include Banque Commerciale pour l'Europe du Nord, or Eurobank in Pairs, Moscow Narodny Bank of London, Ost-West Handelsbank in Frankfurt, and others in Luxembourg, Zurich and Vienna. Western deposits in Soviet-owned banks approximate $5 billion."

What is going on here? Western nations deposit billions of dollars in Soviet banks. Where is the rivalry between Communist and capitalist? The answer is that it is just where the fabled Soviet Empire has been, in Never-Never Land.

American International Corporation continued to exercise a behind the scenes role in U.S. Soviet dealings until World War II, when W.A. Harriman's presence in Moscow to direct Stalin's handling of the war usurped its duties. Standard and Poors shows in 1982 an American International Group, an insurance holding company with $3.4 billion in assets, whose attorneys are Sullivan & Cromwell. It was formed from the Cornelius V. Starr insurance network which was part of the CIA's Asiatic operations. Its directors include Harry Kearns, chmn Eisenhower-Nixon presidential campaign, now chmn American Asian Bank, served as president Export Import Bank 1969-73; William L. Hemphill, pres. United Guaranty, director of Cone Mills (the Hemphill family has been allied with J.P. Morgan for many years); Douglas MacArthur II, diplomat; John I. Howell, chmn J.Henry Schroder Bank, and Schroders Ltd of London; Edwin A. Granville Mentin of England, who was chairman of American International from 1946-1979, now director of the Starr Foundation; and J. Milburn Smith, director of Lloyd's of London.

Prominent American businessmen and political leaders such as W. Averill Harriman do not bother to conceal their pro-Soviet activities. Russian Ambassador Dobrynin casually referred to Henry Kissinger's double role, saying,

> "I am the laughing third man, sitting still. Kissinger is negotiating for us too."

Brezhnev, dictator of Russia, was asked why the Soviet Union did not take a role in Middle East negotiations. He replied,

"We don't need representation. Kissinger is our man in the Middle East."

With this kind of influence, it seems odd that the Communists do not precipitate a coup, and seize absolute power in the U.S., as they did in Russia in 1917. There are 200,000,000 answers to this question, not 200,000,000 Americans, but 200,000,000 guns held privately by American citizens. A confidential Ford Foundation study showed that only 5 to 10% of Americans would actively resist a Communist seizure of power. This was the good news. The bad news was that only 1% of our citizens, armed and opposing the takeover, would defeat it. Since 1948, Americans have asked this writer when the Communists will seize power in the U.S. The answer is that they will seize power after they have confiscated the 200,000,000 guns. Guns are forbidden in the Soviet Union. Only the highest officials are allowed to possess them. Criminals understand only one law - the law of force. The criminal syndicalists who seek to enslave the entire world cannot be defeated by humility or compassion, but only by the most determined and the harshest measures. To examine the American situation in perspective, there are only five hundred men, primarily in the major foundations, who are actively engaged in transmitting international banker-Socialist orders to our government. Beneath them are ten thousand politicians, businessmen, media personalities, and academicians who, with the aid of religious operatives, implement the orders from

London. This is a much smaller number than the members of the Communist Party of the USSR which rules the Soviet Union.

To protect these traitors, the U.S. government has imported 25 million aliens into the United States, which includes 5000 intensively trained terrorists, and 100,000 hardened criminals. This force is intended to neutralize the opposition of the American people to Communism. The government encourages crime, because it is the nationwide criminal force, not the police force, which keeps the population subdued. Americans must devote all their energies to defending themselves against the professional criminals, protecting their homes and families, leaving them no opportunity to organize against the criminal syndicalists of the World Order. This clever plan of subsidizing the criminal element was the sole achievement of the Law Enforcement Administration, a foundation-organized plan which originated at the University of Chicago.

The federal government uses its armed police, the IRS, the FBI, the BATF and the CIA solely to terrorize its American subjects into compliance with the program of the World Order. Most American citizens have had to come to the painful realization that the FBI is not concerned with fighting Communism, but only with battling American anti-Communists. They now realize that the IRS functions as an armed group of terrorists, not to collect funds, of which the government has no need, but solely to extort money by force from American citizens, as part of the program of the World Order. The intent is to render them impoverished and terrorized, so that they will be rendered impotent and unable to organize to resist the World Order. It is the program of *1984*.

Even if they planned otherwise, the five masters of the World Order have now created a situation which must lead to world war, world economic collapse, or both. The thirty-year buildup of the Soviet Union as the next opponent in an ongoing world conflict was noted by Srully Blotnick in *Forbes* magazine, Nov. 7, 1983:

> "A wealthy New York lawyer whose portfolio contained substantial holdings of McDonnell Douglas, Raytheon and General Dynamics, commented, 'It bothers me even to think what would happen if the Russians decided to take us up on

our 5% a year solution to the arms race. Once we started dismantling our strategic weapons, the defense stocks will make the hitech group look stable by comparison. The 60% loss I took on my Fortune computer system could be a hint of things to come.'"

The World Order has no religious, political or economic program except World Slavery. Only by subduing all potential opposition can the parasite guarantee his position of lodging on the host. The World Order sets up countless groups to promote any type of idea, and then sets up other groups to fanatically oppose them, but the masters have no dedication to anything except slavery. As R.E. McMaster wrote in *The Reaper*,

> "The goal of international communism is not to destroy Western international debt capitalism. The goal of international communism is to enslave mankind at the behest of Western international debt capitalism."

This is all you can ever know about the present world situation, and it is all you need to know.

In 1985, in the initial printing of *The World Order*, I posited a worst-case theory for the U.S. economy almost entirely dependent on the "Soviet threat", a Russian revolution would mean the collapse of the U.S. economy. In 1992, we have seen the Soviet Empire collapse, and the U.S. economy is in shambles. Of course the Bush league officials are frantically trying to convince Americans that there is no connection between the two events. In fact, the Soviet Empire is the empire that never was. There was a Russian Empire, under the Romanovs, but after the biggest heist in history, when the richest man in the world, Czar Nicholas, was robbed, and he and his family murdered by thugs who called themselves "Communists", a tremendous propaganda campaign, aided and abetted by the kept press of the world, has sought to convince us that Communism exists, and that the Soviet Empire exists. I have detailed the financial and other support give to the "Soviets" by Americans, and most of all, the American taxpayer, on an ongoing basis since 1917 to the present day. President Bush is now beating the bushes for hundreds of billions of additional aid to Russia. This is nothing new. He is carrying on the tradition established by his grandfather and name sake,

George Herbert Walker, when he became a director of American International Corp., a Wall Street firm set up to finance the Bolshevik Revolution. What really happened in Russia in 1917? Through the furtive acts of British Secret Intelligence Service agents in Moscow, the Romanov government was overthrown, and a provincial government installed. In 1917, Russia joined the United States as a colony of the Bank of England. The Czar's fortune was used, among other things, to purchase the stock of the Federal Reserve Banks for $144,000,000. Today, the rightful owners of that stock are the heirs of the Romanovs. George Orwell envisioned the world of *1984*, in which two rival powers maintained perpetual hostility and martial law but never went to war against each other. *1984* continued in effect until one player, the United States, weakened and could no longer afford to subsidize its rival. What happened to the world Communist threat was that the American taxpayer, looted and betrayed by the minions of the World Order, could no longer afford to pay for Communism in Russia.

The charade came close to collapse during the Burgess-MacLean episode, when these British agents "defected" to Russia. They were followed by their handler, Kim Philby, who became a Lieutenant General in the KGB. This episode almost exposed the behind the stage scenery, in which the British SIS, Mossad, the KGB and the CIA, inhabited a fairy land of their own, and in which harsh reality was never permitted to intrude. Why did these financiers indulge in this charade? For a very simple economic reason. Since 1917, the enormous wealth and potential productivity of the Russian people has been withheld from the world. A great rival has been handcuffed and condemned to prison. The problem which the conspirators of the world now face is how can they continue to hold Russia down?

One reason that this farce ran so long on the Great White Way was the diligence of the CIA in promoting a false image of Russia. We now know that the Russian economy was never more than one-tenth of the annual figures furnished to our officials by the CIA. Financial writers such as Henry Rowen and Charles Wolf, who argued that Soviet production was less than one-third of that of the United States, were shouted down by the CIA statisticians. When Russia showed signs of collapse, World Order leaders were rushed to Moscow to shore up the ruins. President Bush himself made repeated trips to Russia for the Trilateral Commission, to preserve the Soviet dictatorship. At Kiev, on Aug. 1, 1991, Bush exhorted the Ukrainians to be good Soviet citizens, "because the Soviet Union was reforming itself." Eighteen days later, it collapsed. So much for the wishes of the Trilateral Commission. George Bush's passion for Gorbachev cannot obscure the historical fact that the "evil empire" never existed from 1917 to 1990 which survived on gifts from Washington which were exacted from the American taxpayer. When the United States went into a recession, Soviet Russia collapsed.

President Bush made so many trips to Russia to save the Soviet KGB regime that he faces serious problems in winning re-election in his own country. For many months, Bush dedicated himself to maintaining Gorbachev in power as the KGB protege of the World Order. While Bush sneered at Boris Yeltsin, and publicly snubbed him, he profusely praised Gorbachev, noting in his address to the nation, Dec. 26, 1991,

> "I'd like to express my gratitude to Mikhail Gorbachev for years of sustained commitment to world peace and for his intellect, vision and courage."

Bush had been quoted in *USA Today* on Oct. 30, 1991, as reassuring Gorbachev, who daily faced ouster in Russia, that "You're still the master." The Russian people ignored Bush's trilateral recommendation, and chose Yeltsin.

Yeltsin himself quickly came under siege by aspiring agents of the World Order. Aging and discredited Trotskyites crawled out of the woodwork, shrieking that they were still important figures. The *Washington Post* named some of his would-be American agents as Allen Weinstein, who describes himself as "Yeltsin's man in Washington"; a number of refugees from the Hoover Institution in Palo alto; and a street car operator from Washington, D.C. named O. Roy Chalk.

Chapter Four

Franklin D. Roosevelt

The Crash of 1929 and the resulting depression have been exhaustively covered in a previous work (*Secrets of the Federal Reserve*[2], 1983). Roosevelt was elected president in 1932 in a campaign which ignored Hoover's Rothschild connections and his World War I record. Instead, Roosevelt blamed Hoover for a depression which had been set up by the Bank of England. Hoover states in his *Memoirs*,

> "In replying to Roosevelt's statement that I was responsible for the orgy of speculation, I considered for some time whether I should expose the responsibility of the Federal Reserve Board by its deliberate inflation policies from 1925-28 under European influence, and my opposition to these policies."

Hoover remained silent, and was ushered out of office. He later termed Gerard Swope's "economic planning" for the New Deal as "the precise pattern of Fascism". "The New Dealers". by an Unofficial Observer, Literary Guild 1934, noted that the New Deal included W.A. Harriman, administrator in charge of heavy industry, and his sister, Mary Rumsey, who backed *Newsweek* with Vincent Astor, and the *New Deal weekly*, Today. "Observer" also noted that Col. House was the elder statesman behind the New Deal, and that House had only backed two

---

[2] *The Secret of the Federal Reserve*, Eustace Mullins, Omnia Veritas Ltd, www.omnia-veritas.com.

Presidential candidates, Wilson and FDR. Roosevelt continued the Wilson policies (actually the House policies outlined in *Philip Dru, Administrator*), with the same personnel, and ended as Wilson did, by involving America in another World War. Observer states that Col. House's New York apartment was only two blocks from the Roosevelt home on E. 65th St. in New York, and that House was seen there almost every day in 1932. He also visited Roosevelt in New England and on the Roosevelt yacht.

The Council on Foreign Relations had purchased a headquarters building at 45 E. 65th St., next door to Franklin's mansion. With Roosevelt's election in 1933, the idle rich of the World Order swarmed into Washington to amuse themselves with government programs. Ray Tucker reported in *Collier's* magazin,

> "Washington was transformed from a placid, leisurely Southern town, with frozen faces and customs, into a gay, breezy, sophisticated and metropolitan center."

Tucker's use of "gay" proved very prophetic. Arthur Krock of the *New York Times* wrote,

> "They are a merry group, the New Dealers. They like singing and dancing and a fair amount of drinking."

A few years later, Washington had the highest per capita amount of alcohol consumption in the United States. With the World Order crowd came their allies, the Communist. Harold Ware, son of Ella Reeve Bloor, the veteran Communist agitator, came to Washington to organize the infamous Harold Ware cell among government employees, he had spent several years in the Soviet Union, and had returned to the U.S. with personal assignments from Lenin. The cell met in his sister's music studio on Connecticut Ave. As a sign of the times, the Dept. of Agriculture issued an official ruling that

> "A man in the employ of the Government has just as much right to be a member of the Communist Party as he has to be a member of the Democratic or Republican Party."

To consolidate Roosevelt's power, his backers used the typical World Order scheme — they set up his "opposition". In

August, 1934, the principal architects and financiers of his New Deal formed the Liberty League, immediately characterized as an "extreme rightwing" organization. Pierre and Irenee DuPont put up $325,000 for it. The League was also financed by J.P. Morgan, the Rockefellers, J. Howard Pew, and William J. Knudsen (who was later appointed by FDR to an important position!). The backers of Liberty League, who were busily denouncing Roosevelt & his staff as "Communist", which many of them were, were also the organizers of American International Corporation, which had been formed to prevent the economy of the Soviet Union from collapsing. Liberty League successfully corralled the opponents of FDR and branded them as "rightwing nuts". Roosevelt was given the opportunity to rant against his opposition as "economic royalists", "the Old Guard", and "princes of privilege". Gerald L. K. Smith was then brought into the picture, in order to smear Roosevelt's opposition as "anti-Semitic". The ploy operated from 1934 to the 1936 elections, when it effectively destroyed Landon's campaign. No effective political opposition was organized against Roosevelt for the rest of his lifetime in office. It was one of the most successful political hoaxes in American history. Roosevelt then married his son to an heiress of the DuPont dynasty. At the very time that Eugene DuPont, cousin of Pierre, was one of the most active members of the Liberty League, F. D. Roosevelt Jr. was courting his daughter, Ethel! They were married June 28, 1937, in what Time Magazine called the "Wedding of the Year", presided over by Dr. Endicott Peabody. The couple made the cover of Time magazine, the only newlyweds ever to do so.

These measures were necessary because FDR's backers were planning to involve the U.S. in the Second World War. Any popular political opposition to Roosevelt might have swept him out of office in 1940, just when he was needed to bring off the Pearl Harbor attack. On the morning of Pearl Harbor, Gen. Marshall, his Chief of Staff, met secretly with Maxim Litvinoff (married to Ivy Low of England), to assure the Russians that everything was going according to plan. Marshall later testified before Congress that he "couldn't remember" where he was on Pearl Harbor Day.

The "managed conflict" was well on its way. Jacques Rueff points out that Schacht did not invent Hitler's monetary policy; it was imposed on Germany "by American and British creditors to finance war preparations and finally unleash war itself" (*The Monetary Sins of the West*). Rueff also points out that the Standstill Agreement of 1931 allowing Germany a moratorium on war debts through the 1930s was an amicable pact between the London, New York and German branches of the Warburg and Schroder houses. Max Warburg remained Schacht's deputy at the Reichsbank until 1938; Kurt von Schroder then became his deputy. (Schacht's father had been Berlin agent for the Equitable *Life* Insurance Co. of New York.) The industrialist levies for Hitler (the Circle of Friends) were paid into the Schroder Bank.

Throughout the 1930s, Hitler was duped into persevering in his desire for friendship with England, an alliance originally proposed jointly by Theodore Roosevelt and the Kaiser in 1898 between the three Nordic powers, England, Germany and the United States. The Schroders assured Hitler than their Anglo-German Fellowship in England was a hundred times more influential than it actually was. With such figures as the Astors and the Chamberlains supporting rapport with Germany, Hitler was persuaded that war with England was impossible. In 1933 he had announced his discovery that Marx, Lenin and Stalin had all said that before international Communism could triumph, England and her Empire must be destroyed. "I am willing to help defend the British Empire by force if called upon," he declared. In 1936, Hitler arranged for meetings to take place between English and German diplomats, but the desired result was never attained, as the British had only one goal, to lull Hitler into a sense of false security until they could declare war against him.

To lure Hitler into World War II, it was necessary to guarantee him adequate supplies of such necessities as ball bearings and oil. Jacob Wallenberg of the Swedish Enskilda Bank, which controlled the giant SKF ball bearing plant, furnished ball bearings to the Nazis throughout the war. The anti aircraft guns sending flak against American air crews turned on SKF ball bearings. Its American plant, SKF of Philadelphia, was repeatedly put on the Proclaimed List, and each time, Dean Acheson removed it.

President William S. Farish of Standard Oil refueled Nazi ships and submarines through stations in Spain and Latin America. When Queen Elizabeth recently came to the U.S., the only family she visited was the Farishes. Throughout the war, the British paid royalty to Ethyl Standard Corp. on the gasoline used by German bombers who were destroying London. The money was placed in Farben bank accounts until after the war. I. G. Farben was organized by the Warburgs in 1925 as a merger between six giant German chemical companies, Badische Anilin, Bayer, Agfa, Hoechst, Welierter-Meer, and GriesheimElektron. Max Warburg was director of I. G. Farben, Germany, and I. G. Chemie, Switzerland. American I. G. Farben was controlled by his brother, Paul, architect of the Federal Reserve System, Walter Teagle of Standard Oil, and Charles Mitchell of National City Bank. Just before World War II broke out, Ethyl-Standard shipped 500 tons of ethyl lead to the Reich Air Ministry through I. G. Farben, with payment secured by letter of Brown Bros. Harriman dated Sept. 21, 1938.

Throughout World War II, the Paris branches of J.P. Morgan and Chase National Bank continued to do business as usual. At the end of the war, occupation authorities repeatedly issued orders to dismantle I. G. Farben plants, but were countermanded by Gen. William Draper of Dillon Read, which had financed German rearmament in the 1920s.

Winston Churchill remarked of this "managed conflict" in 1945, just before it ended, "There never was a war more easy to stop." (quoted in *Washington Post* June 11, 1984). The only real difficulty had been encountered in getting it started. Churchill succeeded in prolonging the war for at least a year by defeating Gen. Wedemeyer's plan for a Channel crossing in 1943, and by embarking on his ruinous North African-Sicilian swing, a replay of his disastrous Gallipoli campaign of the First World War. *Life* revealed April 9, 1951 that Eisenhower had radioed Stalin through the U.S. Military Mission in Moscow of his plan to stop at the Elbe and allow the Russians to take Berlin. The message had been written by Ike's political advisor, John Wheeler Bennett of RIIA, received by W. Averell Harriman, and delivered to Stalin. In Washington, Gen. Marshall assured President Truman that we were "obligated" to allow the Russians to take Berlin. Senator Joseph McCarthy later called Marshall "a living lie".

The conquered German people were now systematically looted and ruthlessly governed by the occupying powers. Henry Kissinger, John J. McCloy (son-in-law of a J.P. Morgan partner), Benjamin Buttenweiser, partner of Kuhn, Loeb & Co. (his wife was Alger Hiss's lawyer at his trial for perjury), and other Rothschild operatives descended like locusts upon the prostrate nation. Aid to Soviet Russia continued under the guise of the Marshall Plan, a rerun of Hoover's Belgian Relief Commission in World War I. The Marshall Plan originated as a special study by David Rockefeller for the Council on Foreign Relations, "Reconstruction of Western Europe" completed in 1947. It was retitled the "Marshall Plan" and advertised as a great contribution to "democracy in Europe". (Imperial Brain Trust-Shoup). W. Averell Harriman was installed in the Rothschild's Paris mansion, Hotel Talleyrand, as head of the Marshall Plan.

The victorious Rothschilds consolidated their control of world monetary systems by the Bretton Woods pact, a replica of the charter of the Bank of England. It provided immunity from the judicial process, its archives were inviolable and not subject to court or Congressional inspection; no taxation could be levied on any security dividend or interest of the Fund; all officers and personnel were immune from legal processes. The pact systematically looted Western Europe and the United States. On April 3, 1984, AP reported that "British" investments in the U.S. were now $115 billion, and the British held $28 billion in U.S. bank assets. At least one U.S. Senator is a member of the British aristocracy, Malcolm Wallop, (R. Wyo.) son of Hon. Oliver Wallop, whose brother is Earl of Portsmouth (created 1743). Sen. Wallop's sister, Lady Porchester, married Lord Porchester, son of the Earl of Carnarvon. Lord Porchester is the Queen's Master of Horse, and her Racing Manager.

Lord Carrington, for many years British Foreign Minister, is now Henry Kissinger's partner in Kissinger Associates, and was recently appointed head of NATO. He is chmn of GE chmn

Australian New Zealand Bank, director of Rio Tinto, Barclay's Bank, Cadbury Schweppes, Amalgamated Metal, British Metal, and Hambros Bank. His mother was the daughter of Viscount Colville, who was financial secretary of the treasury 1936-38. Richard Davis notes in *The English Rothschilds* that Lionel Rothschild was a frequent visitor at Lord Carrington's house in Whitehall. In fact, Lord Carrington was related to the Rothschild family by marriage. The first Lord Carrington was Archibald Primrose. His son became Viscount Rosebery. The 5th Earl Rosebery married Hannah Rothschild, daughter of Mayer, in 1878. She was given away by Disraeli.

World War II delivered the peoples of the world into the hands of the World Order, with the predictable result that they have been systematically despoiled, terrorized, oppressed and massacred in further "managed conflicts", not the least of which was the Vietnam War, in which American boys with little or no combat training were sent into battle against the highly trained guerilla troops of Ho Chi Minh and General Giap, communist troops whose leaders had been intensively trained by the special OSS Deer team.

The Rothschilds rule the U.S. through their foundations, the Council on Foreign Relations, and the Federal Reserve System, with no serious challenges to their power. Expensive "political campaigns" are routinely conducted, with carefully screened candidates who are pledged to the program of the World Order. Should they deviate from the program, they would have an "accident", be framed on a sex charge, or indicted on some financial irregularity. Senator Moynihan stated in his book, *Loyalties*, "A British friend, wise in the ways of the world, put it thus: 'They are now on page 16 of the Plan.'" Moynihan prudently did not ask what page 17 would bring.

The American citizen works hard and pays taxes, blissfully unaware that at any moment the secret rulers, operating through the Federal Reserve Board, can make a monetary ruling which will place him in onerous debt or bankrupt him. Gary Allen writes in *American Opinion*, Oct. 7, 1979,

> "Whatever the future holds, you can bet it will be unstable with wide swings in the value of the dollar and precious

metals. As long as Volcker's sponsors know in advance what his policies will be, they will make big money."

This accurate prediction was followed by 20% interest and 25% inflation.

Businessweek, Feb. 20, 1984, stated,

> "The worst market for traders is a stable one. Investment banks now have a greater than ever vested interest in market instability. They can rack up enormous profits by guessing right about rapid, wide swings in profits, prices and interest rates."

It is obvious that they can rack up "enormous profits" if they know in advance what the monetary decisions will be. Anyone who seriously believes that no one knows in advance what Federal Reserve decisions will be is too naive to be allowed out on his own; anybody who believes that there is no one who can tell the Federal Reserve Board what its policies are to be is even more out of touch with reality. Many people believed that Lord Montagu Norman ran the Bank of England as a one-man show for thirty years, showing that some people will believe anything. A. Craig Copetas writes in *Harper's*, Jan. 1984,

> "How the Barbarians Do Business" about the 2,000 dealers of the London Metal Exchange, that viewing these people objectively, "you are left with a simple scrap merchant — a rag and bone man, as the British call their junk dealers."

It is the rag and bone men who are running the economies of the world up and down like a window shade, and profiting handsomely on every move of the markets.

Carter Field notes in his biography of Baruch,

> "Baruch got out of the market just before the Crash. But what made Baruch sell stocks and buy tax-exempts at such a favorable time?"

Field offers no answer. Norman Dodd, who was then with Bankers Trust, states that Henry Morgenthau came into Bankers Trust a few days before the Crash, and ordered the officers to close out all securities of his trusts, $60 million, in three days. The officers tried to remonstrate with him, pointing out that if he would sell them over a period of weeks, he would make much greater profits, perhaps five million dollars more than if they were disposed of on such short notice. Morgenthau became furious, screaming at them, "I didn't come here to argue with you! Do as I say!" Black Friday occurred within the week.

On May 30, 1936, *Newsweek* wrote about a Roosevelt appointee to the Federal Reserve Board, Ralph W. Morrison,

> "He sold his Texas utility stock to Insull for ten million dollars, and in 1929 called a meeting and ordered his banks to close out all security. As a result, they rode through the depression with flying colors."

The insiders come through "with flying colors", while millions of victims are ruined, destroyed by forces which they refuse to believe exist. Heartbreak, losses of homes and businesses, breakdowns, suicides, destruction of families, these are the results of World Order economic policies initiated and carried out by "the rag and bone men".

Through its monetary command of the Federal Reserve Board, the World Order determines the outcome of American elections. A news commentator recently pointed out that Paul Volcker would determine whether Reagan would be re-elected. In 1980, the Federal Reserve Board deliberately defeated Carter and elected Reagan. Otto Eckstein noted in *U.S. News*, Sept. 5, 1983, that the prime rate reached 21.5% in late 1980, creating a recession in an election year. Eckstein, head of Data Resources in Lexington, Mass. (he later died suddenly), said,

> "The Federal Reserve had never before made such a move."

One critic pointed out that Volcker has boosted interest rates, which hurts U.S. stocks, making short term U.S. money instruments more desirable than long-term, and bringing about the very instability of foreign capital flows which he claims to fear. Gordon Thether writes in The London *Financial Times*,

> "In all history, there can be fewer instances of a man having inflicted greater damage on the interests of his fellow human beings than Volcker has done with 'benign neglect'

and its all too many malignant manifestations — not the first of which is the ill-conceived gold demonetization campaign Washington has been engaged in since the late 60s. Interest rates rise when gold does not back currency."

Through the London Gold Pool, the Federal Reserve System and the U.S. Treasury disposed of American gold at the giveaway price of $35 an ounce, one tenth of its current value, robbing the American public of billions of dollars. On July 24, 1969, Volcker authorized SDR paper gold, Special Drawing Rights, to replace gold in foreign exchange. He then triumphantly remarked to his fellow bankers in Paris, "Well, we got this thing launched." Secretary of the Treasury Connally then took the Nixon Administration off gold, devaluing the dollar in August, 1971.

On July 17, 1984, Jack Anderson described the Federal Open Market Committee in the *Washington Post* as "a mysterious council of 12", "the enigmatic group" with "excessive secrecy" who, says Anderson, "influence what rates you will pay, how much money will be available for business to borrow and whether inflation once again will eat up your earnings and reduce the value of your bank accounts." Despite the far-reaching importance of "Volcker's" decisions, his testimony before Congress is shrouded in gobbledygook; this writer has gone through hundreds of pages of his testimony without finding a single quotable phrase about his economic intentions. On July 9, 1984, Jack Anderson said of Volcker's meetings with high Treasury officials,

> "One of them, asked if he could recall anything Volcker had said during the high-level meetings, thought a moment and replied, 'I can't remember anything he said that I understood'."

Sen. Moynihan noted in the *New Republic*, Dec. 31, 1983,

> "The Fed does not control the precise money supply and cannot precisely determine interest rates. But it can set the direction and range for both, and this it did. Anyone who tried to dissent was soundly rapped. Its two dozen or so central bankers decided to bust the economy, and bust it they did."

Paul Craig Roberts writes in *Businessweek*, Feb. 27, 1984,

> "Whatever Volcker's intentions, the empirical data show that there has been a deceleration in money growth since last spring and that the Fed has been using open market operations to keep interest rates up... What concerns the financial markets is the eclipse of Reagan's policies by Volcker's.—the most likely result will be higher taxes and higher deficits."

Nevertheless, the press and the Democrats attack Reagan as responsible for the deficit, over which he has no control, and which Volcker creates.

The *New York Times* stated that whoever won the election in Nov. 1984, it has already been decided that taxes will be increased by $100 billion. Here again, why have an election of elected officials who have no influence in economic affairs? Brunner recently interviewed Walter Wriston, retired head of Citibank, who said,

> "I have been through the Fed's actions for the past fifteen years in detail - the Fed has exercised a malign influence on the economy of this country. Its interference in the financial markets of America over the last decade has resulted in persistently excessive money growth, inflation which undermined the financial strength of U.S. corporations owing to the combined inflation and excessive rates of taxation, and record debt."

Forbes pointed out June 20, 1983 in a story about "Tony" Solomon,

> "Solomon may be the most important man in the Federal Reserve System after the chairman, and what he says and does has an effect upon us all."

Perhaps you have never heard of "Tony" Solomon. Certainly you have never voted him into any office, yet what he says and does has an effect upon us all. He is the chairman of the Federal Reserve Bank of New York, a post formerly held by Paul Volcker. This bank represents the New York money market in the Federal Reserve System. Fifty-three per cent of its stock is held by five New York banks whose controlling influence is the London House of Rothschild. The chairman of the FRBNY sits permanently on the FOMC at the right hand of the chairman of the Board of Governors. Sec. 12 As of the 1913 Federal Reserve Act provided that five representatives of the 12 Federal Reserve Banks should rotate on the FOMC. This was quietly amended in August 1943, while World War II was raging, to read, "one elected annually by the board of directors of the Federal Reserve Bank of New York" replacing the provision that "one should be elected annually by the boards of directors of the Federal Reserve Banks of Boston and New York". FRBNY is now the only Federal Reserve Bank with a permanent seat on the FOMC. The American public was never informed of this change.

Chapter Five

The Business in America

John Moody, author of many standard reference works on American finance, stated in *McClure's Magazine*, Aug., 1911, "The Seven Men",

> "Seven men in Wall Street now control a great share of the fundamental industry and resources of the United States. Three of the seven men, J.P. Morgan, James Stillman, and George F. Baker, head of the First National Bank of New York, belong to the so-called Morgan group; four of them, John D. and William Rockefeller, James Stillman, head of the National City Bank, and Jacob H. Schiff of the private banking firm of Kuhn, Loeb Co., to the so-called Standard Oil National City Bank group the central machine of capital extends its control over the U.S.. The process is not only economically logical; it is now practically automatic."

What was true in 1911 is even more true in 1984; the seven men are now, as then, merely American agents for London interests. In 1919, Moody wrote in *Masters of Capital*,

> "All of the great bankers began as dry goods traders, including Junius S. Morgan. Beebe Morgan was a dry goods house. J.M. Beebe Co. of Boston made Junius S. Morgan a partner. Junius Morgan was later invited to join George Peabody & Co. of London, which handled most of the House of Rothschild's trading in American stocks. Junius Morgan's son, J.P. Morgan, later changed the name of the firm to J.P. Morgan & Co., but it continued to one of three representatives of the House of Rothschild in the U.S., the others being Kuhn, Loeb & Co. and August Belmont."

The Morgan group and the National City Bank group held a secret meeting at Jekyll Island, Ga. the week of Nov. 22, 1910 to consolidate their financial power. Present were Sen. Nelson Aldrich (his daughter married John D. Rockefeller Jr.), his private secretary, Shelton, A. Piatt Andrew, Asst. Sec. of the Treasury, Frank Vanderlip, president National City Bank, Henry P. Davison, J.P. Morgan's right-hand man, Charles D. Norton, pres. First National Bank of New York, Benjamin Strong of Liberty Natl. Bank (he later married the daughter of the president of Bankers Trust, became president of Bankers Trust, and chairman of the Federal Reserve Bank of New York) and Paul Warburg, a German immigrant who had joined Kuhn, Loeb & Co.

Although these men were the most influential financiers in the U.S., they were present at Jekyll Island merely as the emissaries of Baron Alfred Rothschild, who had commissioned them to prepare legislation establishing a central bank in the U.S., modelled on the European fractional reserve central banking organizations of the Reichsbank, the Bank of England, and the Bank of France, all of which were controlled by the House of Rothschild.

To enact the Federal Reserve Act into the law of the land, the bankers elected Woodrow Wilson president of the U.S. in 1912 by splitting the Republican Party, defeating the popular William Howard Taft by financing Theodore Roosevelt's malicious Bull Moose third party candidacy. Wilson's academic career at Princeton had been financed by gifts from Cleveland H. Dodge, director of National City Bank, and Moses Taylor Pyne, grandson and heir of the founder of National City Bank. Wilson then signed an agreement not to go to any other college. The Federal Reserve Act was legislated through Congress as the Glass-Owen bill, backed by two Democrats, Congressman Carter Glass of Virginia, and Sen. Robert Owen of Oklahoma. Owen was persuaded to back the bill by Samuel Untermeyer, who had cultivated him while acting as counsel for the Pujo Money Trust investigation. Untermeyer flattered Owen by entertaining him at Greystone, his palatial Hudson River estate. Untermeyer claimed to be a "progressive Democrat", although he lived in feudal splendor, employing 167 men to tend his expanse of orchids and greenhouses. At Greystone, Owen dined with Paul Warburg, Bernard Baruch, and other financiers who had been instructed to get the Federal Reserve Act passed. Owen, a former Indian agent who knew little about finance, was easily persuaded by Paul Warburg's doctrinaire pronunciamentos about "our antiquated banking system", which must be brought up to par with the more modern banking system of Europe.

After the Federal Reserve Act had been passed by Congress and signed into law by President Woodrow Wilson, six New York banks controlled by the Morgan-Standard Oil group bought controlling interest of the Federal Reserve Bank of New York, which they have held ever since. The May 19, 1914 organization chart of the Federal Reserve Bank of New York shows that of the 203,053 shares issued, National City Bank took 30,000 shares; the Morgan-Baker First National Bank took 15,000 shares. These two banks merged into the present Citibank in 1955, giving them one-fourth of the shares in the Federal Reserve Bank of New York. The $134 billion Citicorp is now the largest bank in the U.S. The National Bank of Commerce of which Paul Warburg was a large shareholder, took 21,000 shares; Hanover Bank (now Manufacturers Hanover, of which Lord Rothschild is a director,) took 10,200 shares; Chase National Bank took 6000 shares; Chemical Bank took 6000 shares. These six banks in 1914 owned 40% of the stock of the Federal Reserve Bank of New York. The Federal Reserve System printout of shareholders July 26, 1983 showed that they now own 53%, as follows: Citibank 15%; Chase Manhattan 14%; Morgan Guaranty Trust 9%; Manufacturers Hanover 7%; Chemical Bank 8%. Citicorp Citibank is No. 1 in size in the U.S. No. 3 is Chase Manhattan with $82 billion assets; No. 4 is Manufacturers Hanover, $64 billion; No. 5 is J.P. Morgan, $58 billion; No. 6 Chemical Bank. No. 11 is First Chicago, formerly First National Bank of Chicago, controlled by the Baker-Morgan interests. House Rept. 159362, p. 183 - notes,

> "Next to Baker and Son, Morgan & Co. is the largest stockholder of First National (of New York), owning 14,500 shares; Baker and Morgan together own 40,000 of the 100,000 shares of First National Bank."

The *New York Times*, Sept. 3, 1914, at the time of the Federal Reserve stock was being sold, showed the principal stockholders of these banks as follows: National City Bank — 250,000 shares of which James Stillman owned 47,498; J.P. Morgan & Co., 14,500; W. Rockefeller 10,000; M.T. Pyne 8267; Percy Pyne 8267; J.D. Rockefeller 1750; J.S. Rockefeller 100; W.A. Rockefeller 10; J.P. Morgan Jr. 1000. National Bank of Commerce, 250,000 shares — George F. Baker 10,000; J.P. Morgan Co. 7800; Mary W. Harriman, (widow E.H.) 5650; Paul Warburg 3000; Jacob Schiff 1000; J.P. Morgan Jr. 1100. Chase Natl. Bank— George F. Baker 13,408. Hanover Natl. Bank — James Stillman 4000; William Rockefeller 1540.

During a period when thousands of U.S. banks have gone bankrupt since 1914, these banks, protected by their interest in the Federal Reserve Bank of New York, have grown steadily. A Senate Report,

> "Interlocking Directorates among the Major U.S. Corporations, a staff study of the Senate Committee on Governmental Affairs, June 15, 1978, shows that five of these aforementioned banks held a total of 470 interlocking directorates in the 130 major corporations of the U.S., an average of 3.6 directors per major U.S. Corporation. This massive report is worthy of anyone's detailed study: we can only give the totals here:

CITICORP	97 directorates
J.P. MORGAN CO.	99 directorates
CHEMICAL BANK	96 directorates
CHASE MANHATTAN	89 directorates
MANUFACTURERS HANOVER	89 directorates
Total	470

This centralized control over American industry by five New York banks controlled from London suggests that instead of 130 major U.S. corporations, we may have only one, which in itself is an outpost of the London Connection.

In the early 19th century, the House of Rothschild established a number of affiliates in the U.S. which carried the code identification of City banks, or City companies, identifying them as originating in the financial Centre, the City of London. The City Bank was established in New York in 1812, in the same room in which the Bank of the United States had operated until its charter expired. Later called the National City Bank, its principal for fifty years was Moses Taylor, whose father had been a confidential agent for John Jacob Astor and British intelligence. Like the Morgan-Peabody operation, Moses Taylor doubled his fortune in the Panic of 1837 by purchasing stock in the depressed market with capital advanced by N.M. Rothschild of London. During the Panic of 1857, while many of its competitors failed, City Bank prospered. Moses Taylor purchased the outstanding stock of Delaware Lackawanna Railroad for $5 a share during the panic. Seven years later, it was worth $240 a share. He was now worth $50 million. His son-in-law, Percy Pyne, had come from London to work at City Bank, and married Taylor's daughter. When Taylor died in 1882, he left $70 million. His son-in-law, now paralyzed, became president of the now National City Bank. John D. Rockefeller's brother William invested in the bank, and persuaded Pyne to step aside in 1891 in favor of James Stillman, Rockefeller's associate, to become president. William's son William married Stillman's daughter Elsie; his other son Percy married Stillman's daughter Isabelle. James Stillman also had a London connection - his father, Don Carlos, had been a Rothschild agent in Brownsville, Texas and a successful blockade runner during the Civil War.

The National City Bank acquired several subsidiaries in New York, the National City Co., later renamed the City Co., and City Bank Farmers Trust Co.

The dominance of the Morgan-Kuhn Loeb financial power in New York is shown by a Dow Jones report in the *New York Times* Feb. 11, 1928 that of total offerings of bonds in 1927, J.P. Morgan was first with $502,590,000; National City Co. was second with $435,616,000; Kuhn Loeb was third with $423,988,000. On July 3, 1929, the *New York Times* noted that Charles A. Peabody had joined the boards of National City Co.

and City Bank Farmers Trust. On Aug. 4, 1932, the *New York Times* stated that National City Bank would issue its own currency against U.S. bonds carrying the circulatory power under the new Federal Home Loan Bank Act which empowered National City Bank to issue up to $124 million in currency. The National City Bank had now become a "bank of issue", a function formerly reserved to central banks. On June 8, 1933, James H. Perkins, chmn National City Bank, announced the National City Co., would change its name to City Co. of New York. On Nov. 21, 1933, the National City Bank listed 31 affiliates including City Bank Farmers Trust, City Co. of New York, City Co. of Massachusetts, 44 Wall St. Co. and Cuban Sugar Plantations Inc.

On March 3, 1934, the *New York Times* announced that National City Bank would sell the National Bank of Haiti, a wholly owned subsidiary, on April 29, 1934. The *Times* also noted that National City Bank had organized United Aircraft Feb. 2, 1934, and that its subsidiary, City Bank Farmers Trust had celebrated its 112th anniversary on Feb. 28, 1929.

On June 27, 1934, the City Co. of New York was designated German bond scrip agent in the U.S. On May 22, 1933, City Co. of N. Y. announced its merger with Brown Bros. Harriman, with Joseph Ripley as chairman of the board. The company went through several name changes as Brown Harriman Co., Harriman Ripley, and is now Brown Bros. Harriman once more.

On March 4, 1934, Gen. Billy Mitchell, addressing the Foreign Policy Association, stated that National City Bank and its affiliates control aviation in this country. Allen W. Dulles, introduced as a "specialist in international affairs" announced the profits of international munitions makers were unconscionable.

On March 2, 1955, National City Bank announced it would purchase the stock of First National Bank for $165 million, $550 a share (in the 1929 boom, First National sold for $8600 share). Some market analysts believed the stock should have brought $750 a share in the 1955 sale, suggesting that the Baker family was no longer able to protect its interests. The resulting Citibank became the largest bank in the U.S., with a controlling interest in the Federal Reserve Bank of New York. National City Bank had been in Hong Kong for eighty years; it has a $90 million Citibank Centre there. In 1983, 4% of its annual profits came from the Hong Kong operation, which is the center of the world's drug trade.

Besides its controlling interest in the Federal Reserve Bank of New York, the Rothschilds had developed important financial interests in other parts of the United States. The House Banking and Currency Committee Report May, 1976, "International Banking", p. 60, identified the Rothschild Five Arrows Group and its present five branches: N.M. Rothschild & Sons Ltd. London; Banque Rothschild, France; Banque Lambert, Belgium; New Court Securities, N.Y.; Pierson, Holding & Co., Amsterdam. These five were combined in a single bank, Rothschild Intercontinental Bank Ltd. The House Staff Report discloses that Rothschild Intercontinental Bank Ltd. has three principal American subsidiaries: National City Bank of Cleveland; First City National Bank of Houston (First City Bancorp); and Seattle First National Bank. These Rothschild subsidiaries were ranked in 1983 as follows: First City Bancorp Houston, 23rd in size in U.S., $17 billion assets; National City Corp. of Cleveland, 48th largest in U.S., $6.5 billion assets. National City Corporation of Cleveland has exercised a dominant role in Midwestern industry and politics for many years; First City Bancorp dominates Texas oil and heavy industry as well as Texas politics.

In 1900, Cleveland was the home of Marcus Alonzo Hanna (known as Mark), the legendary political boss of the Republican Party. He twice nominated and elected an Ohio Congressman, William McKinley, to the Presidency of the U.S. He initiated the checkoff system by which banks and corporations were required to make regular political contributions. Hanna founded two companies; M. A. Hanna Co., and Hanna Mining Co., which acquired large steel and iron holdings. In 1953, President Eisenhower named George Humphrey Secretary of the Treasury. Humphrey, president of M.A. Hanna Co., was also chmn National Steel Co. (recently acquired by Nippon Kokan, a Japanese concern); director of Sun Life Assurance Co. (Rothschild), Industrial Rayon Corp., the world's largest manufacturer of auto tire cord (L.L. Strauss of Kuhn, Loeb Co. controlled the firm; Harry Byrd Jr. was also a director. Humphrey was also a director of the National City Bank of Cleveland. Other directors of this bank were C.T. Foster, chmn Standard Oil of Ohio; J. A. Greene, chmn Ohio Telephone Co.; L.L. White, chmn Chicago & St, Louis Rwy.; R.A. Weaver, chmn Ferro Corp.; J.B. Ward, President Addressograph Co.; H.B. Kline, President Industrial Rayon Corp.; and William McAfee, director Standard Oil of Ohio. National City Bank of Cleveland now has $6.5 billion assets, 8,171employees, and seventeen companies. It recently purchased the $500 million revenues bank, BANCOHIO.

In 1978, George Humphrey's son, Gilbert W., was chmn Hanna Mining Co., director National City Bank of Cleveland, Sun Life Assurance, National Steel, Massey Ferguson, General Reinsurance, and St. John del Rey Mining Co. M.A. Hanna Co. the holding company, was liquidated in 1965, and its $700 million assets distributed to its stockholders.

The National City Bank of Cleveland's influence was not limited to the Hanna and Humphrey families. As the Ohio Connection of the House of Rothschild, it guided the careers of two of the nation's best known families, the Tafts and the Rockefellers. The bank financed the Taft family's activities in politics and business, the Taft Broadcasting Co. and other firms. John D. Rockefeller's success began when he obtained the backing of the National City Bank of Cleveland to finance his takeover of his competitors in the oil business. Because J.P. Morgan and Kuhn, Loeb Co. controlled 95% of all railway mileage in the U.S. in the latter half of the 19th century, they offered Rockefeller special rebates on shipping oil through his holding company, South Improvement Co. This enabled him to undersell and ruin his competitors. One of them was a Mr. Tarbell, whose daughter, Ida Tarbell, later wrote the first expose of Standard Oil and was termed a "muckraker" by Theodore Roosevelt, a term which promptly went into the language. The entire Rockefeller empire was financed by the Rothschilds.

When Lincoln Steffens became a Wall Street reporter, he interviewed both J.P. Morgan and John D. Rockefeller on several occasions. He soon realized that these gentlemen, powerful though they were, were mere front men. He noted that

> "No one ever seems to ask the question 'who is behind the Morgans and the Rockefellers?'"

No one else ever asked the question, nor did anyone answer it! Steffens knew the money for their operations was coming from someone else, but never managed to trace it.

In February 1930, one of the few articles on the Rothschilds ever to appear in an American magazine appeared in *Fortune*, which stated,

> "On only one important point did the Rothschilds guess wrong. They never would have anything to do with the U.S. of America. Imagination falters at what the Rothschilds might be today if they had spent on the infant industries of this country one-half the sums they poured into Imperial Austria."

The *Fortune* writer did not know then and probably never knew that the Rothschilds have always controlled the Morgan and Rockefeller operations, as well as the foundations set up by these front men to control the people of the United States.

During the past quarter of a century, many writers have published alarming exposes of the Rockefellers and their control of the U.S. through the Council on Foreign Relations. In 1950, the *New York Times* carried a small notice on an inside page that L.L. Strauss, a partner of Kuhn, Loeb Co., had been appointed financial advisor to the Rockefeller brothers. In short, all their investments must be approved by a partner of Kuhn, Loeb Co. It has always been thus, beginning with Jacob Schiff. Strauss held the position from 1950 to 1953, when it passed to J. Richardson Dilworth. Dilworth, who married Elizabeth Cushing, was a partner of Kuhn, Loeb Co. from 1946 to 1958, when he became director of Finances for the entire Rockefeller family, presiding over all their accounts on the 56th floor of Rockefeller Center. He held the position until 1981. He is now Chairman of the Board of Rockefeller Center, director of International Basic Economy Corp., Chrysler, R.H. Macy, Colonial Williamsburg and Rockefeller University.

The National City Bank of Cleveland continues to dominate Midwestern industry and politics. For many years, its primary law firm has been Jones, Day, Reavis and Pogue of Cleveland. The *Washington Post* announced Dec. 19, 1983 that this law firm was spending $9 million for office space in Washington to house a staff of sixty lawyers, making this Cleveland law firm one of the most potent lobbying groups in Washington.

Hanna Mining Co., despite relatively modest revenues of $333 million exercises an important role, as shown by its board of directors, including such distinguished names as Herbert Hoover Jr. (Under Secretary of State under Eisenhower & Dulles); Stephen D. Bechtel, chmn of Bechtel Group and director of J.P. Morgan Co.; R.L. Ireland of Brown Bros. Harriman; George F. Bennett, treasurer of Harvard University, and Nathan W. Pearson, financial manager of the Mellon family.

Despite the Hollywood image of red-faced Texas oil millionaires driving new Cadillacs, the Texan oil industry has for years been dominated by the London Rothschilds through the billion dollar First City National Bank of Houston, and its fifty-seven subsidiary Texas banks. Chairman of First City is James Anderson Elkins Jr., who is a director of Hill Samuel Co. of London, one of the seventeen merchant banks chartered by the Bank of England. His father was chairman of First City, and founded the Texas law firm of Vinson and Elkins, the primary law firm of First City Bank. This firm dominated national politics through its most well-known partner, John B. Connally, who achieved a reputation as "kingmaker" in Texas politics. He began as administrative assistant to Congressman Lyndon B. Johnson in 1949, then became attorney for the oil millionaire Sid Richardson, and Perry Bass, 1952-61, Secretary of the Navy 1961, Governor of Texas 1963-69; Secretary of the Treasury 1971-72. He was wounded in the Kennedy assassination in Dallas. He is now trustee of the Andrew Mellon Foundation, serves on the President's Foreign Intelligence Advisory Board, and the Advisory Committee on Reforming the International Monetary System. He advised Nixon on devaluing the dollar and going off the gold standard in 1971. He is now director of Superior Oil, and Falconbridge Nickel Mines Ltd.

James Anderson Elkins is also director of Freeport Minerals, whose directors include some of the leading names in American business. Chmn of Freeport is Benno H. Schmidt, managing director of J.H. Whitney Co. Schmidt, who married into the wealthy Fleischmann family — (*New Yorker* magazine etc.) graduated from Harvard Law in 1941, became general counsellor of the War Production Board in Washington 1941-42, and headed the Foreign Liquidation Commission 1945-46, which disposed of billions of dollars worth of property. He is also director of CBS, and Schlumberger, the huge oil field service firm who began business in 1928 when it was awarded its first contract by the Soviet Union — it is said to have important Anglo Swiss intelligence connections. Other directors of Freeport Minerals are William McChesney Martin Jr., Chairman of the Federal Reserve Board 1951-1970, now director of J.P. Morgan U.S. Steel, Eli Lilly, General Foods, Royal Dutch Shell, IBM, American Express, Riggs National Bank, and Scandinavian Securities (the Wallenberg firm); Donald S. Perkins, of Morgan Guaranty Trust, *Time* magazine; John B. Madden, partner Brown Bros. Harriman; Godfrey S. Rockefeller; Norborne Berkeley Jr., director Uniroyal, and Anglo-Energy Ltd.

Other directors of First City Bancorporation include Anne Armstrong, U.S. Ambassador to Britain 1976-77, co-chmn Reagan-Bush Campaign 1980, director of General Foods, General Motors, trustee Hoover Institution, Guggenheim Foundation, Atlantic Council, Council on Foreign Relations, Halliburton Co.; George R. Brown, director of Halliburton — he founded the huge contracting firm, Brown & Root, which financed Lyndon B. Johnson's political campaigns, subsequently receiving billion dollar contracts to construct naval bases and airfields in Vietnam, which are now being used by the Soviet Navy and Air Force. Brown married into the Pratt family, founded Texas Eastern an oil firm, and is director of ITT, TWA, and the Brown Foundation. The Brown-Johnson association began in 1940, when Johnson secured a lucrative contract for Brown & Root in to build a large naval base at Corpus Christi, Texas; it was said then that any course chosen by Johnson would be paved by money from Brown & Root. J. Evetts Haley pointed out that Brown & Root prospered on government contracts after

Johnson helped them and rapidly became a worldwide operation. In 1940, the Internal Revenue Service found that large contributions given to Johnson by Brown & Root and its subsidiary, Victoria Gravel Co., as much as $100,000 each, were taken by Brown & Root as tax deductions. Haley states,

> "Brown & Root were in control of Texas politics; that L.B. Johnson was in control of IRS; that records had been burned at IRS to get Brown off the hook in 1954. Johnson and Connally then picked up a government plant for a small sum which became a giant wartime contractor, the Sid Richardson Carbon plant at Odessa, Tex., in which Mrs. Lyndon B. Johnson had a one-fourth interest."

In 1955, Johnson suffered a major heart attack on his way to George Brown's palatial Middleburg Va. estate.

As mentioned, Brown is a director of Halliburton, whose primary law firm is also Vinson & Elkins. In 1981, Halliburton had $8.3 billion revenues, 110,398 employees, and daily monitors most U.S. oil wells. In addition to George Brown and Anne Armstrong, directors of Halliburton include Lord Polwarth of Scotland, who is Governor of the Bank of Scotland, director of Canadian Pacific, Sun Life Assurance Ltd. and Brown & Root UK which interlocks with George Wimpey Ltd., the largest construction firm in England, through Brown & Root Wimpey Highland Fabricators. Lord Polwarth, Henry Hepbume Scott, is a descendant of James Hepburn, Earl of Bothwell, who was married to Mary, Queen of Scots. The first Baron Polwarth (1641-1724) was Sir Patrick Hume, first Earl of Marchmont, and William of Orange's closest advisor. He accompanied William in 1688 on his voyage to take possession of the throne of England, and became his privy councillor, in which office he advised William to grant the charter of the Bank of England. He became a peer of Scotland 1689, Lord Chancellor of Scotland 1696-1702, and Earl of Marchmont 1697. He passed the Act of Succession on to the House of Hanover, and was reappointed by King George I.

John Pickens Harbin, president of Halliburton, is a director of Citicorp. Another director of Halliburton is William E. Simon, Secretary of the Treasury 1973-77. He is a director of Citicorp,

Citibank, and United Technologies. As director of Citibank, he interlocks with Lord Aldington of London (Toby Low), who is also director of Citibank and chairman of Sun Life Assurance, the keystone of the Rothschild fortune. Lord Aldington is chairman of Grindlay's Bank, London, director of General Electric Ltd., Lloyd's Bank, United Power Ltd., and National Discount Corp.

During a national "oil crisis" government officials complained they could not obtain any records from oil companies on production and reserves, yet Halliburton received this information on a daily basis.

As director of United Technologies, William Simon again interlocks with Citibank, the only corporation which has four officers on the board of directors of Citibank— Harry Gray, chmn of United Technologies, Simon, William. Spencer, who is president of Citibank, and Darwin Eatna Smith, chmn of Kimberly Clark.

Other directors of United Technologies are Robert F. Dee, chmn & CEO of the Smith Kline drug firm; T. Mitchell Ford, general counsel CIA 1952-55, now chmn of the $1.8 billion Emhart Corp., and director of Travelers Insurance; Richard S. Smith, exec, vice-pres. National Steel, was with First National Bank New York 1952-62, and treasurer of M.A. Hanna Co. 1962-63, and director of Hartford Fire Insurance, and Hartford Accident & Indemnity; Charles W. Duncan, Jr., dep. Sec. Defense, 1977-79, Sec. Dept of Energy 1979-81, chmn Coca Cola International, chmn Coca Cola Europe, director Humble Oil Co.; Melvin C. Holm, pres & CEO Carrier Corp., director N.Y. Telephone, Mutual of New York SKF Industries; Antonia Chandler Hayes, wife of Abram Hayes, who was law clerk to Felix Frankfurter, later joined Covington & Burling, Washington 1952-55 , wrote the Democratic Natl. Platform 1960, legal adviser Sec. of State 196 1-64, director of foreign policy Democratic Natl. Committee 1972; Jacqueline Wexler, pres. Webster College 1965-69, pres. Hunter College since 1969, leader of the feminist movement; and Robert L. Sproull, with the Dept. Defense 1963-65, pres. Univ. of Rochester since 1970, lecturer at NATO, director of Xerox, General Motors, pres. Telluride Assn.

Other directors of First City Bancorporation are John Diesel, pres. of Tenneco, which interlocks with the George Bush oil firm, Zapata Oil Corp., whose chmn John Mackin is a director of Tenneco; Randall Meyer, pres. Exxon; MA. Wright, former chmn Exxon 1966-76, now chmn Cameron Iron Works.

Other directors of Halliburton Corp. include James W. Glanville, former ptnr. Lehman Bros, and Lazard Freres, was with Humble Oil 1945-59, Lehman Bros. 1959-78, had been with Lazard Freres since 1978, and is director of International Mining & Chemical Co. Other directors of Lazard Freres include its senior partner, Michel David Weill, head of the Paris house of Lazard Freres; Donald C. Cook, SEC financial examiner 1935-45, director Office of Alien Property Custodian for Dept. of Justice, 1946-47, commissioner SEC 1949-53, and is now director of ABC, Amerada Hess, chmn of the board American Electric Power and director of General Dynamics, the defense oriented firm; Felix Rohatyn, born in Austria, came to U.S. 1942, married Jeannette Streit, daughter of Clarence Streit, head of Union. Now with England; Rohatyn joined Lazard Freres in 1948, is director of Schlumberger, MCA, American Motors, Owens Illinois, Engelhardt Mining & Chemical, Pfizer, ITT, and Rockefeller Bros. Fund; he is chmn Municipal Assistance Corp., which bailed New York City out of its approaching bankruptcy; Frank C. Zarb, asst. to President of the U.S. 1974-77, administrator Federal Energy Administration 1974-77, now director of Philbro Corp., Engelhard Mining & Chemical, and the Energy Fund.

The Houston-Cleveland axis interlocks with many political figures, including W. Michael Blumenthal, Secretary of the Treasury 1977-79, who interlocks with the axis through Chemical Bank, Equitable Life and the Rockefeller Foundation; Robert B. Anderson, Secretary of Treasury 1957-61, partner of the law firm of Stroock Stroock & Lavan which administers the Warburg family finances, and interlocks with this group through Equitable Life, ITT and PanAm; G.William Miller, chmn Federal Reserve Board of Governors 1978-79, Secretary of the Treasury

1979-81, interlocks with this group through Textron and First City Bancorporation, was chmn of U.S.-U.S.S.R. Trade & Economic Council, now director of Federated Dept. Stores whose directors include three directors of Chase Manhattan Bank and interlocks with Citibank and Kuhn, Loeb Co.

The political power of this Rothschild-controlled axis was demonstrated by the ease with which they financed the campaigns of two governors of supposedly conservative Southern states, John D. Rockefeller IV. in West Virginia, and Charles Robb, son-in-law of Lyndon B. Johnson, in Virginia, heir to the Connally-Brown & Root First City Bancorp political clout.

The May 1976 staff rept. of the House Banking & Currency Committee noted another Rothschild affiliate (p.60),

> "The Rothschild banks are affiliated with Manufacturers Hanover of London (in which they hold 20% interest, a merchant bank, and Manufacturers Hanover Trust of N. Y."

Manufacturers Hanover recently bought the giant CIT Financial Corp. for $1.6 billion in October, 1983.

Despite his reputed wealth, the elder J.P. Morgan did not leave one of the great American fortunes when he died in 1913; it was first estimated at $75 million, then 50, and finally disclosed there were only $19 million of securities in the entire estate, of which $7 million was owed to the art dealer Duveen. J.P. Morgan Jr. (known to a very few intimates as Jack) was embarrassed to find he had to sell off many of his father's art treasures to pay the debts of the estate. Most of the huge sums handled by J.P. Morgan went directly to the Rothschilds. In 1905, the *New York Times* noted in its obituary of Baron Alphonse de Rothschild that he possessed some $60 million in American securities, although the Rothschilds, according to most financial authorities, had never been active in American finance.

Lincoln Steffens noted,

> "Senator Aldrich is a great man to me; not personally, but as leader of the Senate. He, Aldrich, bows to J.P. Morgan. The other day J.P. Morgan came to Washington, and he and I and Aldrich had a conference. And I noticed how he,

Morgan, addressed himself to me, not to Aldrich. Morgan talked to me, while I talked to Aldrich, who talked to Morgan."

Morgan's partner, George W. Perkins, worked furiously to obtain Theodore Roosevelt's nomination as McKinley's running mate. During Roosevelt's presidency, his closest advisor was George W. Perkins. Despite Roosevelt's nickname of "trustbuster", he protected Morgan's interests throughout his term of office. His successor, William Howard Taft, was opposed to Morgan, and introduced anti-trust legislation to control two Morgan trusts, International Harvester and U.S. Steel. Perkins then created the Progressive Party in 1912 to split the party and defeat Taft.

J.P. Morgan's apex of power was attained in the Panic of 1907, when he assumed control of Wall Street. Oakleigh Thorne, president of the Trust Co. of America, a victim of the "panic", testified before a Congressional Committee that

> "his bank had been subjected to only moderate withdrawals, that he had not applied for help, and that it was Morgan's sore point statement alone that had caused the run on his bank... that Morgan interests took advantage of the unsettled conditions during the autumn of 1907 to precipitate the panic, guiding it shrewdly as it progressed so that it would kill off rival banks and consolidate the preeminence of the banks within the Morgan orbit."

Morgan's financial power came from control of the enormous cash flow of the nation's biggest life insurance companies. He gained control of Mutual Life, New York Life, Metropolitan Life, and with George F. Baker and James Stillman, bought controlling interest in Equitable from Thomas Fortune Ryan, who had acquired it from the Hyde family. Hyde originally set Equitable up while acting as a front for Jacob Schiff and James Speyer.

On June 7, 1933, Nation noted

> "J.P. Morgan is generally regarded as the most prominent banker in the world."

Paul Y. Anderson mentioned in this article that testimony before the Senate Banking Committee showed that Morgan and his partners, including Thomas W. Lamont and E.T. Stotesbury, paid no federal income tax in 1931-32; the partners paid a total of $48,000 in 1930. Anderson remarked,

> "Is there any mystery as to why the Marines were dispatched against Haiti, San Domingo, and Nicaragua when those countries defaulted, or threatened to default, on the debt payments to American banks? It has been shown that the Morgan firm had a certain selected list of 'clients' to whom it sold stock at figures substantially under market prices. In the case of the Allegheny Corp. these fair-haired boys got the stock at 20, when the market was 35."

Anderson pointed out that these fortunate few could have sold the stock immediately for almost double what they had paid. Among the recipients of these Morgan favors he listed Senator McAdoo, Justice Owen Roberts, Secretary Woodin, Owen D. Young, and John J. Raskob.

In *Nation*, June 21, 1933, Anderson continued,

> "When Ft. Sumter was fired on, gold began to leave the country. The man who later said 'Don't sell America short' then took a flyer on the short side of America. He borrowed 2 million in gold coins and shipped it to London. This was really a blow behind the lines. Then he went to the 'gold room' to watch the effect. There was a scramble for gold to pay commitments abroad and this patriotic American with 2 million in eagles in London sold at his own price."

In March, 1929, perhaps in preparation for the coming storm, two Morgan banks merged, the National Bank of Commerce, which, according to the *New York Times* had "important foreign connections", and Guaranty Trust, forming a $2 billion institution. On Feb. 26, 1929, the *New York Times* noted,

> "The Guaranty Trust has long been known as one of the 'Morgan group'. The National Bank of Commerce has also been identified with Morgan interests."

J.P. Morgan's longtime associate, George Fisher Baker, was one of the founders of First National Bank, purchasing 30 shares in 1863 for $3000. He also was cashier, and later became president. Sheridan A. Logan's book, *George F. Baker and his Bank*, privately printed, 1981, noted that

> "a European syndicate headed by N.M. Rothschild was represented in New York by August Belmont and First National Bank to refund the Government debt. Baker wrote a letter Aug. 29, 1876, 'I have to advise you that our negotiations with the Treasury Dept. resulted in a contract between Messrs. N.M. Rothschild & Sons and others and the Secretary of the Treasury for the purpose of forty million dollars of U.S. 41.2 per cents of 1891, with an option on the remainder, $260 million. In this contract the bank participated to the extent of 10%, $4 million'."

Logan also states that

> "In 1901 Baker sold to J.P. Morgan $23 million stock in Central Railroad of New Jersey. The mutual confidence and respect which developed between Mr. Baker and Mr. Morgan cemented their increasingly close relationship and the First National Bank became more and more the unswerving ally and valuable source of mobile funds for the work of J.P. Morgan & Co."

In 1901, Baker increased the stock of First National Bank from $500,000 to $10 million by a 1900% stock dividend. He organized First Security Co., a holding company, with this dividend. During the 1929 boom, Baker's personal fortune reached the $500 million mark. His son, George Jr. pleaded with him to pay of the $29 million owed on stocks in First Security's $80 million portfolio. Baker, then 89 years old, had not been informed of the planned credit contraction, possibly because the insiders feared he might gossip about it. He continued to refuse to sell any stocks; the crash of 1929 reduced his fortune to $200 million. When he died in 1931, the estate was appraised at $73 million; his son, George Jr. inherited $30 million. His health had been shattered by the strain of working with his father during the desperate days of 1929, and he died of a heart attack in Honolulu, aged 59. His son, George F. Ill was found shot at Horseshoe Plantation, Fla. in 1977. George Ill's son, Grenville, was found shot at Tallahassee, Fla. in 1949, at age 33. George Jr.'s daughter,

Edith Brevoort Baker, married Jacob Schiff's grandson; John Mortimer Schiff, in 1934, uniting two of America's largest fortunes. George Baker F s daughter Florence had married Howard Bligh St. George in 1891, member of one of England's oldest families. Their grand daughter Priscilla married Angier Biddle Duke in 1937, and second, Allen A. Ryan Jr. in 1941, a relative of the Delanos.

In 1935, Gen. Smedley D. Butler wrote in the Nov. issue of *Common Sense* of his Marine career,

> "I helped make Mexico and especially Tampico safe for American oil interests in 1914. I helped make Haiti and Cuba a decent place for the National City Bank boys to collect revenues in... I helped purify Nicaragua for the international banking house of Brown Bros, in 1909-12. In China in 1927 I helped see to it that Standard Oil went its way unmolested. In 1899 J.P. Morgan floated the first important foreign loan on behalf of the Mexican Government. In 1901 he lent $50 million to the British Government to fight the Boer War. But it was mainly into the countries of Spanish America that American capital found its way."

Butler continued his revelations in the Dec. 1935 issue,

> "In 1910, six months after the Nicaraguan Revolution which ousted President Zelaya, his successor, Dr. Madris, grew cold towards the Nicaraguan investments of Brown Bros, and Seligman Co. Another revolution immediately 'occurred'."

Butler mentions the Latin American activities of Brown Bros., now Brown Bros. Harriman, a firm little known to most Americans. In 1801, a linen auctioneer from Belfast, Alexander Brown, established a banking house, Alexander Brown & Co. in the slave trading port of Baltimore. It is now the oldest banking house in the U.S. Its English branch, Brown Shipley, also became influential, its most well-known member being Lord Montague Norman, Governor of the Bank of England for many years, 1907-44, longer than any other man in history. *Current Biography* 1940, noted,

> "There is an informal understanding that a director of Brown Shipley should be on the board of the Bank of England and Norman was elected to it in 1907."

In expanding Rothschild investments in U.S. railroads, Kuhn, Loeb Co. found a useful agent in E.H. Harriman. A young man on the make, Harriman married the daughter of the president of a small New York railroad, and soon looked for more worlds to conquer. George Redmond writes in *Financial Giants of America*

> "He (Harriman) early won the confidence of Kuhn, Loeb Co. and established relations which later became most advantageous to both."

Kuhn, Loeb financed the Union Pacific takeover by Harriman.

H.J. Eckenrode notes in *E.H. Harriman*,

> "In his takeover of UP, Harriman had behind him tremendous financial force — not only Kuhn, Loeb Co. with funds from Frankfurt and Berlin, but the National City Bank, 'the greatest source of cash in the country'".

Harriman employed Judge Robert Scott Lovett as general counsel for Union Pacific. When Harriman and Otto Kahn were summoned by the ICC in 1897, Lovett advised them to refuse to answer all questions about their stock operations. In 1908, the Supreme Court upheld their refusal to talk. The records of this case, SC No. 133 US v. UP Ry, later disappeared from the Library of Congress. In 1911, the Equitable Life Insurance building, which contained all the records of the UP RR, burned, destroying all UP papers to that date. Lovett's son, Robert Abercrombie Lovett married Adele Brown, daughter of a partner of Brown Bros, and became partner in 1926. He was Special Asst. Sec. of War 1940-45, under secretary of state, 1947-49, dep. secretary of Defense 1950-51, secretary of Defense 1951-53. It was Lovett who took the then Secretary of Defense James Forrestal, of Dillon Read Co. to Fishers Island to persuade him to change his stand against U.S. Middle Eastern policies. Forrestal refused, and was placed in a mental ward at the National Institute of Health, where he fell out of the window. Lovett then replaced him as Secretary of Defense.

Brown Bros, backed the B & O steamship line in 1887, and went into joint venture with J & W Seligman Co. on a number of South American loans. In 1915, Brown Bros, combined with J.P. Morgan to float a series of Latin American loans, which in many instances were followed by revolutions in the respective countries. In the *Nation*, June 7, 1922, Oswald Garrison Villard noted,

> "The Republic of Brown Bros with J & W Seligman had reduced Haiti, Santo Domingo, and Nicaragua to the status of colonies with ruinous loans. Most of the loans were repaid in 1924."

In 1931, W. Averell Harriman, son of E.H. Harriman, merged his banking house, W.A. Harriman & Co. with Brown Bros, to form the present firm of Brown Bros. Harriman. In 1933, Brown Bros. Harriman backed the expansion of CBS, in which they have maintained a large position. The Brown Bros, firm occupied offices on the corner of Wall Street and Hanover which had been occupied by J.L. & J.S. Joseph Co., the American representatives of the Rothschilds. Josephs went broke in the Panic of 1837, having been cut loose by the Rothschilds, who were now operating through August Belmont and George Peabody & Co. W. Averell Harriman brought to the new firm his vice president, Prescott Sheldon Bush, who had been with him since 1926. Bush became chairman of the Board of Pennsylvania Water & Power Co., director U.S. Rubber, PanAm, CBS, Dresser Mfg Co. Vanadium, U.S. Guaranty, Prudential Insurance and partner Brown Bros Harriman. He was chmn National War Fund 1943-44 and chmn USO. His son George Bush is now president of the U.S. George Herbert Walker, grandfather of George Bush, who was named after him, became president of W.A. Harriman Co. in 1928 - now Brown Bros. Harriman). He was director of Belgian-American Coke Ovens Corp., chmn Habershaw Cable Corp., chmn International Great Northern Railway, director Certain Teed Products, American Shipping & Commerce Corp., American International Corporation, Cuba Railway Co., Pennsylvania Coal & Coke. He was the donor of the Walker Cup, the prestigious golf trophy, and president of the U.S. Golf Association. In 1925, he financed the building of Madison Square Garden. His son, George H. Walker Jr. became chmn

Walker-Bush Oil Corp., and Zapata Petroleum (George Bush's firm), Silesian Holdings, with W.A. Harriman City Investing Corp., Westmoreland Coal. Co. and West Indies Sugar Co. He is a trustee of Yale. George H. Walker III merged the firm of G.H. Walker Co. with Laird & Co. and White & Weld in 1974. He is now a senior vice pres. of White & Weld.

Some Americans see George Bush's rapid rise to the Presidency as evidence of the power of the Trilateralists. But Bush's stars go back much farther than the Trilaterals. He is a distant cousin of the Queen of England, the Black Nobility which traces its power back some five thousand years, and his family firm, Brown Brothers Harriman, has represented the Bank of England here since the early 1800s. Through service to the Harrimans, the Bush family achieved the position of a third rank family in the hierarchy of dynastic families. The World Order dynastic families of the first rank are the Rothschild, and the ruling aristocracy of England and Europe, most of whom have owned stock in the Bank of England since 1700. The second rank of dynastic families consist of those who serve as courtiers to the first rank. The second rank includes families such as the Rockefellers, the Morgans, and the Harrimans, By becoming servants of a dynastic family of the second rank, the Harrimans, the Bush family entered the ranks of the third group of dynastic families of the World Order. When Averill Harriman began doing business with Moscow in 1921, he dealt directly with Felix Dzerzhinsky, head of Cheka, now known as the KGB. Harriman and other Western financiers linked to the terrorist activities of Dzerzhinsky became known as The Trust. They worked through a number of firms located in the Equitable Trust Building at 120 Broadway in New York's financial district. These firms included E.H. Harriman Co., American International Corp., Dresser Industries, J.P. Morgan Co., and Equitable Trust. As members of the Trust, the owners of these firms served as a colonial government of the Soviet Union, as illustrated by the fact that Averill Harriman spent most of the Second world War at Stalin's side in Moscow, directing the Russian war effort.

George Bush's assets are held in a blind trust while he serves as President of the United States. The blind trust is handled by a family friend named William Stamps Farish II. His father founded Humble Oil Corp. in 1917, raising capital for the venture from Walter C. Teagel, president of Standard Oil. Farish later succeeded Teagle as president of Standard Oil, and has always been known as "a Rockefeller man". He married into the wealthy Rice family of Houston, whose progenitor had been murdered by his secretary and a crooked lawyer in order to prevent his fortune from being donated to Rice Institute. The killers were sent to prison, and the institute was built. William Farish II and the Queen of England have much in common; their families collected royalties on each gallon of gasoline burned by the Nazi planes which nightly bombed London. Because of these memories, Queen Elizabeth stays in only one private home in America when she visits here - the Farish home. Each autumn, President Bush hunts quail on the 10,000 acre Lazy F. Ranch at Beeville, Texas, one of Farish's many lavish estates, he is a director of Pogo Producing, formed as a spinoff of Pennzoil by Chemical Bank, and Manufacturer's Hanover Bank (Rothschild).

When George Bush formed Zapata Oil Co. with Hugh and Bill Liedtke in 1953, the partners were unwilling to choose a name from American history, such as Washington or Lee. Instead, they named their firm after one of Mexico's most blood thirsty Communist terrorists, General Emiliano Zapata. From its outset, the firm was involved heavily in CIA activities. In 1961, when the CIA planned the Bay of Pigs invasion, George Bush resided in Houston, where he worked secretly with George de Mohrenschildt, an oil man who is now believed to have been a Soviet plant. An entry in de Mohrenshildt's personal phone book show Bush, George H. W. (Poppy) 1412 W. Ohio, and also Zapata Petroleum Midland. This phone book was found after de Mohrenschildt's "suicide". The top secret name for the CIA Bay of Pigs plan, known only to a few top people, was Operation Zapata. Col. Fletcher Prouty, formerly with the Chiefs of Staff, was responsible for securing ordinance for the Bay of Pigs invasion. He obtained two ships from the Navy which were sent to Elizabeth City, N.C. to be remitted for the invasion. New names were painted on these ships, Barbara, and Houston, J. Edgar Hoover wrote a memorandum on Nov. 29, 1963 after the JFK assassination that Mr. George Bush of the CIA was assessing the reaction of Cuban exiles in Miami. Bush had begun service with the CIA in 1960, using his oil business as a cover. Zapata Oil may have been one of the CIA (The Company) firms from its outset.

Besides Farish, Bush's other close friend is Nicholas Brady, senior partner of Dillon Read, a New York investment house. Brady was the personal protege of C. Douglas Dillon, head of the firm, who has an enormous estate at Short Hills, N.J. Brady was brought up on the neighboring estate, a 4,000 acre spread only a few miles from Manhattan. Dillon Read was founded by Clarence Dillon (Lapowski) of Texas, who bought the firm from William Read of New York. His son served as Secretary of the Treasury for years. He is one of America's silent billionaires, his enormous fortune never reported in the press. Bush appointed Nicholas Brady as his Secretary of the Treasury. He confers daily with Brady.

Harriman was the go-between of Churchill and Roosevelt's World War II alliance. The two leaders did not know or particularly like each other; each of them conferred with W. Averell Harriman about how to talk to the other, and carefully followed his advice.

W. A. Harriman served as U.S. Ambassador at large during World War II, principally in Moscow with Stalin; his brother E. Roland was president of the American Red Cross, Robert A. Lovett was Secretary of Defense. Harriman was related by marriage to Wild Bill Donovan, founder of the OSS.

Brown Bros, has always maintained close relations with British firms. James Brown, partner from 1935-50 was director Northern Assurance of London, Sun Insurance, pres. British Empire Club and National Bank of Nicaragua. Thatcher M. Brown, another partner, was director of Manchester Land Co., National Bank of Nicaragua, chairman of the board of Liverpool and London Insurance Co. Ltd., Globe Indemnity Co., Royal Insurance, British and Foreign Marine Insurance Ltd., American London & Empire Co., Ocean Accident & Guaranty of London, and Thames & Mersey Marine Insurance Co.

The *New York Times* noted May 29, 1928,

> "Dr. Rudolf Roesler, representative of the New York banking house of Brown Bros, said Germany for a number of years to come would be a borrowing nation. Brown Bros, had loaned the City of Berlin $15 million on 6% 30 yr. bonds and Mr. Roesler, who completed details of the transaction said that 'it was the biggest loan to a city in Europe since 1914'."

The *New York Times* later noted,

> "Word was received here yesterday by J. Henry Schroder Banking Corp., representative in the U.S. for Capt. Alfred Lowenstein, that a corporation organized by the Belgian capitalist and French associates, whom it has offered the public in Paris, had been oversubscribed twenty-five times."

The holding company for artificial silk shares was offered at $117.50 and promptly went to 200. This good news was somewhat palled by the *Times* report that a syndicate had been formed to handle this stock since

> "Capt. Alfred Lowenstein whose reported death through a fall from an airplane in the English Channel July 4th has been surrounded by mystery. J.Henry Schroder is to purchase $25 million of bonds of International Holding and Investment Corp. through Albert Pam, of J.Henry Schroder London, and Albert Svarvasy, head of British Foreign and Colonial Corp., British investing company."

The July 5, 1928 *New York Times* headlined, CAPT. LOWENSTEIN FALLS FROM PLANE. Known as Mystery Man. Alfred Lowenstein was known as a Croesus.

> "The 'mystery man of Europe', the successor to Sir Basil Zaharoff as a man of mystery, in European finance. The pilot informed the authorities that while the plane was crossing the sea, Capt. Lowenstein, wishing to go to the washroom, opened the wrong door and fell out. His valet and two stenographers as well as the pilot and mechanic of the plane were present, but did not notice what happened."

The story added that Lowenstein owned eight villas in Biarritz, an estate in Lancashire, a castle in Brussels, and a townhouse in London.

Informed observers believed it was Zaharoff himself who dethroned the pretender to his title as "mystery man of Europe". Lowenstein had become involved in a desperate struggle with Zaharoff and his associate, Dreyfus Clavell, to control the artificial silk industry in Europe. After Lowenstein's accident, his two associates in this struggle also died mysteriously. M.M. Ayrich had an automobile accident on a deserted road, with no witnesses. Lowenstein's third associate, Prince Radziwill, was poisoned by a woman friend, according to a French journal, *La Crapouille*.

The Robert Maxwell case parallels in many ways the Lowenstein affair. After Maxwell's sudden death in a "fall" from his yacht, more than two billion dollars was found to have been siphoned from his many enterprises. The money will never be recovered. Maxwell had been identified as an agent of Mossad, Israeli Intelligence, shortly before his demise. It is believed Mossad had him disposed of to prevent him from testifying about his operations for Mossad.

W. Averell Harriman was 78 when his wife died. A year later, Katharine Meyer Graham, publisher of the *Washington Post*, invited him to a party to meet Pam Churchill, daughter of Lord Digby, an English horse fancier. She had been married to Randolph Churchill, and was mother of the present Winston Churchill. She then married into the first family of Hollywood, producer Leland Hayward, formerly married to actress Margaret Sullavan. In *Haywire*, her autobiography, Brooke Hayward describes her stepmother as "a cold-blooded golddigger who made off with her mother's jewels". Pam dated Elie de Rothschild before deciding to marry Harriman. They are now the dominant figures in the Democratic Party. Harriman has given $15 million to the Russian Institute at Columbia, (now the Harriman Institute).

Another prominent banking house is the firm of Dillon Read. Clarence Dillon (1882-1979) was born in San Antonio, Texas, son of Samuel and Bertha Lapowsky or Lapowitz. He graduated from Harvard in 1905, married Anne Douglass of Milwaukee, whose father owned Milwaukee Machine & Tool Co. They went abroad from 1908 to 1910.

Their son, C. Douglas Dillon, was born in Switzerland in 1909. In 1912, Dillon met William A. Read, founder of a well-known Wall Street bond brokerage, through a Harvard classmate. They became partners. Read died suddenly in 1916, and Dillon bought control of the firm. During World War I, Dillon served as Bernard Baruch's right-hand man at the War Industries Board. In 1915, Dillon had set up American & Foreign Securities Corp. to finance the French Government's purchases of munitions in the U.S. His right-hand man at Dillon Read was James A. Forrestal, who later died while serving as Secretary of Defense. Dillon Read played a crucial role in rearming Hitler during the preparation for World War II. In 1957, *Fortune* Magazine listed Clarence Dillon as one of the richest men in the U.S. ($150-200 million). By normal growth rates, his son C. Douglas Dillon should be worth over $1 billion, but nobody knows. C. Douglas Dillon worked with John Foster Dulles on the Dewey campaigns, and served as Under Secretary of State, helping Bechtel Corp. obtain its first large Saudi Arabian contracts, which later became a $135 billion operation. Dillon was Ambassador to France 1953-57, later became Secretary of the Treasury. He was chairman of the Rockefeller Foundation from 1971-75, then chairman of the Brookings Institution. To organize his estate, he sold Dillon Read to the Bechtel Corp. He is considered to be one of the ten wealthiest men in the U.S. and one of the three most powerful.

Second to the Rothschilds, the Warburgs were considered the most important international banking family of the 19th and 20th centuries. In 1798, two sons of Marcus Gumprich Warburg, Moses Marcus and Gerson W. founded M.M. Warburg Co. in Hamburg. They were descendants of Simon von Cassel, a 16th century moneylender and pawnbroker. They were also direct descendants of Abraham del Banco, largest banker in Venice. When they moved north, they took the name of Warburg, after Cassel settled in this Westphalian town. In 1814, the Warburgs became one of the first affiliates of N.M. Rothschild of London. They were related to the leading banking families of Europe, the Rosenbergs of Kiev, the Gunzburgs in St. Petersburg, the Oppenheims and Goldschmidts in Germany. Moritz Warburg was apprenticed to the Rothschilds in Italy and Paris, and later married Charlotte Oppenheim, whose family were diamond merchants in Frankfort. They had five sons, known as "the Five Hamburgers"; the oldest, Aby, founded the Warburg Institute; Max financed the German struggle in World War I and later, the Nazi regime; Dr. Fritz Warburg was German commercial attache in Stockholm during World War I; Paul and Felix emigrated to America and joined the firm of Kuhn, Loeb & Co. with Jacob Schiff, who had been born in the Rothschild house in Frankfort. Paul wrote the Federal Reserve Act and saw it through Congress. He represented the U.S. at the Versailles Peace Conference, while his brother Max represented German interests.

The Memoirs of Max Warburg state,

> "The Kaiser thumped the table violently and shouted 'Must you always be right?', but then listened carefully to Max's view of financial matters."

M.M. Warburg Co. closed during World War II but reopened in 1970. George Sokolsky noted in *We Jews*,

> "Even in Hitler Germany the firm of Max Warburg was exempted from persecution. Max left for the U.S. in 1939, unhampered by supposed restrictions on Jews."

The U.S. Naval Secret Service Report Dec. 2, 1918 noted:

> "PAUL WARBURG. German, nationalized U.S. citizen 1911, decorated by Kaiser, handled large sums furnished by German bankers for Lenin & Trotsky. Has brother Max who is director of espionage system of Germany."

In partnership with Walter Teagle of Standard Oil, Paul Warburg organized the international dye trust, I.G. Farben and Agfa Ansco Film Trust. At the second annual convention of the American Acceptance Council, Dec. 2, 1920, President Paul Warburg said,

> "It is a great satisfaction to report that during the year under review it was possible for the American Acceptance Council to further develop and strengthen its relations with the Federal Reserve System."

He did not add that as vice chairman of the Federal Reserve Board from 1914-18, he had organized the Federal Reserve System, or that he served as president of the Federal Advisory

Council from 1918-27, which actually formulated policy for the Board. He was director of Union Pacific, B&O Rys, National Railways of Mexico, Western Union, Wells Fargo, American IG Chemical, Agfa Ansco, Westinghouse, Warburg Banks in Amsterdam, London and Hamburg, and chairman of the board of International Acceptance Bank. His brother Felix was chief financial banker of the Zionist Organization of America, Palestine Economic Corp., National Railways of Mexico, Prussian Life Insurance of Berlin, and many other companies. Felix's son Edward M.M. Warburg succeeded Gen. Donovan as Coordinator of Information in 1941 and later served as special political advisor to Gen. Eisenhower at SHAEF, London during World War II. His other son Frederick was Herbert Lehman's right-hand man in organizing the Lehman Corp., and was later known as "the foreign minister of Kuhn, Loeb" because of his many contacts around the world. He retired as a country gentleman at his estate Snake Hill, Middleburg, Va. His partner, Lewis L. Strauss had a magnificent estate nearby at Brandy Station, site of the Civil War engagement which was the largest cavalry battle in U.S. history.

Dept. of Commerce figures show that Kuhn, Loeb controlled 64% of all railroad mileage in the U.S. in 1900, which dropped to a mere 41% by 1939. In 1900, Kuhn, Loeb and J.P. Morgan, representing the Rothschilds, controlled 93% of all railway mileage in the U.S. Speyer & Co. controlled N.Y. real estate and South American minerals, Seligman & Co. sugar, public utilities, and Latin American loans, August Belmont, the New York subway system, Lazard Freres, gold and silver, specializing in international gold movements.

U.S. News May 14, 1984 listed Who Runs America; the first ten included Weinberger and Shultz of Bechtel Corp.; the second ten included Sulzberger of the *New York Times*, vice pres. Bush, David Rockefeller; the third ten included Katharine Graham and Henry Kissinger. Former president Gerald Ford was not listed; he is now director of GK Technologies, a $1.19 billion firm with large defense contracts.

Other leading defense firms are United Technologies; Scovill Corp. whose chairman Malcolm Baldrige is now Secretary of

Commerce; directors include Daniel Pomeroy Davison of J.P. Morgan bank and president U.S. Trust; Olin Corp., $1.85 billion; and General Dynamics, controlled by the Crown family of Chicago.

When Texaco swallowed the $12 billion Getty Oil corp. after its founder died, it showed the financial power of the London Connection; Directors of Texaco included Willard C. Butcher, former chmn of Chase Manhattan; Earl of Granard (*Forbes*) (the first baronet had reduced Sligo for William III), and grandson of Ogden Mills, Secretary of Treasury U.S. 1932-33; Thomas H. Moorer, chmn Joint Chfs of Staff 1970-74, director Fairchild Bunker Ramo; Robert V. Roosa, director Brookings Institution, Trilateral Commission.

The Rothschild Houston-Cleveland axis brought off one of its greatest coups when its agent John Connally, then Secretary of the Treasury, persuaded Nixon to abandon the gold standard.

The *New York Times* headlined, Aug. 16, 1971,

> "SEVERS LINK BETWEEN DOLLAR AND GOLD. President Nixon announced tonight that henceforth the U.S. would cease to convert foreign held dollars into gold — unilaterally changing the 25 year old international monetary system. The President said he was taking the action to stop 'the attacks of foreign monetary speculators against the dollar'. The change in the world monetary system brought about by the Presidential decision to cease converting foreign held dollars into gold is entirely uncertain. That was the word used by Secretary Treasury John B. Connally. Mr. Connally said he did not know what would happen."

The *Times* noted that

> "Advice to impose some controls has been given the President from such sources as David Rockefeller, chmn of the $23 billion Chase Manhattan Corp., and the Organization for Economic Development, a group representing 22 nations."

The *Times* editorially stated,

"We unhesitatingly applaud the boldness with which the President has moved on all economic fronts — an admiration for the completeness with which the President has junked the do-nothing approach that immobilised the country and sapped the national will."

Volcker conferred with leading European financial officials here today on President Nixon's new policy to meet the dollar crisis. He hinted broadly that the U.S. would be happy if other countries let their currencies float in the exchange markets. Their value would presumably rise in relation to the dollar. Mr. Volcker said he had found a 'very good understanding' in his meeting. But at the end of a confusing day in European ministries and banks, few thought they could see a clear way out of the immediate monetary chaos caused by Mr. Nixon's moves.

Advance knowledge of such a far-reaching change in the monetary system would be worth billions of dollars.

On 17 Aug. 1971, the *Times* quoted Paul Volcker, Under Secretary of the Treasury, who, when asked if other currencies would rise in relation to the dollar, replied,

"I think we are in no position to object."

EUSTACE MULLINS

CHAPTER SIX

THE CIA

On May 24, 1979, a 14 ft. bronze statue of General William J. Donovan was dedicated in front of Columbia University's Law School. The dedication speech was delivered by John J. McCloy, who had been Asst. Sec. of War when Donovan founded the Office of Strategic Services in World War II. When Donovan died on Feb. 8, 1959, the Director of the Central Intelligence Agency, Allen W. Dulles, sent a message to all CIA stations around the world,

> "Bill Donovan was the father of central intelligence. He was a great leader."

International intelligence, or, as it was formerly known, espionage, was not founded by either Donovan or Dulles, who were merely employees of the World Order. The Order founded international espionage to protect their far reaching investments and dealings in slaves, drugs and gold, the commodities on which their wealth was built.

On Nov. 17, 1843, the Port of Shanghai was opened to foreign traders. Lot No. 1 was rented by Jardine Mathieson & Co. Other entrepreneurs were Dent & Co., and Samuel Russell, an American who represented Baring Brothers. Captain Warren Delano, Franklin D. Roosevelt's grandfather, became a charter member of the Canton Regatta Club, and entered into dealings with the Hong Society. Dr. Emmanual Josephson states,

> "Warren Delano, Frederic A. Delano's father, founded his fortune on smuggling opium into China."

His son, Frederic A. Delano, was born in Hong Kong, and later became the first vice chairman of the Federal Reserve Board in 1914.

Although he was the son of an Irish ward heeler, William J. Donovan studied law at Columbia from 1903 to 1908. His grades were said to be "atrocious", but one of his professors, Harlan F. Stone, took a liking to him. Another protege of Stone was J. Edgar Hoover. As Attorney General Stone shocked Washington by naming Hoover director of the Bureau of Investigation. Another Columbia professor who liked Donovan was Jackson E. Reynolds, later president of the First National Bank of N.Y. who backed Donovan's selection as head of OSS. One of Donovan's Columbia classmates was Franklin Delano Roosevelt.

In 1910, Donovan met Eleanor Robson, an actress who later married August Belmont, American representative of the Rothschilds. There was no question of their marriage — he was looking for a rich wife, she was looking for a rich husband — they began a relationship which lasted for years. Donovan also courted Blanche Lopez, of a wealthy tobacco family, who lived in Rumson, N.J. He then returned to Buffalo, where he opened a law practice. He met Ruth Rumsey, and abruptly dropped Blanche Lopez, never contacting her again. Ruth Rumsey was heiress of one of the richest families in America. Her father, Dexter Rumsey, and her uncle Bronson owned 22 of Buffalo 43 square miles. In 1890, Dexter Rumsey was worth $1 million. His wife was a member of the wealthy Hazard family of Rhode Island, who had owned one thousand slaves, and were the largest slave owners in America. The Rumseys were Masters of the Genesee Valley Hunt, the most exclusive hunt club in the U.S. Dexter Rumsey died in 1906, leaving his son and daughter 121.2% each of his fortune intrust. Bill Donovan's courtship of Ruth Rumsey was complicated by the reappearance in Buffalo of Eleanor Robson, now Mrs. August Belmont. She turned up at the Studio Club, an acting group run by Katharine Cornell's father, where Donovan had the juvenile lead. La Robson requested that Donovan come to her suite in New York each weekend for "drama lessons". Donovan then took the long train ride to New York City each weekend, causing considerable gossip in Buffalo, where he was already widely known for his philandering. Nevertheless, Ruth Rumsey had determined to marry him, probably because her family was so strongly opposed. Friends of the family stated that had Dexter Rumsey lived, he would never have allowed this marriage to take place, because of Donovan's age; he was 31; his religion, Irish Catholic; and his philandering. The Rumseys were Episcopalian, but Donovan persuaded his wife to bring up their children as Roman Catholics. His brother was a priest. After the marriage, Donovan and his wife moved into the Rumsey family mansion at 742 Delaware Ave. in Buffalo.

Because of his New York connections, the Rockefeller Foundation selected Donovan to go to Europe on a "War Relief Mission" in 1915, the first of many assignments from the World Order. He was to be separated from Ruth Donovan continually during the next three years. While in London, he worked with Ambassador Walter Nelson Page, William Stephenson, who later "advised" him on setting up the OSS, and Herbert Hoover. Donovan spent five weeks in Belgium as an observer with Hoover's Belgian Relief Commission.

When the U.S. entered World War I, Donovan helped organize the "Rainbow" Division, and was given command of the "Fighting 69th". He fought at Landes et Landes St. George, in the Meuse-Argonne sector, where, although wounded, he charged a German machine gun squad on Oct. 15, 1918 with his bayonet. For this feat, he was awarded the Congressional Medal of Honor. His bravery was the subject of wide publicity in the American press, and Current Biography later stated he was the most famous man in the A.E.F. He was with Joyce Kilmer, the poet, when Kilmer was shot down. In 1919 and 1920, Donovan was sent on secret missions to China and Siberia.

After the war, J.P. Morgan established the Foreign Commercial Corp. to float $2 billion in bonds in postwar Europe. In February, 1920, he asked Donovan to make a secret tour of Europe to obtain intelligence relating to these bonds. Cave Brown described this mission,

> "Having helped to finance the war, Morgan wished to help finance the peace by expanding the House of Morgan's

interests widely... These activities required the best intelligence from the best sources in Europe. Donovan and the Rainbow Division intelligence officer, Grayson Mallet-Prevost Murphy, had been retained by John Lord O' Brian's firm to obtain that intelligence, working in secrecy."

Morgan reportedly paid Donovan $200,000 for this operation.

During his European reconnaissance, Donovan met Adolf Hitler at Berchtesgaden, and spent an evening with him in his room at Pension Moritz. Donovan later claimed he had not known who Hitler was, but that he found him a "fascinating talker".

In 1922, Donovan was appointed U.S. District Attorney for New York. In 1924, Atty. Gen. Harlan F. Stone, Donovan's Columbia law professor, asked him to come to Washington as Asst Atty Gen. Donovan and his wife bought a house in Georgetown (later the home of Katharine Meyer) at 1637 30th St. Donovan's first official act was to demand that Stone fire J. Edgar Hoover from the Bureau of Investigation. Instead, Stone, who was Hoover's patron as well as Donovan's, appointed Hoover Director of the Bureau of Investigation Dec. 18, 1924. Donovan also became involved in another political football, the prosecution of Senator Burton K. Wheeler. Wheeler was defended by Senator Tom Walsh, one of the most powerful politicians in Washington, but Donovan, against all advice to the contrary, insisted on proceeding with the prosecution. It was said that the charges against Wheeler were "ludicrous", and Stone asked Donovan to drop the case, but he stubbornly proceeded to indict Wheeler before a District of Columbia grand jury. When the case was tried in Great Falls, the jury deliberated only ten minutes before bringing in a verdict of acquittal for Wheeler.

Such a boner would have destroyed the careers of most men in Washington, but Donovan was under the protection of Herbert Hoover, his associate from World War I. Between 1924 and 1928, he was Hoover's closest associate. Hoover took him to the Bohemian Club, the sacrosanct West Coast powerhouse where he was the directing figure. Hoover then persuaded President Coolidge to appoint Donovan to the Colorado River Commission, a seven state authority which organized the proposals for the Hoover Dam (later renamed the Boulder Dam by FDR, and still later, renamed the Hoover Dam by Act of Congress in 1947.) During the 1920s, Republican politicians favored the nomination of Dawes for president. Although it seemed that he was backing a sure loser, Donovan worked as Hoover's top strategist for four years. When Hoover was nominated on the first ballot at the Republican Convention (a tribute to the power of the Rothschilds), Donovan wrote his acceptance speech. It was understood that Donovan was to be Hoover's running mate. However, Hoover immediately realized that because he was running against Al Smith, a Roman Catholic, he would lose the massive anti-Catholic vote if he picked Donovan, also a Roman Catholic, as his running mate. Hoover had no intention of losing his trump card in the forthcoming election. He cast Donovan aside without a second thought, and even refused to consider him for a cabinet post, such as Attorney General, probably the only time in American politics that the architect of a successful Presidential campaign was denied a position on the team or in the Cabinet.

The disheartened Donovan decided to forego political life. In 1929, he organized the law firm of Donovan, Leisure, Newton and Irvine, with offices at 2 Wall St. He also took a 23 room suite at the Shoreham Hotel for the firm's Washington offices. During ensuing years, Donovan rarely saw his wife, although they were never legally separated. Dunlop's biography of Donovan notes that

> "He always had his pick of feminine admirers. To many of the women he met, Donovan was irresistible."

Ruth Donovan stayed at their summer home on the South Shore of Massachusetts, or at their New York apartment on Beekman Place.

Despite his disappointment with Hoover, Donovan continued to take an active role in national politics. He ran Knox's campaign for the Republican nomination in 1936, and his firm defended American Telephone and Telegraph in an anti-trust suit by the government. Donovan won handily, which brought in a new influx of business to his firm.

In 1937, Donovan renewed his association with the Rothschilds. The Viennese branch of the family had lost extensive holdings in Bohemia when the Nazis moved into Czechoslovakia. Because Donovan had already established a network of informants in the highest echelons of the Nazi government, including Admiral Canaris, the Rothschilds asked him to salvage their interests. He went to Germany to argue their case, but despite his important contacts, he was defeated by Hitler's view of the Rothschilds as a symbol of what he hoped to achieve in his battle against "the international bankers". The Rothschilds were not overly concerned; they knew that World War II was on its way, and that the outcome had been decided in advance.

Donovan won another important legal victory in 1937, when he and a staff of 57 lawyers defended IS oil firms against anti-trust charges. His clients were let off with nominal fines, and once again Donovan was considered the winner.

His German contacts now invited him to observe the Nuremberg maneuvers, as a guest of the German General Staff. He also accompanied them on a trip to observe the progress of the Spanish Civil War. Although he was there as an invited guest of "the Fascists", Donovan was soon to build the OSS around the hard core of the Communist Lincoln Brigade. He met Kim Philby in Spain, who was writing about the Civil War as a "pro-Nazi" journalist, a pose he carried off successfully despite his recent marriage to Litzi Friedmann, a fanatical Communist and Zionist provocateur.

On April 10, 1940, Donovan's daughter, Patricia wrecked her car near Fredericksburg, Va. and was killed. She was his only daughter; there was also one son, David, who married Mary Grandin, Patricia's roommate at boarding school, and heiress of a wealthy Philadelphia family. Associates said that Donovan never got over his daughter's death. Because he had received the Congressional Medal of Honor, Patricia was buried in Arlington National Cemetery. His grief-stricken wife left for a round the world cruise on Irving Johnson's ship, Yankee.

On May 29, 1940, William Stephenson arrived in New York with a letter to Donovan from Admiral Blinker Hall, a British Naval Intelligence officer whom Donovan had met in 1916. The letter proposed an American intelligence agency, although we were not at war. Franklin D. Roosevelt sent Donovan to London with orders to develop this program, as an "unofficial observer". Despite efforts at secrecy, there was widespread journalistic speculation about his mission for Roosevelt. He then made a tour of southeast Europe for the President, gauging the status of the German occupied countries. Although this was an obvious espionage mission, the Germans placed no obstacles in his path. They were anxious to maintain good relations with the United States.

After Donovan delivered his report to the President, he was named Coordinator of Information by the White House. Because he had had no experience in propaganda work, the office was later split into the Office of War Information, Executive Order 9128, and the Office of Strategic Services, Military Order of June 13, 1942. Donovan was placed in charge of the OSS.

The "new" agency was from the outset merely an outpost of British Intelligence. On Sept. 18, 1941, Col. E.I. Jacob, Churchill's military secretary, was informed by Maj. Desmond Morton Church, Churchill's liaison with the British secret service,

> "Another most secret fact of which the Prime Minister is aware is that to all intents and purposes U.S. Security is being run for them at the President's request by the British. A British officer sits in Washington with Mr. Edgar Hoover and General Bill Donovan for this purpose. It is of course essential that this fact should not be known."

For some months, Donovan had been living in a suite at the St. Regis Hotel in New York. He and William Stephenson had been meeting regularly since 1940 to organize the new agency. Stephenson was working directly under Col. Stewart Menzies, head of Special Operations Executive, the top British intelligence agency. As cover, Menzies was Colonel in the Life Guards, the escort troop of the King. Stephenson was head of SIS, (Special Intelligence Section). When Donovan had left for London July

15, 1940 on his mission for Roosevelt, Stephenson had wired London,

> "Col. Wm. J. Donovan, personally representing the President, left yesterday by clipper. U.S. Embassy not repeat not being informed."

This was a replay of the House-Wilson-Wiseman operation during World War I. Not only were the American people left in the dark, but concerned agencies were never told what the conspirators had planned. Donovan's London mission was a slap in the face to the U.S. Ambassador, Joseph Kennedy. Roosevelt called Donovan "my secret legs", and he assured Stephenson in a private interview, "I'm your biggest undercover agent."

In *A Man Called Intrepid*, Stephenson is quoted as saying that after April, 1939, "The President was one of us." It was also in 1939 that Roosevelt privately told Mackenzie King, Prime Minister of Canada and a longtime Rockefeller agent, "Our frontier is on the Rhine." This same book quotes Churchill as saying, on the eve of war, "We need Rockefeller and Rothschild." Stephenson replied, "I can find the Rockefellers and they'll support us. We can offer our secret intelligence in return for help."

Indeed, the Rockefellers gave Stephenson an entire floor rent free at Rockefeller Center, where the agency has operated ever since. A later book, *Intrepid's Last Case* notes that

> "What some would later call the secret SIS Secret Occupation of Manhattan began in 1940. By 1941, J. Edgar Hoover was complaining that the Rockefeller Center headquarters of British Security Coordination controlled an army of British secret agents, a group of nine distinct secret agencies. Attorney General Biddle was quoted as saying 'The truth is nobody knows anything about what Stephenson does.'"

Had "anyone" known, Stephenson would have had to be arrested and deported. German sailors were being deliberately murdered by Stephenson's provocateurs in New York as acts designed to force Hitler to declare war against the United States.

The INTREPID file in SOE (Stephenson's cover name) described it as

> "a reign of terror conducted by specially trained agents and fortified by espionage and intelligence in Occupied Europe."

Every act of Donovan and Stephenson was a violation of American neutrality. Donovan's law office at 2 Wall Street was next to the Passport Control Office. He had special passports prepared for Stephenson's British agents. Stephenson had offices at three locations, Hampshire House, Dorset Hotel, and Rockefeller Center. Allen Dulles had opened a branch office of Coordinator of Information at Rockefeller Center in 1940. He evicted all the tenants on the 25th floor of 30 Rockefeller Plaza, which was the floor above the UK Commercial Corporation, whose president was William Stephenson. This agency was set up after Stephenson complained on April 14, 1941 that Standard Oil was supplying the Germans through Spain, and that it was acting as a hostile and dangerous agency of the enemy. A 400 page report by Stephenson listing Standard Oil and other American corporations' dealings with the Germans was turned over to the FBI in 1941. J. Edgar Hoover prudently buried it.

Nelson Rockefeller, as Coordinator of Inter-American Affairs, covered up the supplying of German military forces from his South American subsidiaries. Listed in the Stephenson Report were Standard Oil, I.G. Farben, a subsidiary of Standard Oil; Ford Motor Co.; Bayer Aspirin (Sterling Drug); General Aniline and Film; Ansco; and International Telephone and Telegraph. Co. Sosthenes Behn, head of ITT, had hosted a lavish conference of German intelligence operatives at the Waldorf Astoria in 1940. The German director of ITT was Baron Kurt von Schroder, of the Schroder banking family of Cologne, London and New York, who was Hitler's personal banker.

The OSS was actually set up by four members of the British Chief of Staff: Lord Louis Mountbatten (formerly Battenberg), a cousin of the King, and related to the Frankfurt banking families, Rothschild and Cassel; Charles Hambro, director of Special Operations Executive, and director of Hambros Bank; Col. Stewart Menzies, head of Secret Intelligence Service; and

William Stephenson, in charge of SIS American operations. An ancestor of Col. Menzies had been a notorious Jacobite double agent during the last days of James IPs reign. The present Menzies was the son of Lady Holford; he married Lady Sackville, daughter of the 8th Earl de la Warre, of the Sackville-West family which owned historic Knole; second, he married Pamela Beckett, daughter of J. Rupert Beckett, chmn of Westminster Bank, now National Westminster Bank, one of England's Big Five. Menzies' mother-in-law was the daughter of Lord Berkeley Paget, Marquess of Anglesey. Menzies' daughter married Lord Edward Hay, Marquess of Tweedsdale, Earl of Kinoull, related to Countess of Errol. The present Sir Peter Menzies is a director of National Westminster Bank, treasurer of the giant Imperial Chemical Industries, and director of Commercial Union Assurance Co. In the British Who's Who, 1950, Col. Menzies noted that he had been appointed "C", head of MI6 from 1939-51, but in later editions, he omitted this information.

Ford states in his *Acknowledgements*,

> "Lord Mountbatten of Burma was a close personal friend of Donovan as one of the four members of the British Chief of Staff Committee which helped Donovan in the formation and operation of Office of Strategic Services."

The "American" secret service was never anything but a British operation, directed at all levels by representatives of the British Crown. OSS agents received advanced training for the European theater at Bletchley Park, British espionage headquarters. This site was chosen because it was only ten miles from Woburn Abbey, where Lord Beaverbrook's agent, Sefton Delmer, operated the British "dirty tricks" center and other propaganda activities. Woburn Abbey was the ancestral home of the Duke of Bedford, Marquess of Tavistock. The British Bureau of Psychological, Warfare operated as the Tavistock Institute.

The membership list of CFR members in 1946 reveals the names of many OSS and OWI operatives; Lyman Bryson, who was with the American Red Cross in Paris, 1918-19, chief of special operations, OWI, 1942, and a director of CBS; Thomas W. Childs, Rhodes Scholar, Paris representative of Sullivan &

Cromwell (the Dulles law firm), exec. asst. to British Govt. War Supply US, British Embassy, Washington, 1940-45, partner Lazard Freres 1945-48, holds Order of the British Empire, leader in English-Speaking Union; Nicholas Roosevelt, American Commission to Negotiate Peace, Paris, 1919, OWI, 1942-43; Joseph Barnes, director OWI's Foreign Operations, organized Willkie's world tour 1942, coined the phrase "One World", identified as a Communist agent; Elmo Roper, the famed pollster, OSS agent 1942-45; Gaudens Megaro, chief Italian Section OSS 194 1-45; Henry Sturgis Morgan, son of J.P. Morgan, director Pullman, General Electric; Shepard Morgan, London director OSS 1943-44, was with Federal Reserve Bank of New York 1916-24, director reparations payments Berlin 1924-30 supervised by Chase Natl Bank, later chmn Natl Bureau of Economic Research, the Rockefeller propaganda operation; John Gardner, OSS Europe 1944-45, then joined the Carnegie Corp.; Allen W. Dulles chief OSS Europe, director J. Henry Schroder, later first director CIA; John Haskell, OSS 1943-44, formerly with Natl City Co. 1925-31.

Another son of J.P. Morgan, Junius, was placed in charge of OSS finances. Paul Mellon and his brother-in-law, David Bruce joined OSS — Bruce was in charge of the London office, later was Ambassador to France. OSS also had operatives from the Vanderbilt, Archbold, DuPont and Ryan families, giving rise to the quip that OSS meant "Oh So Social". James Paul Warburg, son of Paul (who had written the Federal Reserve Act), was Donovan's personal assistant in setting up OSS. William J. Casey, present head of CIA, was chief of secret intelligence OSS Europe.

In Feb. 1981, OSS veterans held a gala reunion in New York. Present were Margaret Thatcher, Prime Minister of England; Julia Child; Beverly Woodner, Hollywood designer; John Shaheen, who had been chief of OSS Special Projects now a wealthy oil man; Ernest Cuneo, who had been liaison between OSS and FDR; Arthur Goldberg, labor lawyer and Zionist leader, later Supreme Court Justice and U.S. Ambassador to the U.N.; Bill Colby, later chief of CIA; and Temple Fielding, the travel authority who began his travel expertise with OSS. One of OSS' most famous agents who didn't show up, was Ho Chi Minh.

OSS agents became prominent members of "the new class" in Washington; Archibald MacLeish became Librarian of Congress; Ralph Bunche became U.S. Representative to the U.N.; S. Dillon Ripley became head of the Smithsonian.

Donovan had been chosen to head the OSS because of two decades in which he carried out secret missions for the Morgans, the Rockefellers and the Rothschilds. When he staffed the agency with known Communists, they offered no objection. He had earlier provided unpaid legal help for members of the Communist mercenary force, the Abraham Lincoln Brigade. Now he welcomed these veteran "anti Fascists" into OSS. Ford writes,

> "In the OSS employment of pro-Communists was approved at very high levels. OSS often welcomed the services of Marxist enthusiasts."

When J. Edgar Hoover, eager to embarrass a rival, sent agents to Donovan with FBI dossiers on Communist OSS employees, Donovan replied, "I know they're Communists-that's why I hired them." Donovan loaded OSS with such fanatical Communists that they became a joke in Washington. He appointed Dr. Maurice Halperin Chief Latin American Div. OSS. Halperin regularly altered the information which came across his desk to fit the current party line. He often kept his office locked, causing other OSS employees to joke that "Halperin must be having another cell meeting." After the war, J. Edgar Hoover testified before Congress about Halperin's Communist background. Halperin later moved to Moscow, then to Havana.

Despite the damning dossiers which J. Edgar Hoover maintained on leading Communists in the OSS, he could find no politician willing to buck FDR's three White House assistants, Hiss, Currie and White. Eleanor Roosevelt had been one of the most frenetic activists on behalf of the Lincoln Brigade. Joe Lash gave her a small bronze of a Communist soldier, which she kept on her desk for the rest of her life. Donovan even appointed Irving Goff head of OSS in Italy after the Salerno landing. Goff had been commander of the Lincoln Brigade, and was later chairman of the Communist Party in Louisiana and New York.

The Spanish Civil War had created an alliance between American "intellectuals" and the Communists. In *Passionate Years*, Peter Wyden reports that Archivist Victor A. Berch, of Brandeis University, said 40% of the Lincoln Brigade were Jewish. Oddly enough, the "Fascists", the Falange, was led by two Marranos, General Franco and his financial backer, Juan March. March paid for Franco's return to Spain with a $2 million credit at Kleinwort's of London. In July, 1936, March placed $82 million of securities in Nationalist accounts. He deposited $1.5 billion in gold at the Bank of Italy, 121.5 metric tons greater than the gold reserve of most nations.

The Communists stole the Spanish gold reserve and shipped it to Russia. NKVD General Alexander Orlov, on orders from "Ivan Vasilyevitch", a rare code name for Stalin, loaded Spain's gold reserve on the Soviet ship Komsomol Oct. 25, 1936; it arrived in Odessa Nov. 2, and was trucked to Moscow's Precious Metals Deposit, Gohkran, $788 million. $240 million had also been shipped to France from Spain.

The Lincoln volunteers surrendered their passports to NKVD officers when they arrived in Spain. These passports were then routinely used in Communist espionage. The murderer of Trotsky was arrested in Mexico with a Canadian passport issued to Tony Babich, who was killed in the Civil War. Gouzenko later exposed a Communist agent in Los Angeles using the passport of Ignacy Witczak. Witnesses saw stacks of these Lincoln passports stacked in the Lubianka prison, waiting to be used.

Ernest Hemingway wrote that "The Spanish Civil War was the happiest time of our lives." He modelled his hero in *For Whom the Bell Tolls* on Robert Merriman, a Moscow agent who was receiving a $900 a year fellowship from the University of California. Hemingway wrote and produced a film, *The Spanish Earth* to raise money for the Communists, aided by Archibald Macleish, Dashiell Hammett and Lillian Hellmann. Hemingway put up $2750 for the film, and donated all his royalties. He toured Hollywood to raise funds for the Communists, an effort reciprocated when they named his book *For Whom the Bell Tolls* a book-of-the-Month Club selection and a multi-million dollar Hollywood production. This was how one achieved "artistic success" in the 1940's.

The English contingent fighting in Spain for the Communists included Virginia Woolf's nephew, Julian Bell, who was killed, and Eric Blair, later known as George Orwell. He was in the front line for 112 days before being wounded. He later wrote *1984* a propaganda coup for the World Order which claimed no one would be able to withstand their power. He concluded *1984* with the observation that the future would be marked by a jackboot being stamped into the human face forever.

Journalists to a man rallied to the Communist cause. A.M. Rosenthal, executive editor of the *New York Times*, said of his brother-in-law, George Watt, Commissar of the Lincoln Battalion,

"God, how I admired that man. He was my hero."

Herbert L. Matthews wrote in 1946,

"Nothing so wonderful will ever happen to me again as those two and a half years I spent in Spain. There learned that men could be brothers. Today, Wherever in this world I meet a man or woman who fought for Spanish liberty I meet a kindred soul. Nothing will ever break that bond. We left our hearts there."

Despite his despair, Matthews was able to relive the glory of Spanish years when he promoted Castro and a band of six guerillas into the dictatorship of Cuba, through a frenetic propaganda barrage in the *New York Times*.

Kim Philby, later active with the OSS and CIA as British Liaison also was prominent in the Spanish Civil War. Son of the famed Arabist, Sir Harold Philby, he joined the Cambridge Socialist Society in 1929. He worked for the British Treasury in 1932-33 and was recruited by the communist party. In 1934, in Vienna, he married Litzi Friedmann, a communist agent. Witness at the marriage was Teddy Kollek, later a fundraiser for the Israeli terrorists, now Mayor of Tel Aviv.

Working as a Soviet mole, Philby was financed by the Schroder Bank in 1934 to publish a pro-Hitler magazine for the Anglo-German Fellowship. The *Times* then sent him to Spain to cover the Civil War. He took as his mistress the divorced wife of Sir Anthony Lindsay Hogg, Frances Doble, a Falangist sympathizer whose Salamanca palace became his Spanish headquarters. The daughter of a Canadian banker, Doble lavishly entertained the Falangist leaders. Philby frequently met General Franco there.

Philby was recruited for the British SIS in 1940. In 1942, he helped Norman Holmes Pearson, a Yale professor who specialized in the work of Ezra Pound, to set up the London office of OSS with Charles Hambro chief of SOE. In 1949, Philby was sent to Washington as SIS liaison officer with the CIA and FBI. J. Edgar Hoover frequently lunched at Harvey's Restaurant with Philby and James Angleton of the CIA. While CIA station chief in Rome, Angleton worked closely with the Zionist terrorists Teddy Kollek and Jacob Meridor, and later became chief of the Israeli desk at the CIA, helping Philby to set up the lavishly funded international Mossad espionage operation, all paid for by American taxpayers. A senior CIA security official, C. Edward Petty, later reported that Angleton might be a Soviet penetration agent or mole, but President Gerald Ford suppressed the report.

Top secret files of the CIA and FBI were opened to Philby, despite widespread claims that he was a Soviet agent. Although he helped Burgess and MacLean defect to Russia in 1951, he continued to work for SIS until 1956, under the protection of Harold MacMillan, who defended him publicly in parliamentary debate. In 1962 an Englishwoman at a party in Israel said, "As usual Kim is doing what his Russian Control tells him. I know that he always worked for the Reds." Miles Copeland says that Philby placed a mole in deep cover in the CIA known as "Mother". Philby was quoted as saying, "Foreign agencies spying on the U.S. Government know exactly what one person in the CIA wants them to know, no more and no less." Philby was finally exposed by a defector, Michael Goleniewski. On Jan. 23, 1963, Philby left Beirut and defected to Moscow, where he became a Lt. Gen. in the KGB. On June 10, 1984, Tad Szulc wrote in the *Washington Post* that Philby was never a Soviet agent, according to CIA memoranda introduced in a lawsuit, but that he was a triple agent. This explains curious paradoxes in the supposed rivalry between the CIA and the KGB, when certain charmed souls float easily back and forth between the two services. Agents of either service are "eliminated" when they find out more than is good for them about this odd arrangement.

Intrepid's Last Case states that

> "For 38 years there was an official NKVD mission in London whose agents were assisted by both British Special Operations and the American OSS. Only now is it clear that Moscow had received hundreds of top secret OSS research studies; and that the British had supplied guerilla warfare expertise to the chief of the NKVD's subversive operations, Col. A.P. Ossikov!"

In 1943, Donovan was sent on a special mission to Moscow, to establish a permanent alliance between the OSS and the NKVD. Donovan, W. Averill Harriman, and Lt. Gen. Fitin and Maj. Gen A.P. Ossikov of the NKVD worked out a plan to establish offices of the NKVD in key American cities. On Feb. 10, 1944, J. Edgar Hoover sent a confidential message to Harry Hopkins,

> "I have just learned from a confidential source that a liaison arrangement has been perfected between the OSS and the NKVD whereby officers will be exchanged between the services; the NKVD will set up an office in Washington."

Hopkins was forced to contact Atty. Gen. Biddle to alert the Dept. of Justice to this operation; because of the coming election, Roosevelt prudently withdrew his support for the plan.

Because of their cooperation with the NKVD and the prominent Communists in OSS, General Douglas MacArthur refused to allow any OSS agent in his theater of operations in the Pacific. Donovan went to MacArthur's headquarters on April 2, 1944 and made a personal appeal to him, but was rebuffed. MacArthur considered the OSS agents more dangerous to American Security than any military opponents. In Donovan's Washington headquarters, Estelle Frankfurter was caught stealing confidential OSS reports. She was discharged, although her brother, Justice Felix Frankfurter, was Roosevelt's closest confidante. As organizer of the Harold Ware cell, Frankfurter had placed Soviet operatives in many Government agencies, and had put his personal protege, Alger Hiss, in FDR's office. Frankfurter's brother, Otto, served a sentence in Anamosa State Prison, Iowa for Fraud.

While Joseph E. Davies was Ambassador to Moscow, the State Dept. in 1937-38 was ordered to destroy all of its irreplaceable files on the Soviet Union. The Russian Division of the State Dept. was abolished, and the last anti-communist survivors were summarily fired.

Since 1935, seven Soviet networks of espionage had been active throughout Europe. Known by their German name, *die Rote Kapelle*, the Red Orchestra, they were run by Grand Chief Leopold Trepper, who later emigrated to Israel. In January, 1942, Allen Dulles enlisted die Rote Kapelle to form an anti-German group led by Baron Wolfgang von Pultitz, who later arranged for the defection to East Germany of Otto John, head of West Germany's FBI. During World War II, both von Pultitz and John had worked under Charles Hambro at Britain's SOA.

General Alfred E. Wedemeyer later testified that in 1942 he had proposed a guaranteed plan to shorten the war by at least a year, invading France across the Channel. Winston Churchill argued for his "soft Underbelly" approach through North Africa and Sicily. Gen. Marshall called Wedemeyer before Churchill and Roosevelt to explain his plan, on which he had worked for months, perfecting every detail. Churchill persuaded Roosevelt to postpone the Wedemeyer plan for another year, while the Churchill plan was put into action in North Africa in Nov. 1942. Wedemeyer's plan was vindicated in 1946 by Gen. Franz Haider, Chief of Staff of the German Army, who said the Wedemeyer cross-Channel invasion would have been a decisive and timely blow which would have shortened the war by at least a year. However, ending the war in 1943 would have cost the munitions manufacturers many billions in profits. Ezra Pound broadcast on July 17, 1943.

> "I reckon my last talk was the most courageous I have ever given. I was playing with fire. I was openly talking about how the war may be prolonged, by fellows who were scared that the war might stop. I mean they're scared right out of their little gray panties, for fear economic equity might set in as soon as guns stop shooting or shortly thereafter. The stage scenery fell with a flop, simultaneously with some anti-Axis successes."

What was Pound talking about? Stage scenery — what a cynical way to describe a world conflagration in which one hundred million people were dying. Pound exposed the charade. Early in the war, a British Secret Service operation, Operation Ultra, had obtained the German coding machine. They were able to read every secret order from Hitler and the German General Staff. It was like shooting fish in a barrel. F.W. Winterbotham, chief of Air Intelligence, SIS, wrote about his operation of Ultra, "The Ultra Secret". He says,

> "On Aug. 2 (1944) which I remember, covered two whole sheets of my Ultra paper, Hitler told Kluge not to pay any attention to the American breakout. He then outlined his master plan for handling the entire invasion."

Had Hitler had access to all secret communications of the Allies, he would have had an unbeatable advantage. The Allies listened to all of his orders, and reacted accordingly. Early in the war, Ultra informed them that the Germans were planning a massive bombing raid on Coventry. If they evacuated the city, it would show the Germans they were listening to their plans. Churchill ordered the British to do nothing. The Germans bombed Coventry, killing thousands of women and children. The Ultra secret was protected at the cost of many British lives.

The British also had a double agent, Baron Wilhelm de Ropp, who was Hitler's personal confidante on British policy. DeRopp had lived in England since 1910. He married an English wife, but maintained an apartment on the Kurfurstendamm, as a journalist moving between Germany and England. His closest friend in England was F. W. Winterbotham, chief of Air Intelligence. In Feb. 1934, deRopp took Winterbotham to Germany, where he conferred with Hitler, Rudolf Hess, and von Milch, head of the German Air Force. Winterbotham writes,

> "By 1934, I had obtained personal contact with the Head of State, Hitler, and with Alfred Rosenberg, the official Nationalist Party Philosopher and Foreign Affairs expert, and Rudolf Hess, Hitler's deputy. From my personal meetings with Hitler I learned about his basic belief that the only hope for an ordered world was that it should be ruled by three superior powers, the British Empire, the Greater Americas, and the new Greater Reich. I felt that his desperate desire for peace was no bluff. (At Dunkirk) Hitler told his General Staff exactly what he had told me in 1934; it was necessary that the great civilization Britain had brought to the world should continue to exist and that all he wanted from Britain was that she should acknowledge Germany's position on the Continent."

Hitler failed to comprehend the depravity of the behind the scenes figures of the World Order who had gained control of the British Empire with the South Africa wealth they had won in the Boer War. This hoard of gold and diamonds represented the greatest influx of new purchasing power into Europe since the Spanish galleons brought in the gold of the Incas. The resistance encountered in this war caused the planners to resolve that in the future, wars would be managed as precisely as any other business operation. Their philosophy of Hegelian determinism called for setting up two opposing forces, thesis and antithesis, which would be thrown against each other in conflict to produce an outcome, synthesis.

Between the two World Wars, it was necessary to rearm Germany, and also to back a German Government strong enough to prepare the nation for another war. The same people who had supplied Germany from 1916 to 1918 in order to keep World War I going now backed the Nazis to produce a Second World War. The Schroders and Rothschilds had set up Hoover with the Belgian Relief Commission, in partnership with Emile Francqui, "the Beast of the Congo", later the U.S. Food Administration, run by selfless men who inexplicably amassed sudden fortunes in sugar, grain and shipping. Two of these men, Prentiss Gray and

Julius H. Barnes, then became partners in Schroder Co. The *New York Times* Dec. 11, 1940 noted that

> "Baron Bruno von Schroder died at his home here, Dell Park, Englefield Green, Surrey. He came to England in 1900 and was naturalized in 1914. He established J. Henry Schroder & Co. in London 1904 and in New York, 1923. His son Helmut W.B. Schroder now becomes head of the firm. His partner Frank Cyril Tiarks has been a director of the Bank of England since 1912. In 1923, Baron von Schroder bought the Baghdad Railway. The deal was the biggest ever made under cover of the Lausanne Conference disposing of former German concessions in Turkey, and the Rothschilds and Lloyd's Bank shared with Baron Schroder in the syndicate that advanced $25 million to start the rebuilding of the lines."

The importance of the Schroder firm between the two world wars is shown by the following excerpts; *New York Times* Dec. 3, 1923;

> "The first installment of capital for the new currency bank which will grow out of the Rentenbank was issued in Berlin today in the shape of checks in pounds sterling, to the value of 25 million gold marks ($6,250,000) from the London bankers Schroder & Co., whose share in the capital loan is 100,000,000 gold marks, ($25,000,000). Baron Henry Schroder who is the head of the firm, has long been closely connected with German financial interests in the international field."

New York Times Nov. 25, 1928;

> "J. Henry Schroder Banking Corp. Finance and Trade Commentary states, 'If, in the forthcoming reparations conference, the external obligations of Germany are fixed at some reasonable figure, it would be an important step in Germany's whole economic recovery."

New York Times, Nov. 2, 1928

> "J. Henry Schroder Co. floats a $10,000,000 6% loan to Prussian Electric Power Co. in partnership with Brown Bros Harriman."

New York Times, Nov. 14, 1929;

> "The Prussian State has arranged a $5 million loan from J. Henry Schroder Co. to extend Stettin Harbor."

New York Times, Jan. 27, 1933;

> "The City Co. of New York and the J. Henry Schroder TrustCo. have been designated as German bond scrip agents by the Gold Discount Bank of Berlin. Representatives of American houses of issue said yesterday that they were without direct advice from Berlin, where the Germans and representatives of other creditors are now conferring. The bankers are represented there by John Foster Dulles of the law firm of Sullivan and Cromwell."

New York Times, April 19, 1940;

> "The J. Henry Schroder Banking Corp. has succeeded Speyer & Co. as fiscal and paying agent for city of Berlin 25 years 61.2% gold bonds due in 1950."

A leading economist, Professor von Wiegand, has gone on record criticizing the present writer for statements about the Schroder Co. claiming the firm had little or no connection with Germany, apparently because he had not researched the subject in the *New York Times*. The president of J. Henry Schroder also issued a denial in 1944 that they had done any business in Germany.

Adolf Hitler had joined the German Workers Party in 1919 because it was supported by the Thule Society, an influential German society of aristocrats and financiers. In 1921, Hitler met with Admiral Schroder, commander of the German Marine Corps. In Dec. 1931, the circle of Friends was formed, twelve prominent German businessmen who promised to donate regularly to the Nazi Party. Baron Kurt von Schroder, partner of J.H. Stein Co. Cologne bankers, was the leader of this group. J.H. Stein then became Hitler's personal banker. Hitler's aide, Walther Funk, met with Schroder to discuss the real views of Hitler on questions concerning the international bankers. Funk was able to satisfy Schroder, and the financial support of the Nazi Party continued.

Maj. Winterbotham points out that Lord Montagu Norman, Governor of the Bank of England for more than thirty years, was

Hjalmar Schacht's best friend. Schacht, Hitler's Finance Minister, named his grandson Norman because of the friendship. Paul Einzig, in *Appeasement Before, During and After the war*, says,

> "On May 29, 1933, Mr. F.C. Tiarks of the British Banking Delegation met with Dr. Schacht, and found Dr. Schacht's attitude wholly satisfactory."

Mr. Tiarks was a longtime partner of J. Henry Schroder and director of the Bank of England since 1912. His granddaughter married the present Duke of Bedford.

On p.78, Einzig says,

> "Towards the end of 1936 a new firm was registered in London under the name of Compensation Brokers Ltd. which was controlled by the banking house of J. Henry Schroder & Co., and Hambro's Bank Ltd., with the declared object of assisting with barter transactions between Germany and various parts of the English Empire."

When Alfred Rosenberg came to London, he was introduced to many leading figures, including Geoffrey Dawson, editor of the *Times*, Walter Eliot, M.P. Lord Hailsham, secretary for War, and the Duke of Kent, brother of king Edward VIII and George VI. The Duke of Coburg, a close friend of Hitler, had three long talks with King Edward VIII on his accession in January 1936. Edward assured the Duke of his sympathies with the Third Reich. In 1965, the then Duke of Windsor remarked, "I never thought Hitler was such a bad chap." The story behind Edward's sudden abdication was that his advisers realized he would not sign the papers for mobilisation against Germany. An American divorcee was brought into the picture. She led Edward off to the Rothschild castle in Austria, while his "slightly retarded" brother George was installed as King of England.

During the mid-thirties, three isolationist groups were active in England, "The Link", led by Admiral Sir Barry Domvile, and composed of genuinely patriotic Englishmen; the Anglo-German Fellowship, organized by J. Henry Schroder Co. with the help of the Soviet mole Kim Philby to lull Hitler into the belief that England would never declare war on him; and "the Cliveden

Set", who met at Lord Astor's palatial castle, Cliveden, to promote "appeasement".

On Jan. 4, 1933, Hitler met with the Dulles brothers at the Cologne home of Baron Kurt von Schroder to guarantee Hitler the funds needed to install him as Chancellor of Germany. The Dulles Bros, were there as legal representatives of Kuhn, Loeb Co., which had extended large short-term credits to Germany, and needed a guarantee of repayment. Allen Dulles was later ensconced in Switzerland by the OSS during World War II. Still later, he became Director of the CIA. He had been a director of J. Henry Schroder Co. for many years.

On June 11, 1934, Lord Norman and Schacht met secretly at Badenweiler in the Black Forest, and again in Oct. 1934, to guarantee loans to National Socialist Germany. The J.H. Stein Bank of Cologne and the London and New York branches of Schroder Bank were correspondent banks often involved in transactions throughout the Hitler regime. Baron Kurt von Schroder was a member of the Herrenklub, the most influential group in Germany, and the Thule Society, which had launched Hitler's career in 1919. He was director of all of ITT's German subsidiaries, SS Senior Group Leader, Deutsche Reichsbank, and many other high-ranking positions (listed by the Kilgore Committee, 1940).

On Sept. 30, 1933, the financial editor of the *London Daily Herald* wrote about

> "Mr. Montagu Norman's decision to give the Nazis the backing of the Bank of England."

Norman's biographer, John Hargrave, writes,

> "It is quite certain that Norman did all he could to assist Hitlerism to gain and maintain political power, operating on the financial plane from his stronghold in Thread needle Street."

Another Hitler supporter was Sir Henry Deterding, of Royal Dutch Shell, which had been founded by the Samuel family. In May, 1933, Alfred Rosenberg was a guest at Deterding's large estate, Buckhurst Park, Ascot, one mile from Windsor Castle.

Oswald Dutch writes that in 1931 Sir Henri Deterding and his backers, the Samuel family, gave Hitler 30 Million pounds. Deterding then divorced his wife, and married his secretary, an ardent Nazi and German.

Otto Strasser wrote that Schroder agreed to "foot the bill" for the Nazi Party at a secret meeting, and guaranteed their debts, ending up collecting a generous amount of interest on his original capital. (Senate Hearings, Committee for Military Affairs, 1945).

In England, journalist Claud Cockburn led the fight against the "Cliveden Set", seemingly unaware that three of the Astors had founded the Royal Institute of International Affairs. He wrote indignantly,

> "The Astors and others clustered around Chamberlain were a set of appeasers who saw Hitler's regime and their collaboration with it as necessary to maintain the social order they preferred."

The Cockburns are too self-limited to understand that the "appeasers" collaborated with Hitler only to obtain the world war which was essential to their world program. Hitler was duped into going into the Rhineland, duped into going into Czechoslovakia, and duped into attacking Poland. The advertised belief is that he was amazed at the weakness of the opposition to these moves; in fact, he had been promised there would be no opposition, until he went into Poland and discovered he had been duped.

Once Hitler had served his purpose, these same bankers plotted to assassinate him. We know the names of Count von Stauffenberg and Fabian von Schlabrendorff, aristocrats who tried to kill Hitler, but on July 22, 1984, the *Washington Post* revealed the name of the mastermind, Axel von dem Bussche. He married the daughter of the Earl of Gosford, Baron Acheson, air attache at the Paris Embassy. Baron Acheson had married the daughter of John Ridgely Carter, a partner of J.P. Morgan Co., whose father, a Baltimore lawyer, had been legal counsel for the Pennsylvania Railroad and many other railroads. John Ridgely Carter married Alice Morgan, was secretary of the American Embassy, London, 1894-1909, and was partner in J.P. Morgan

Co. 1914, and also the Paris branch, Morgan Harjes Co. Dean Acheson, a cousin of the Gosfords, also worked for J.P. Morgan Co. and later became Secretary of State. The 2nd Earl Gosford had been Gov. Gen. of Canada and governor-in-chief of all British North America. Richard Davis notes in *The English Rothschilds* that the Earl of Gosford was a frequent house guest of the Rothschild family. This may explain why his American cousin, Dean Acheson, was plucked from obscurity to become secretary of State.

The cast of characters is really quite small in number. The grandson of a J.P. Morgan partner masterminds the plot against Hitler, cooperating with Schroder partner Allen Dulles from his Swiss redoubt of the OSS. Admiral Canaris, in charge of the Abwehr, Hitler's intelligence services had made contact with the British Secret Service in London as soon as he assumed that post, through Frankfurt lawyer Fabian von Schlabrendorff, a key member of the plot, aided by Count Helmut von Moltke, a member of the German BAr and also a member of the Inner Temple of London, von Moltke's mother was Dorothy Innes, related to the Schroder banking family.

During his first two years with the OSS, Bill Donovan accepted no salary. In 1943, he was promoted to Major General, and received pay for that grade. In 1943, OSS had a $35 million budget, with 1651 employees, which increased tenfold the following year to 16,000. By the end of the war, there were 30,000 agents and sub-agents, many of whom were involved in looting, blackmail, and other money-making schemes. Airplanes were often commandeered for mysterious flights to haul huge sums in gold, diamonds, paintings and other treasure. From the outset, the OSS had been dealing in large sums in gold. In the spring of 1942, $5 million in gold coins was sent to North Africa to finance secret operations. After the North African invasion, certain bankers who had been holding francs worth 100 million were suddenly worth 500 million. Large scale currency transactions were handled for the OSS by an underworld figure named Lemaigre-Dubreuil, who was shot by unknown gunmen at his Casablanca home.

The political advisor to the Supreme Allied Commander, Mediterranean was Robert D. Murphy, whose wife was a manic-depressive, and whose daughter committed suicide. He was having an affair with the Princess de Ligne, official representative of the Comte de Paris, a Bourbon and pretender to the throne of France. She deeply involved Murphy and the OSS with her principal associate, a Syrian Jew named David Zagha, who dealt in million dollar estates, gems and antiques. He had large holdings in Damascus, and he laundered millions of dollars of OSS funds through Lemaigre-Dubreuil, until that worthy's assassination in Casablanca.

The wheelings and dealings have also characterized the operations of OSS' sucessor, the CIA' often called "the Central Investment Agency", because of its many nefarious dealings. V. Lada-Mocarski, president of J. Henry Schroder, was chief of secret intelligence operations for OSS Italy 1943. The OSS secret files later turned up in the hands of Propaganda Due, P-II, a secret Masonic organization which included many prominent figures in Italy. The go-between for P-II and the CIA was Michael Sindona, the conduit for $65 million which the CIA pumped into Italian elections. He was connected with the Nixon law firm, and with John McCaffrey, chief of resistance forces in Europe for British intelligence during World War II, and later representative of Hambro's Bank, and also with Prince Borghese. Although Borghese had been condemned to be executed during World War II, he was rescued by James Angleton, later Vatican consultant for the CIA. Sindona, McCaffrey and Borghese were partners in an Italian bank, Universal Banking Corp. which was a front for Meyer Lansky and the Mafia. The collapse of Banco Ambrosiano cost the Vatican a billion dollars (later reduced to $250 million), ending in the murder of its president Roberto Calvi, found hanging from Blackfriars Bridge in London. He was declared a "suicide", but a judge later rendered the finding he had been murdered by "persons unknown".

Gen. Donovan also had an important family connection with the Harrimans. His wife's cousin, Charles Rumsey, had, married W. Averell Harriman's sister Mary. The Harrimans had been brought up on their New York estate, Arden, which had 30,000 acres, a 150 room house, and a crew of 600 working constantly to keep things in order.

Harriman's other sister married Robert Livingston Gerry, son of Commodore Elbridge Gerry. Their son, El bridge Gerry, is a partner of Brown Bros Harriman.

In 1939, Donovan had purchased a farm near Berryville, Chapel Hill Farm. In 1945, he sold his Georgetown house to Katharine Graham, of the *Washington Post* family. The farm was taken over by the Rumsey Trust. Donovan lived at 1 Sutton Place, New York, the address made fashionable by Bessie Marbury, the queen of the international homosexual set who, as the leading power in the Democratic Party, had made it possible for Franklin D. Roosevelt to become Governor of New York.

In 1921, developer Eliot Cross sold Marbury's "wife", Elsie de Wolfe, No. 13 Sutton Place. The *Times* soon noted a "curious migration", headlining that Mrs. K. Vanderbilt and Anne Morgan had bought homes in Sutton Place, "a little known two block thoroughfare". Mrs. Vanderbilt paid $50,000 for her home; Anne Morgan, daughter of J.P. Morgan, and member of the de Wolfe-Marbury "Hellfire" set, paid $75,000. They then spent several hundred thousand dollars renovating these homes. The *Times* characterized the "Sutton Place curious migration" as a malicious dig at the well-known proclivities of the new settlers, who would soon make Manhattan notorious as the world headquarters of the homosexual movement.

Donovan's surviving son had refused to enter the law firm or to have anything to do with the OSS. He had a distinguished wartime career as a Navy captain in charge of landing operations at Sicily and other invasions. At a New Years Eve celebration, 1946, his five year old daughter Sheila accidentally drank silverpolish and died. His wife died after an overdose of sleeping pills.

Intrepid's Last Case notes that

> "apolitical decision forced the OSS to surrender to Moscow the captured Soviet military and diplomatic code books on intelligence from the Nazis."

The greatest intelligence coup in history came to naught after Roosevelt's three Communist associates demanded that this complete set of Soviet code books be returned to Stalin.

On May 17, 1945, Donovan became special assistant to Justice Robert H. Jackson, U.S. prosecutor at the Nuremberg Trials. Although the captured German leaders were accused of many things, they were never accused of having accepted money from the Bank of England, or of being financed by the Schroder Bank. Baron Kurt von Schroder had been arrested and transferred to a British detention camp. A German denazification court later fined him 1500 RM and sentenced him to three months detention. Since he had already been held for that period, he was released. The *New York Times* on Feb. 29, 1948 demanded that he be tried by an Allied Military Tribunal — "von Schroder is as guilty as Hitler or Goering".

In May 1945, William Stephenson formed the British American Canadian Corp. in New York, later changed to a Panamanian registry as the World Commerce Corp. April 2, 1947. When Germany surrendered, the London office of OSS had ten million dollars on hand, deposited in Hambro's and Schroder's Banks. This money could not be "returned" to the U.S. Government without stating where it had come from. As proceeds from dealings in gold and jewels, an inquiry could provoke a Congressional investigation. The principals decided to hold it in abeyance for future operations in the new corporations, whose officers were Stephenson, Donovan, Sir Charles Hambro, Edward R. Stettinius, Russell Forgan of Glore Forgan Co., nephew of James Forgan, first president of the Federal Advisory Council of the Federal Reserve Board, and successor to David Bruce as chief of OSS Europe; Sidney Weinberg, head of the Special OSS Mission to Moscow; Nelson Rockefeller; Col. Rex Benson Menzies of SIS and chairman of Robert Benson Co. merchant bankers; John J. McCloy; Richard Mellon; Sir Victor Sassoon; Lord Leathers; Sir William Rootes of Rootes Motors; Sir Alexander Korda; Olaf Hambro; Brig W.T. Keswick head of Jardine Mathieson Co., director of Hudson Bay Co. Hong Kong Shanghai Bank and chief of Special Operations Executive in Asia, World War II; Sir Harold Wemher, British industrialist; Ian

Fleming of the Kelmsley Press; David Bruce; Joseph C. Grew, nephew of J.P. Morgan; and L.L. Strauss of Kuhn, Loeb & Co. The new firm operated closely with Morgan Grenfell, Jardine Mathieson, and British and Western Trading Co.

In 1950, Donovan listed World Commerce Corp. as the only firm in which he held an interest. The president at that time was Frank T. Ryan, director John J. Ryan, both of Bache & Co; other directors were Alfred DuPont, Russell Forgan, Jocelyn Hambro, Joseph Grew and William Stephenson, who gave his address as Plaza Hotel. N.Y. with residence in Jamaica, and listed himself as chairman of the board of Caribbean Cement Co. and Bermuda Hotels Corp.

President Truman disliked the idea of a secret service, and dissolved OSS at the end of the war. 1600 of its operatives went to the State Dept. Intelligence & Research Bureau, others went to the Defense Dept. where Robert McNamara set up the Defense Intelligence Agency in 1961. Truman set up the Office of Policy Coordination in 1948, which by National Security Council directive 10/2 merged into the CIA Jan. 4, 1951 with the Office of Special and Clandestine Services. Although Truman had dissolved the OSS on Sept. 20, 1945, his 1948 directive appointed three men to supervise the organization of a new intelligence agency, Allen W. Dulles, of the Schroder Bank; William Harding Jackson, a Wall Street lawyer who married into the Lyman family, became a lawyer with Cadwalder, Wickersham and Taft, and later with Carter, Ledyard & Milburn (J.P. Morgan's attorneys). In Jan. 1944, Jackson had been named head of intelligence at American Military Headquarters in London. He was chief of intelligence for Gen. Jacob Devers, and later headed G-2 intelligence for Gen. Omar Bradley. He Became a partner of J.H. Whitney Co. New York in 1947, served as deputy director of the CIA 1950-51, and later was spec. asst. to Pres. Eisenhower for national security; the third man on Truman's team was Mathias F. Correa, also a Wall Street lawyer, whose mother was of the Figueroa family; his father was head of real estate and investments for the Brooklyn Diocese, and his brother was spec. asst. to the Atty Gen of the U.S. 1946, general counsel ODM 195 1-52, and vice-pres. RCA. Truman later came to be deeply suspicious of the CIA. He told Merle Miller, "Plain Speaking",

> "Now, as nearly as I can make out, those fellows in the CIA don't just report on wars and the like, they go out and make their own."

Allen Dulles placed a verse from the Bible (John 8;32) in the entrance to the CIA building, "And ye shall know the truth, and the truth shall make you free." Allen W. Dulles was chief of the new agency; Frank Wisner was his deputy; it grew from 5000 to 15,000 personnel by 1955. In 1974, it had 16,500 agents and a $750 million budget; in all, the National Security Agency had $6 billion to spend for "intelligence".

The CIA has often been called the Central Investment Agency, not only because of the Wall Street backgrounds of Donovan, Dulles and many other principals, but because of the many commercial operations in which it has engaged (the CIA is always referred to, not by accident, by its insiders, as "the company"). A great deal of stock trading is based upon inside CIA information, buying and selling on the basis of secret intelligence gathered by the CIA all over the world.

The CIA has also spent billions to influence foreign elections, always for candidates inimical to the interests of the people of the United States, but dedicated to the program of the World Order. However, its principal influence has been through its control of foundations and universities. The American people remain blissfully unaware that their Constitutional government with its separated powers of legislative, judicial and executive departments, has been entirely superseded by the foundations, which generate basic policy for all three branches. Monetary policy is generated by the Brookings Institution and implemented through the Federal Reserve System independent of Congress, which has constitutional power to regulate the monetary system. Social policies, originated by the Ford and Rockefeller Foundations, are enacted into law by Congress and upheld against all challenges by the Supreme Court. Foreign policy, a prerogative of the executive branch, is entirely based on foundation "studies" and recommendations. Staffs of all three departments are heavily infiltrated by foundation operatives. The

CIA functions as the coordinating agency between the foundations and the departments of government. The *Washington Post* of Dec. 8, 1984 verified this with an obituary of Don Harris, relating that he came to Washington in 1950 as an economist with the Brookings Institution, then moved to the CIA as chief of the Far East and the West Europe staffs for three years. He then joined the Defense Intelligence Agency's directorate of plans and policy, where he served until 1983.

McGeorge Bundy, in *The Dimensions of Diplomacy*, 1964, noted,

> "All area study programs in American universities after the war were manned, directed or stimulated by graduates of the OSS: there is a high measure of interpenetration between universities with area programs and information gathering agencies of the government of the U.S."

As head of the Ford Foundation, Bundy was in a position to know about the interpenetration.

The *Washington Post*, April 21, 1984, noted that the CIA was funnelling money to many universities through Air Force intelligence grants or other "defense" operations, including Duke, Stanford, Univ. of Texas and many others. The chancellor of the University of Pittsburgh, Wesley Posvar, had received many Air Force intelligence grants as a retired Air Force intelligence colonel, funnelled through Maj. Gen. James F. Pfautz, head of Air Force intelligence. Posvar is a member of the German Marshall Fund.

The CIA has spent millions to fund newspapers, magazines, and publishers to promote the program of the World Order. Frederick A. Praeger Co. N.Y. an "émigré" publishing firm, admitted in 1967 it had published "15 or 16" books for the CIA. Many writers and journalists have been liberally subsidized by the CIA with travel expenses, a villa in France or Switzerland, and other perks, to produce propaganda for the CIA and its ulterior goals.

The *National Review* is considered the most influential CIA publication. It consistently puffs Jean Kirkpatrick, Milton Friedman, and another cognoscenti of the intelligence community and the Viennese School of Economics. The *New York Times*, Dec. 8, 1984, noted the marriage of William Buckley's son Christopher to Lucy Gregg, daughter of 31 year CIA official, Donald Phinney Gregg, who is now personal adviser on national security to President Bush. Buckley founded the *National Review* with Morrie Ryskind and George Sokolsky, funding the publication with ample funds from the Central Investment Agency and its Wall Street connections. Buckley's only known employment was his stint with the CIA under Howard Hunt at the CIA's station in Mexico City, immediately after Buckley graduated from Yale. Buckley became godfather to Hunt's children, "en skids" NSCIDS No. 7 gave the CIA power to question Americans in the U.S. about their foreign travel and to make contracts with American universities. J. Edgar Hoover's influence gave rise to the National Security Act of 1947, which forbade the CIA to exercise any internal security functions or police powers in the U.S. (FBI territory) but Hoover lived to see the act continually flouted by the greater finances of the CIA.

On March 12, 1947, the Truman Doctrine was announced as America's new foreign policy. On June 5, 1947, the Marshall Plan was announced. Both "doctrines" had originated in foundation studies subsidized by the CIA and were to be implemented under close CIA supervision.

The "new" CIA continues its close ties with the Schroder Bank and other linchpins of international intelligence. Allen Dulles, a director of J. Henry Schroder, and lawyer for the bank as attorney with Sullivan and Cromwell, chose Schroder to handle the vast disbursements of the CIA's "discretionary fund", whose financial dealings remain cloaked in secrecy. Secretary of War Robert Patterson was a director of Schroder, as was Harold Brown, Carter's Secretary of Defense. Paul H. Nitze, our chief arms negotiator, not only was a director of Schroder, but married into the Pratt family of Standard Oil who donated their New York mansion as the headquarters of the CFR.

John McCone, later director of the CIA, was partner of Bechtel McCone, giant war contractor financed by Schroder-Rockefeller Co. Richard Helms also a director of CIA, is a consultant with Bechtel. Although from a family of modest means, Helms was educated at the world's most exclusive prep school, Le Rosey of Switzerland, where he became a friend of the Shah of Iran. The Schroder-CIA connection was revealed in a lawsuit in which documents were filed showing a payment of $38,902 to Edwin Moore, on orders from Richard Helms.

Gordon Richardson was chairman of Schroder from 1963 to 1973, when he was named Governor of the Bank of England, where he served for ten years. Richardson, also a director of Lloyd's Bank and Rolls Royce, maintained a New York address on Sutton Place near Donovan's residence.

The Cabot family of Boston, descended from Sebastian Cabot, who was an early member of the World Order, has maintained a close relationship with the CIA. The founder of the family, Giovanni Caboto of Genoa, became John Cabot when he moved to England in 1448 under Henry 7th. His son Sebastian accompanied him on his North American trip in 1497. Sebastian had been born in Venice in 1476; he moved to England in 1551, was granted a pension and founded the London Muscovy Company which developed overland routes across Europe to Russia. Thomas D. Cabot, honorary chairman of Cabot Corp. was director of Office of Inter-American affairs for the State Dept. 1951, president of United Fruit, and set up Radio Swan on Swan Island for the CIA; he went on a special mission to Egypt in 1953. His brother John was in the foreign service from 1926, served as Consul Gen. Shanghi, ambassador to Pakistan, Finland and Colombia, Brazil and Poland; he was U.S. delegate to Dumbarton Oaks in 1944, and was secretary to the United Nations organization in San Francisco in 1945 under Alger Hiss. Paul Cabot is director of J.P. Morgan Co., Ford, Continental Can, Goodrich, and M.A. Hanna Co. Lord Harold Cacciais also a director of Cabot Corp. He served on the Allied Control Commission in Italy 1943-44 as political advisor, Ambassador to Austria 1951-54, Ambassador to U.S. 1956-61; he is also on the board of Orion Bank, National Westminster Bank and Prudential Assurance. He is chairman of Standard Telephone & Cable.

An earlier member of the Cabot family, George Cabot (1752-1823) owned 40 privateers and letters of marque in 1777-78, and became the first Secretary of the Navy.

High level CIA policy was regularly determined at secret meetings at Pratt House, CFR headquarters in N.Y., as revealed by Vic Marchetti, in *Cult of Intelligence*, he describes a top level meeting at Pratt House Jan. 8, 1965 at 5 pm, chaired by C. Douglas Dillon, chmn of Dillon, Read. The main speaker was Richard Bissell, director of CIA clandestine operations. This was the third meeting at this address. William J. Barnds was secretary; his father was Episcopalian Bishop of the Dallas Division. Present were Frank Altschul, partner of Lazard Freres, who married into the Lehman Family. Altschul was chmn National Planning Assn, director of Ford Foundation, China Institute in America, American Institute of International Education, and vice pres. Woodrow Wilson Foundation; Robert Amory, dep. Dir CIA 1952-62, National Security planning Board 1953-61; Meyer Bernstein; Col. Sidney Berry former military asst. to Secretary of Defense 1961-64, now deputy chief of personnel operations U.S. Army; Allen W. Dulles; George S. Franklin Jr., lawyer with Davis Polk and Wardwell, asst. to Nelson Rockefeller in 1940, intelligence Dept. State 1941-44, executive div. council on Foreign Relations 1945-71, national secretary of the Trilateral Commission 1972, member Atlantic Council, Ditchley Foundation, American Council on United Europe; Thomas L. Hughes, head of the Carnegie Endowment for International Peace (Alger Hiss' former post); Joseph Kraft, newspaper columnist *Washington Post, L.A. Times* etc. Eugene Fubini, naturalised U.S. 1945, technical adviser U.S. AF, Army and Navy on radio techniques, was with CBS 1938-42 with the Secretary of Defense since 1961, National Security Agency since 1965, chmn Defense Intelligence Agency, Harry Howe Ransom, Vanderbilt professor, Rockefeller Foundation, Institute of Strategic Studies London; Theodore Sorensen, Pres. Kennedy's assistant 1957-61, now attorney with Paul Weiss and Rifkind; David B. Sage, prof. Bennington, trustee Russell Sage Fund and 20th century Fund. Bissell, the principal speaker, had been educated at Groton, Yale and London School of Economics, was economist with War Shipping Board 1942-45; Harriman committee for President 1947-48, ECA 1948-51, Ford Foundation 1952-55, dep dir. CIA 1954-64, consultant to Fortune, U.S. Steel, and Asiatic Petroleum.

CIA financial operations continually surface and are quickly forgotten. Jack Anderson noted in a column July 30, 1984 that two OSS pals in World War II, Joe Rosenbaum, a venture capitalist, and William J. Casey, present head of the CIA had been involved in a huge Mid East pipeline deal with former Secretary of the Navy William J. Middendorf, now U.S. Ambassador to the Organization of American States. Middendorf is a director of First American Bank of VA. which handles many financial dealings for the CIA. Directors of First American are Eugene R. Casey, Lt. Gen. Elwood Quesada, who married into the Pulitzer family, asst chief of air on the General Staff, now director of the munitions firm Olin Industries; Stuart Symington, who married into the Wadsworth family, was formerly Secretary of the Air Force and Senator from Missouri, chairman of Emerson Electric, a defense contractor; Lt. Gen James M. Gavin, director Guggenheim Foundation, chairman of Arthur D. Little Co., (said to be a branch of CIA operations).

In *Spooks* Jim Hugan exposes another firm with CIA ties, Quantum Corp., based at Rockefeller owned L'enfant Plaza in Washington which sold arms to both sides in the Arab-Israeli conflict; chairman was Rosser Scott Reeves III, heir to an ad fortune; his father sold Eisenhower like soap with a series of brilliant TV ads. Reeves III married into the Squibb family, was with Lazard Freres from 1962-7, and Military Armaments Corp. 1972-4. His father was a limited partner of Oppenheimer Co. Other members of Quantum were Mitch Wer Bell III, a CIA operative who had the rank of General, U.S. Army; Edmund Lynch; Stewart Mott; Lou Conein, a Union Corse operative known throughout Southeast Asia as Black Luigi; Walter Pforzheimer, former aide to Allen Dulles; he kept two apartments at Washington's most expensive address Watergate; one was filled with his documentation on intelligence activities; he was found murdered at Watergate; and Paul Rothermeil, liaison between CIA and FBI who was sent on a special mission to H.L. Hunt's headquarters in Dallas to destroy the Hunt Oil Co. After millions of dollars vanished, and the Hunt Oil Co. was on the verge of bankruptcy, the Hunts sued him, but were unable to prosecute because of "national security".

The sinking of the USS Liberty, a government intelligence ship, by the Israelis in the 1967 war exposed the close collaboration between the CIA and Mossad, Israeli Military Intelligence. The CIA representative at the U.S. Embassy, Tel Aviv, reported to the senior office CIA at McLean VA. June 7, 1967 that Israel had decided to sink the U.S.S. Liberty. The CIA refused to warn the doomed American sailors. With President Johnson in the White House at the time were Mathilde and Arthur Krim, Johnson's liaison with the Israeli Govt. Mathilde was a former Irgun terrorist who had served on terrorist strikes with Menachem Begin, who boasted he had introduced terrorism to the entire world.

Andrew Tull, in *The Super Spies*, reveals another CIA cover-up. The entire operational plan for the Soviet invasion of Czechoslovakia in July 1968 was obtained by a German operative in May; he delivered the plans to Lt. Gen. Jos. F. Carroll, dir. Defense Intelligence Agency in Berlin. Carroll outlined a plan to "leak" this intelligence, which would force the Soviet Union to abandon the operation. Ambassador to West Germany Henry Cabot Lodge was briefed on the "leak", but received direct orders from Washington to cancel it from Secretary of Defense Clark Clifford. The World Order did not wish to interfere with the planned invasion. The Soviet Union was aware of the discovery, and postponed the invasion from July to August 21. During this period, they were assured by Washington officials that the U.S. would not interfere. With this top level go-ahead, the Red army's conquest of Czechoslovakia was successfully implemented.

We have mentioned the CIA-Mossad connection of James Angleton. The State of Israel was largely created by a Hungarian Jew named Tibor Rosenbaum, who procured arras and money through his Swiss base for both the Haganah and Stern gangs of terrorists, through his control of the International Credit Bank in Switzerland. International Credit Bank was the foreign bank for Meyer Lansky's Mafia operations, and also handled Mossad's

European funds for secret operations. Rosenbaum was the mastermind of Bernie Cornfield's operation. Cornfield's successor at IOS, Robert Vesco, later fled to Central America with $224 million of IOS fund, and is now the partner of Fidel Castro in a huge drug operation which netted $20 billion profit between 1980-84. Castro's cut, $50 million, has been deposited in Swiss banks.

In 1965, the CIA correspondent in Africa was Michael King, partners with Dr. Joseph Churba in Consultants Research Associates, 509 Fifth Ave. N.Y. He is now Meir Kahane, member of the Israel Knesset and head of the terrorist Jewish Defense League. Part of their CIA duties was to mobilize campus riots against the Vietnam War at Columbia and Adelphi College. King's girlfriend, Donna Evans, fell or was thrown from the Queensborough Bridge in July, 1966.

Another important CIA figure was Robert Maheu, who was Liaison between the CIA and J. Edgar Hoover of the FBI. Maheu later became head of Howard Hughes "Las Vegas operations". His code name in the CIA was "Stockholder".

In *OSS, the Secret History*, R. Harris Smith states that Ho Chi Minh had made contact with OSS Col. Paul Helliwell at Kunming in World War II and was recruited as an agent. Ho's reports soon received top priority at OSS Headquarters in Washington, and were placed directly on Gen. Donovan's desk. Helliwell, who later became consul for the Thai government in Miami, and Major Austin Glass, a Socony Oil official, sent arms to Ho for his revolutionary struggle. Another early Ho supporter from OSS was Lt. Thibaut de Saint Phalle, nephew of a prominent Paris banker.

Journalist Robert Shaplen was later told that an official of Chase Manhattan Bank was parachuted into Ho's remote headquarters, where he found the guerilla leader dying of malaria and dysentery. With only a few hours to live, he was saved when an OSS medic Paul Hoagland, was flown in. He saved Ho's life by administering the new sulfa drugs and quinine. He later served at CIA headquarters until the 1970's, where he was always known as "the man who saved Ho's life". After Ho was out of danger, a special OSS contingent, the Deer Team, was sent to Ho's headquarters in Nov. 1945. The members of this team were unanimous in their denunciation of the French "imperialists", the colonial government. They boasted that it had been decided at the highest levels in Washington that the French had to go. A prominent member of this team was Capt. Nicholas Deak, a Hungarian, now president of Deak Pereira. He has controlling interests in Swiss and Austrian banks, and operates currency exchanges in the U.S. Canada and the Far East.

The French were dismayed to learn that their "American allies" were training and arming Ho's Viet Minh forces. Ho was informed that General Donovan represented large economic interests (the World Commerce Corp.) which planned to rebuild Vietnam's railroads and highways, in exchange for "economic privileges" in Indochina. In Oct. 1945, the OSS sponsored the "Vietnam Friendship Association" headed by OSS Lt. Col. Carleton H. Swift. The OSS armed Ho Chi Minh's forces with the latest weapons, and gave intensive training in infiltration and demolition to 200 selected men of General Giap's Army. It was these men who later led the attacks against American troops in the Vietnam War. The OSS sponsorship of the Viet Min and other terrorist groups around the world led Robert Welch to charge that

> "The OSS has thrown the weight of American supplies, arms, money and prestige behind the Communist terrorist organizations of Europe and Asia."

The Deer team claimed that Ho was a great statesman whose nationalism transcended his Communist loyalties.

To supervise the developing political situation in southeast Asia, Donovan was appointed Ambassador to Thailand by Secretary of State John Foster Dulles on Aug. 12, 1953. Donovan's assistant was William J. van den Heuvel. After his return to the U.S. Donovan had a stroke in 1956. He kept to his apartment in Sutton Place and rarely went to his law office. In 1957, another stroke left his brain atrophied. He lingered for several years, finally going to Walter Reed Hospital, where he died in Feb. 1959.

The OSS trained forces of Ho Chi Minh kept up a steady onslaught against the French Colonial Government. John Foster Dulles, playing a double game, met with Georges Bidault, and urged the French to make a stand. "We will provide support", he promised. When the French forces were surrounded at Dien Bien Phu, Bidault, to explain his strategy, read Dulles' commitment to the French parliament. Dien Bien Phu collapsed after a 77 day siege, and the French government was lost. Le Figaro claimed that the State Dept., the White House and the Kremlin, had made a secret deal to partition French Indo China into U.S. and Soviet zones, as had been done in Korea. Whatever agreement may have been reached, it is a fact that the Soviet Army and Navy now have full use of the billion dollar Da Nang airport and the vast naval facilities built in Viet Nam by Lyndon B. Johnson's financial backers, Brown & Root.

One explanation of the fall of French Indo China was a behind the scenes struggle to control the dope trade in Asia. Alfred McCoy points out that during World War II, Lucky Luciano and Meyer Lansky secretly worked for the OSS. Through their influence, the OSS became deeply involved in dope running. After the war, Lansky moved the headquarters of the dope traffic to Miami, where Paul Helliwell, OSS chief of special operations in Asia, was his front man. Helliwell also operated a CIA front in Miami called Sea Supply, Inc.; one of his agents was Howard Hunt. Helliwell later served as paymaster for CIA sponsorship of the Bay of Pigs operation. He opened secret accounts for American mobsters in Miami banks, working closely with Sandro Trafficante and Louis Chesler. Chesler handled Meyer Lansky's real estate investments.

The involvement of the Mob in dope running goes back to well before the murder of Arnold Rothstein. Although Rothstein was widely known as a gambler, this was a cover for his rise to eminence as Mr. Big of the U.S. drug trade. After he was shot in 1928, Louis Lepke, head of Murder Inc., confiscated over $5 million worth of heroin from Rothstein's hotel room.

Former OSS Col. Paul Helliwell became head of the prestigious-Miami law firm, Helliwell, Melrose and DeWolf. His partner, Mary Jane Melrose, was attorney for Resorts

International, a Vesco-Lansky operation in which Nixon's friend Rebozo was said to have an interest. Helliwell opened the Castle Bank in the Bahamas to launder drug payoffs for Thailand poppy growers. As Thai consul, his Washington correspondent was Rowe and Cork, close advisors to President Lyndon B. Johnson, and representatives of United Fruit (a Cabot-CIA connection), Libby and other large firms. Helliwell was also attorney for General Development Corp., Lansky's real estate firm which was run for him by Louis Chesler. As counsel for Miami Natl Bank, Helliwell laundered mob funds through Swiss banks. One of his associates was Wallace Groves, who served several years for mail fraud. Helliwell died one Christmas Eve, 64 years old, and had never been charged with a crime. Protected by powerful friends in the Mob and the CIA he epitomized the ties between organized crime, intelligence agencies and the national government, all overseen, of course, by the World Order.

This cozy arrangement was for a time epitomized by the operations of the BCCI, now popularly known as "the Bank of Crooks and Criminals International". Originating as an Arab bank in the Orient, it soon became the bank of choice for many types of surreptitious financial dealings, including financing drug operations in many countries, handling secret funds of many intelligence organizations, including the CIA, and financing political activities throughout the world. Through veteran Washington insider Clark Clifford, personal adviser to many Presidents since Harry Truman, with whom he began his career in the White House, BCCI bought First Virginia Bank in Washington, a bank which had long close CIA ties. Although BCCI carried out its multitudinous assignments with great aplomb, Israel became jealous of its growing importance, and the Bank of England suddenly precipitated its collapse, citing as its reason financial practices which Middle Eastern banking experts have assured this writer were quite acceptable, and of which the Bank of England has been aware for several years, the reason behind the scenes was probably another of those sudden financial coups which reap great rewards for a few insiders, while leaving depositors and investors holding an empty bag.

Miami Natl Bank, which is now owned by Citibank was known for many years to be controlled by Meyer Lansky. The bank financed the Outrigger Club, which became a meeting place for Santos Trafficante Jr., Philadelphia mobster and members of the Gambino family. Chase Natl Bank lost $20 million in this operation, but chose not to make any complaint about it. Citibank was also deeply involved with City Natl Bank of Miami, whose director Max Orovitz was a longtime associate of Meyer Lansky. The president of City Natl, Donald Beazley, had previously headed Australia's Nugan Hand Bank, a CIA drug operation. Other directors of City Natl included Polly de Hirsch Meyer, Robert M. Marlin, who operated Marlin Capital Corp. and Viking General Corp.; among stockholders of American Capital are Samuel Hallock DuPont Jr., and Paul Sternberg. Sternberg is also on the board of City Natl. While Marlin controlled City Natl Bank, it picked up the mortgage on the Miami Cricket Club, which was owned by Alvin Malnik, widely reputed to be Lansky's heir apparent. Another director of City Natl was Sam Cohen, a Lansky associate who controlled Miami Natl Bank.

In 1973, a bank was established in Australia under the name of Nugan Hand. Its principals were an Australian named Frank Nugan and an American, Michael Hand, a former Green Beret and CIA operative in Asia. Bernie Houghton, an undercover agent for U.S. Intelligence, who represented Nugan Hand in Saudi Arabia, has disappeared, whereabouts unknown. The attorney for Nugan Hand Bank was Bill Colby, director of the CIA. Directors of Nugan Hand were Walter McDonald, deputy director of the CIA, Guy Pauker, a CIA adviser, and Dale Holmgren, who represented both the CIA and Nugan Hand Bank in Taipei. The president of Nugan Hand Bank was Rear Adm Earl Buddy Yates, former chief of strategy for U.S. operations in Asia. Also on the board were Edwin F. Black, a retired general who had commanded U.S. troops in Thailand during the Vietnam War, formerly an OSS operative in World War II and asst. army chief of staff in the Pacific; he served as president of the Nugan Hand Bank branch in Hawaii; Edwin Wilson, who is now in prison for arms deals; and Don Beazley, now of Miami.

Nugan Hand Bank expanded as Australasian and Pacific Holdings Ltd., a front for Air America and other CIA "investments". General Erie Cocke Jr., a Washington public relations officer, was Nugan Hand's Washington representative. From the outset, the bank was actively engaged in the drug trade. Lernoux says the bank controlled the $100 million "Mr. Asia" heroin syndicate which arranged a number of contract murders. Hand boasted that Nugan Hand Bank was paymaster for CIA operations anywhere in the world. In Saudi Arabia, Nugan Hand Bank handled the huge outlays of Bechtel Corp. in its billion dollar operations. Bechtel employees were told they must bank with Nugan Hard. The Manila office of Nugan Hand was run by Lt. Gen. Leroy J. Manor, who had been Chief of Staff of U.S. forces in Asia. The CIA station chief at Bangkok, Red Jansen represented Nugan Hand in Thailand. We may recall that Gen. Donovan, founder of the OSS, had gone to Thailand in 1953 as U.S. Ambassador. Nugan Hand's important contacts with government officials, perhaps greased with handouts from its huge drug operations, shielded it from investigation. In 1978, despite repeated complaints about Nugan Hand's international drug operations, the Australian Federal Bureau of Narcotics refused to investigate. When increasing public pressure was brought to bear on the Bureau to investigate Nugan Hand Bank, the Bureau disbanded in 1979! It was controlled by the Australian Secret Intelligence organization, which in turn was dominated by the CIA.

Veteran Washington political analysts have voiced doubt that President Bush's "War on Drugs" can be taken seriously. These experienced observers of the political scene point out that the CIA's sudden emergence as the directing influence of the world's drug commerce coincided with George Bush's period of service as Director of the CIA. Although all of the machinery was in place when he assumed command, and the CIA was actively engaged in this commerce, it was during Bush's time on watch that every restriction on this trade was removed and that the CIA overnight became the world's preeminent force in the drug trade. Such an overnight Full Speed Ahead could only have come from orders issued at the highest levels.

Inquiry Magazine revealed that while director of the CIA, William Colby laundered many millions of dollars of CIA funds through Nugan Hand to support political parties in Europe; the Christian Democratic Party in Italy was a principal recipient of this largesse, but other political parties in Europe also received millions of dollars. The World Order saw to it that funds were given only to those politicians who would carry out their program. On August 15, 1984, the *Washington Post* revealed that the CIA had dominated the San Salvador elections by giving $966,000 to the Christian Democratic Party, and $437,000 to the National Council Party, to prevent D'Aubuisson, a militant anti-communist, from being elected.

Donald Beazley, a former Federal Reserve Bank examiner, was introduced by Admiral Yates at a bankers' meeting as "the finest young banker I know". Before the debacle of Nugan Hand Bank, Beazley was found to have transferred $200,000 from Nugan Hand to his Florida bank account. He could not remember what this transaction was for. An Australian Royal Commission proved that the bank regularly transferred funds from Sydney to southeast Asia as payment for heroin shipments to the U.S. West Coast via Australia. It was a regular conduit for payments made by Santos Trafficante, underworld boss and Florida based heir to the Luciano drug empire.

Although exposure seemed imminent, Frank Nugan continued blithely with his deals as a big spender. He was closing the deal for a $2.2 million country estate for himself the day he was found shot through the head in Jan. 1980. He was in his Mercedes on a country road. By his side was the rifle he supposedly shot himself with, although in his last moments of life he apparently decided to wipe off all fingerprints. Police investigators found none on the gun. The investigators also decided that Nugan would have had to be a contortionist to shoot himself with the rifle in his car. Donald Beazley went to Florida; his other associates, CIA operatives Michael Hand and Bernie Houghton, disappeared. They have not been seen since 1980.

For many years, the principal American intelligence agent in China was Cornelius V. Starr. Born in 1892, he organized the Asia Life Insurance Co. in Shanghai in 1919. He also owned the

English language newspaper in China, the Shanghai Evening Post, which gave him a dominant role in propaganda activities. He was chairman of the board of U.S. Life Insurance Co. and other companies, as the leading American businessman in China. He was also an OSS agent, and his financial power in China gave the OSS and later the CIA their entree into drug smuggling. After his death, his insurance companies were absorbed into the American International Group.

The American "free press", known to the cognoscenti as "the drug press" because of Luce's longstanding China connection, consistently portrays the source of the world's drugs as "The Golden Triangle", an area of Laos, Thailand and Burma. However, this is merely a staging area for the world's drug trade. Review of the News in 1970 indentified Red China as the world's largest producer of opium, its usual source of hard currency from non-communist nations. The refined opium reaches the "free world", that is "the cash world", through Canton and Hong Kong. It also includes heroin, which had been synthesized from opium in 1898 by the Bayer Co., and became one of their most important products.

Red China's mutterings about taking over Hong Kong when the present lease expires in 1997 allows insiders of the World Order opportunity to increase their fortunes in the volatile Hong Kong real estate market. Red China has to allow the British to operate in this trading area to assure the supply of hard currency from the drug trade. When the British took over this trading area in 1843, they maintained control of the local population through the Triads, the Assassins, as the Hong Society was known, also called the Honorable Society, and the Society of Heaven, Earth and Man. Dan E. Mayers wrote in *Fortune*, Aug. 6, 1984,

> "British colonial rule in Hong Kong is not democracy. Britain rules by decree in all matters of importance. Hong Kong Chinese don't have democratic rights."

Opium began as a cash crop in the poppy fields of Asia Minor, particularly in Turkey, where it is still an important crop today. In 1516, opium was the official monopoly of the Great Mogul in Kuch Behar. When opium reached China, about 1729, Emperor Yung Chen prohibited its use. In 1757, with Clive's great victory at Plassy, the East India Co. took over the opium monopoly as part of its spoils from the Indian Moguls. When the British promoted the use of East India's opium in China, as payment for raw materials needed by their Industrial Revolution (they had been paying in silver), the Emperor Tao Kwang repeatedly warned them to stop selling opium in his country. When these warnings were ignored, the Emperor burned 20,291 chests of opium in 1831, a hoard valued at 2 million pounds. This precipitated the British Opium Wars of 1839-42 and 1856-60.

Because the Communists were financed by the international bankers, the sale and use of drugs have always played an important role in the forward march of Communist hegemony. In 1928, the Chinese Red Army began planting large areas of poppies in areas of China over which they had won control. By 1935, the Ynan Headquarters ruled over vast field of poppies. In 1983, Red China had 9 million acres of poppies under cultivation. The Beijing Government has 101 narcotics factories in operation, which refine from 50% to 70% of the world's drugs.

In 1977, Edward Jay Epstein revealed the true story behind Watergate. Nixon's Domestic Council was a group of aggressive young men trying to outmaneuver each other with new programs. Gordon Liddy, trying to break into this circle, conceived an ambitious program called operation Intercept. It was not a surveillance program, but was designed to "intercept" the flow of drugs into the U.S. Nixon in his 1968 campaign had promised to "move against the source of drugs". A special Presidential Task Force Relating to Narcotics, Marijuana and Dangerous Drugs had been formed, but had taken no action. Liddy got Egil Krogh, Nixon's Presidential Deputy for Law Enforcement, to introduce the program at a meeting of the Domestic Council. Richard Helms director of the CIA, was among those present. The plan was officially approved by Erlichman in July, 1970 as a major operation against the heroin traffic. There still was no real program, merely a public relations ploy, but, senior staff people at CIA panicked. They feared that their vast Asia operations, funded by their drug operations, could be wiped out. Liddy, meeting with State and CIA officials, says,

"I pressed CIA on the problems of the Golden Triangle of Burma; Richard Helms replied 'Any move in that area would be impractical.'"

Liddy had set up ODESSA, Organisation Der Emerlingen Schutz Staffel Angehorigen, which was ready to begin operations. The CIA resolved to counterattack by setting up the Watergate operation, hoping to neutralize Nixon's staff. James McCord and other CIA operatives worked out of Mullen Co., a CIA front across the street from CREEP Headquarters. The Watergate job was scheduled for May 26, 1972, but these "highly trained" black baggers couldn't get in; they came back on May 27 with no success, but got in on May 28 and photographed a number of documents in the Democratic offices. Then they were told to return on June 16; by this time the entire setup was ready, and they were arrested.

Future historians will refer to the Vietnam War as "the drug war" akin to the British Opium Wars of the nineteenth century. In 1964, the number of U.S. addicts had dropped to 48,000 down to 60,000 in 1950. Then 15% of all American soldiers in Vietnam returned home as addicts. The drug monopoly was back in business. Two of the leading CIA operatives in Vietnam during that war are Mitch Werbell from Powder, Ga., and Three Fingered Louie Conein, who wore a gold decoration from Union Corse, the Sicilian Mafia, around his neck.

After the collapse of the Nugan Hand Bank and the disappearance of its principals, the CIA used the 17 international offices of a Honolulu investment firm, Bishop, Baldwin, Rewald, Dillingham and Wong as its Asian network. The firm handled some $1 billion in CIA covert funds, laundering huge sums for the Gandhi family in India, and worked closely with Marcos' right hand man in Manila, Enrique Zobel, one of the ten wealthiest men in the world, who handled the investment fund of the Sultan of Brunei. After $22 million disappeared, Rewald was arrested. The resulting litigation is being handled by U.S. atty John Peyton, former chief of litigation for the CIA in Washington, from 1976-81.

CIA headquarters underwent a change after the arrival of a reputed KGB defector. Yuri Nosenko had been sent to the U.S.

to assure American intelligence that Lee Oswald had no KGB connection, even though he had married the niece of a KGB major. Nosenko's story was "verified" by another defector, Fedora, another double agent who had wormed his way into J. Edgar Hoover's confidence; both the FBI and the CIA now had a resident authority on Communist espionage who had been identified as a double agent. The Nosenko caused the CIA staff to split into two camps, pro-Nosenko and anti-Nosenko. William Colby, director of the CIA, was in the pro-Nosenko camp, giving rise to rumors that he and James Angleton were double agents, and that Colby had been recruited while serving in Vietnam. Angleton was forced to resign.

Chapter Seven

The Bechtel Complex

When President Eisenhower concluded his term, he warned the nation in a parting message about the rapid growth of the "military industrial complex". The American people did not know what he was talking about. As a military man, Eisenhower had seen firsthand the growing political and economic power of two giant construction firms, Brown & Root of Houston, Texas, and the Bechtel Group of San Francisco. Brown & Root put its man in the White House, Lyndon B. Johnson. The Bechtel Group has put its own man in the White House, Ronald Reagan, whose presidential campaign in 1980 was run by George Pratt Shultz, president of Bechtel, and Caspar Weinberger, vice president and general counsel of Bechtel. They were appointed Secretary of State and Secretary of Defense. The *New York Times* reports July 15, 1982,

> "Shultz is the fourth member of Bechtel Group serving in Reagan's cabinet. Treasury Secretary Donald T. Regan was chairman of Merrill Lynch, whose White Weld unit is investment advisor to the Saudi Arabian Monetary Authority. Atty. Gen. William French Smith's California law firm, Gibson, Dunn & Crutcher, has branch offices in Washington and Riyadh (capital of Saudi Arabia) and represents the Saudi Ministry of Finance and National Economy."

On Dec. 5, 1980, the *New York Times* noted in a headline story, Business Section,

> "Mr. Bechtel, a reclusive 55 year old engineer, informed his subordinates that 'we encourage and applaud the active participation of our employees in the democratic process'. Bechtel, a privately held concern at work on 130 projects in

21 countries, all of them budgeted at more than $25 million, has for decades struggled to keep a low profile and the affairs of its management private... Also working for Bechtel as consultant are Richard Helms, the former Director of Central Intelligence, and former Ambassador to Iran, and Frank Jungers, former Chmn of Arabian American Oil Co. On the basis of its $6.4 billion revenues last year, the company ranked as the third largest engineering and construction concern in the U.S., after Brown & Root Inc. and the Fluor Corp. Bechtel's contracts are largely in huge industrial and energy-related projects that Larry Thomas, a Bechtel spokesman, refers to as 'mega-Projects'. At present, the company is under a 25 year contract for construction of a city for more than 3,000 people and an industrial complex at Jubail, Saudi Arabia, and to engineer a hydroelectric project at James Bay in Canada that would include a network of dams and earth-filled dikes large enough to substitute for 10 conventional power plants. Bechtel is also the country's leading builder of nuclear power plants."

Many Bechtel projects have been characterized as huge boondoggles. Many nuclear power projects have either failed to come "on line" or have been abandoned, causing billion dollar write offs and shaky financial markets. Bechtel has built such problem-plagued ventures as BART (Bay Area Rapid Transit System) in San Francisco, METRO, the Washington D.C. subway system (the *Washington Post* recently noted it was already $200 million in the red and will ultimately cost $12 billion), and Jubail, called "the biggest boondoggle in history".

Time, July 12, 1982, wrote of Jubail,

> "Bechtel has spent $35 billion and plans to spend $100 billion more. Bechtel's original contract had been for a modest $9 billion."

Jubail is described as lying 324 miles northeast of the Saudi Arabian capital, Riyadh, with 100 plus temperatures most of the year, a desolate area of salt flats washed by the Persian Gulf. 1600 Bechtel employees live on the site in 3 bedroom ranch houses built for $300,000 each, directing the activities of 39,000 construction workers. *Time* says,

> "The infant city could wind up being an enormously expensive ghost town, as marching dunes are expected to cover it by the year 2000."

Christopher Reid, who worked for Bechtel, says,

> "Jubail is a massive WPA project, the biggest boondoggle in history."

He predicts that the sands of the Dahana Desert will shift and cover Jubail before the end of this century. Saudi officials have stated they do not know who will live in Jubail, because of the hot temperatures, the isolation of the area, and the desolate surroundings. Historically, the dunes of the Dahana Desert shift massively every few years. Engineers expect the Jubail area to be completely covered by the year 2000. Future archeologists will be puzzled by this strange ruin, not realizing that the entire project resulted from the huge oil price increases inflicted upon the American people, and pressures compelling the Saudi Arabian leaders to return much of their profit to wealthy entrepreneurs such as the Bechtel Group.

The *New York Times* reported July 26, 1982,

> "Pres. Reagan's special Middle East envoy, Philip C. Habib, is also serving as a private consultant to Bechtel Group, Inc. He had been hired by George P. Shultz while Shultz was president of Bechtel. State Dept. spokesman Dean Fischer said Mr. Habib's retention by Bechtel did not compromise U.S. diplomatic efforts in the Middle East. 'It doesn't strike me as a problem anymore for Habib than it would be for Weinberger or Shultz,' Mr. Fischer said."

Who's Who shows Philip C. Habib has been a career State Dept. official since the 1950s, receiving a Rockefeller public service award in 1969, senior adviser to the Sec. of State, 1979-80, resident fellow Hoover Institution from 1980 to present. Hoover Institution, Stanford, and the Bohemian Club are an interlocking power structure dominating the Washington political scene. These arrogant and omnipotent overlords take their cue from Oriental despots of yore; like the Moguls of the fallen Indian Empire, they are characterized by an insolent half-smile, often seen on the likes of George Pratt Shultz and David Rockefeller. It is known as "the insider's smirk."

On July 27, 1982, the *New York Times* noted further praise for Habib from the White House and State Dept. Senator Alan Cranston and other luminaries.

> "A spokesman for the Israeli lobby voiced confidence today in Pres. Reagan's Special Envoy to the Middle East Philip C. Habib; Thomas A. Dine, executive director of American Israel Political Action Committee, said he had the highest regard for Ambassador Habib's integrity."

A letter to the *Times* July 27, 1982 from Gen. F. P. Henderson noted that when Count Bernadotte raised support for Palestine refugees in 1948, the largest contributors were Arabian American Oil Co. $200,000, and Bechtel International, $100,000. (UN Records No. 11A648).

The revelation of Habib's connection with Bechtel alarmed some Israeli leaders, because of Bechtel's contracts with the Arabs, and Sen. Larry Pressler, R., So. D. called for his resignation. The *New York Times* reported,

> "British officials offered no immediate reaction to the news of 'Habib's departure' nor would they comment on his replacement by George Pratt Shultz, whose reputation as an economist is well known here. Lord Carrington said. 'Mr. Shultz is known to everyone, and I am sure they will work with him.' Israeli Foreign Ministry spokesman said, 'Israel deeply regrets the resignation. Israel respected Mr. Habib as an outstanding statesman and faithful friend of the State of Israel!'"

The *Times* failed to get the comments of any Arabs about Mr. Habib.

On July 10, 1982, Shultz a member of the Standard Oil Pratts, was reported by the *New York Times* to have promised he would "divest" himself of his Bechtel holdings by putting them in a blind trust. Bechtel is a privately held company, 40% of the stock held by the family, the rest by its executives, who sign an agreement that when they leave the firm or die, the company has first option to repurchase their stock, which option is always exercised. The *New York Times* reported Jan. 18, 1979,

> "Increasingly sensitive to accusations of secretiveness, the privately held Bechtel group of companies took a new step in implementing a policy of disclosure today when it issued for the first time something approaching an annual report. Since all stock is held by top executives and members of the Bechtel family, this took the form of a report to the 30,000 employees around the world rather than a report to stockholders."

The *Times* commented in 1982 that "Bechtel does not disclose its earnings". Informed estimates are that Bechtel earned 5% net profit on its $11.6 billion revenues in 1982. Stephen D. Bechtel Sr., now in his eighties, is said to be worth $750 million. His son, Stephen Jr. now head of the firm, is said to be worth $250 million. When his father dies, the younger Bechtel is expected to become a billionaire.

Newsweek reported Dec. 29, 1975,

> "The Bechtel group of companies is hardly a household word. As a privately held corporation, it has operated for 77 years behind a wall of secrecy that is considered unequally impenetrable in the competitive world of heavy construction. Its revenues are estimated at $2 billion a year, equal to General Mills or Standard Oil of Ohio. Bechtel got that way by wheeling and dealing not only in private operations but with governments themselves. The company is building a new 34 story building on Fremont St. in San Francisco. The company, says one Federal energy official, is putting together a modern version of a military industrial complex machine, and they have an inside track on the growth market of the future. It will be called the new General Motors before the century is out."

Bechtel began in 1898 when a Midwestern farm boy, Warren (Dad) Bechtel, came to California to seek his fortune. He began with a mule team hauling dirt on small construction projects. In 1918, with war prosperity, his income increased. His first important project was building a railroad for Hutchinson Lumber Co. at Orotillo, Cal. His three sons, Warren, Steve and Ken joined him in the growing business. In 1928, he was elected president of Associated General Contractors of America, a powerful lobbying group. In 1931, Dad Bechtel became president of Six Companies, a consortium formed to build the $49 million Boulder Dam. It was incorporated in Delaware in Feb. 1931 by H.J. Kaiser Sr. and Jr.; Felix Kahn of MacDonald and Kahn; Henry W. Morrison of Morrison-Knudsen; W. A. Bechtel Co.; J. F. Shea of Los Angeles, which built the Pacific Bridge at Portland, and General Construction Co., Seattle. MacDonald and Kahn had built the Mark Hopkins Hotel; Morrison was a trustee of Stanford and close friend of Herbert Hoover and Leland Cutler.

Between 1931 and 1936, the consortium built the Bonneville Dam, the San Francisco Bay Bridge, and other projects. During the construction of Hoover (Boulder) Dam, a steel salesman, John McCone, called on Bechtel. He had been a friend of Steve Bechtel at the Univ. of California in 1922. Steve was now head of the firm, due to the mysterious death of Warren Bechtel in Moscow August 29, 1933. Dad Bechtel, 61, had come to Russia to inspect the Magnitogorsk Dam, on a 3 days tour which also included the Dnieperstroy Dam. He had been instructed by the Soviet authorities to come alone, and he left his wife in Vienna. While staying at the National Hotel in Moscow, before leaving on the tour, Dad Bechtel died suddenly of "an overdose of medicine". There was no autopsy. Someone in the Kremlin, perhaps Stalin, had changed his mind about allowing Bechtel to inspect the dam.

Stephen Bechtel found a ready ally in the aggressive business acumen of John McCone. They formed a separate company, Bechtel McCone, in the nick of time before World War II broke out. In Dec. 1940, they got an order of $21 million for sixty British freighters, to be built in alliance with Admiral Vickery of Bath Iron Works. McCone and partners later made $44 million profit on Liberty ships built at their Sausalito plant. They also owned California Ship building, a Los Angeles yard which turned out 467 ships during the war, as well as Marin ship, the Oregon Shipbuilding Co. They owned Joshua Hendy Corp. an ironmonger which built the engines for Liberty ships. By Sept.,

1943, they had more than $3 billion in shipbuilding orders. The crews of Liberty ships made wry jokes about the propensity of these hastily flung together productions to break in two during high seas. Many of them were torpedoed before they could fall apart. *Time* noted that

> "Marin ship turned out 460 freighters and 90 tankers at breakneck speed."

The partners also built the colossal Army modification center at Birmingham Ala. to handle the B-24 output from Willow Run; they built the Alaskan Military Highway, and other projects. During this defense activity, Bechtel and McCone prudently remained in the background, allowing their protégés, the Kaisers, to be publicized as the important figures. Fortune pointed out that Kaiser was never more than a standing for Bechtel. Kaiser, after having been snubbed by AGC, became president of Associated General Contractors after the Bechtel's recommended him. At the end of World War II, Bechtel Group held 20% of Kaiser Permanente Metals, which owned Richmond Shipbuilding, the Kaiser firm. The youngest son, Ken Bechtel, ran the Marin Shipyard.

Bechtel's rush program of building Liberty ships considerably antedated Pearl Harbor. Roosevelt (Dr. Win the War) issued his emergency shipbuilding order in January 1941; by Sept. 27, the first Liberty ships were being launched. FDR, as Asst. Sec. of the Navy in 1916, had done the same thing, awarding Navy contracts long before we entered World War I. "Preparedness". The Bechtel-McCone alliance, being short of capital, invented the ingenious "cost-plus" contract arrangement. Under this generous stipulation, the government guaranteed war contractors all costs of production, plus a guaranteed 10% profit. The more the contractor spent, the greater his profit. It was the greatest boondoggle for the fortunate few since the Federal Reserve System started printing paper money with no backing except paper bonds.

The free-flowing profits led to an inevitable intelligence connection. John McCone became president of the Air Pollution Committee in 1947, and in 1948, became deputy Secretary of Defense. Ralph Casey of the General Accounting Office later testified that while holding this office, McCone gave contracts to Standard Oil and Kasier, firms in which he had large investments. McCone went on to become Under Secretary of the Air Force 1950-51, Chairman of the Atomic Energy Commission 1958-60, and Director of the Central Intelligence Agency 1961-65, resulting in a close connection between Bechtel and the CIA. While McCone served as chairman of the Atomic Energy Commission, Bechtel became the largest contractor of nuclear plants in the world. Bechtel completed the world's first nuclear plant at Ara, Idaho in 1951. McCone later became a director of Pacific Mutual Life, Standard Oil of California, and ITT.

The Bechtels were now counted among the most influential wheeler-dealers in Washington. Stephen Sr. and Jr. and John McCone were key members of the small group of millionaires who regularly played golf with President Eisenhower and Arthur Godfrey at the mecca of all lobbyists, Washington's Burning Tree Country Club. When George Pratt Shultz became a Washington official, he regularly played golf with Stephen Bechtel Jr. at Burning Tree, which led to his being named president of Bechtel Group.

The Bechtels had come a long way from the anxious days of 1931, when a small sand and gravel contractor was asked to put up $8 million working capital for the Boulder Dam job. They did manage to come up with $5 million, financed by the Schroder-Rockefeller group. Their later success has been due principally to their connections with the international financiers.

Bechtel had been rescued in its time of need by J. Henry Schroder and Avery Rockefeller. John Lowery Simpson, vice president of J. Henry Schroder, was placed on Bethtel's board as chairman of its finance committee, in total charge of the company's financial arrangements. Huge government contracts followed this connection as naturally as night follows day.

The *New York Times* announced the debut of Schroder-Rockefeller on July 9, 1936, with Avery Rockefeller, son of Percy, and godson of William, allied in a new holding company. Avery's grandfather was James Stillman, who built the National City Bank to a giant concern. Avery Rockefeller held 42% of the stock in Schroder-Rockefeller; Baron Bruno von Schroder of London and Baron Kurt von Schroder of Cologne (who was Hitler's personal banker) held 47%.

On June 3, 1954, the *New York Times* announced that Stephen Bechtel, chmn of Bechtel Corp. had become partner of J.P. Morgan Co. In 1955, *Fortune* reported that as Under Secretary of State, C. Douglas Dillon had arranged important contracts for Bechtel with the Saudi Arabian government, culminating in the present $135 billion Jubail operation.

Allen Dulles, director of the CIA, was also a director of Schroder Co. The vice president of Bechtel, Saudi Arabian operations C. Stribling Snodgrass, also ran a CIA firm called LSG Associates.

Bechtel built the 1100 mile long Trans Arabia Pipeline for $100 million, the largest contract let to that time. A worldwide construction firm, with entree to many countries, can also be a conduit for intelligence agents. In 1980, Bechtel was building apartments in Saudi Arabia, a hydropower complex in Quebec, a coal fueled power project in Utah, an oil refinery in Indonesia, a $500 million tourist resort in Malaysia, a copper and gold mine in Paua, New Guinea, and a $250 million palace for the Sultan of Brunei. It was an ideal operation for the CIA, even without the ubiquitous Schroder connection.

Bechtel was awarded the billion dollar contract for cleaning up the situation at Three Mile Island. In 1979, about half of its business derived from nuclear power activity, despite many complaints about its faulty construction in this field. Bechtel made a $14 million settlement of complaints from Consumers Power Co. that the Palisades nuclear plant leaked radioactive water into the steam generating system. At Bechtel's Midland, Mich, nuclear power station, the reinforcing bar joints were found to be defective. Bechtel settled out of court with Portland General Electric, which had charged Bechtel with "negligent design" in its Trojan nuclear power plant at Rainier, Oregon. Nevertheless, when Brown & Root was removed from construction at South Texas Nuclear Project, Bechtel took over. A commentator noted at that time,

"Bechtel is politically untouchable. So anybody who gets Bechtel on its side is assured of protection."

In January, 1975, *Fortune* pointed out that Bechtel had never been in the red for a single year, because "Its engineering projects are invariably financed by its clients." These clients are usually governments, a lesson which may have been learned from the Rothschilds. The Export Import Bank frequently steps in and offers to finance the huge projects proposed by Bechtel. The American taxpayer finances many Bechtel projects through the World Bank and the International Monetary Fund. It could be said that every American has a stake in Bechtel. The president of Export Import Bank, William H. Draper III, resides at Palo Alto, California home address of the Hoover Institution and Hewlett-Packard Co., and Stanford University, the present headquarters of the Reagan-Bechtel complex. Draper's sponsor for internal auditing during the time in question. It said two audits were cancelled at Bechtel in 1980 'at the insistence of Cho; those audits would have revealed the large undocumented cash advances being paid to Cho'. At the time of the bribery, Secretary of State Shultz was president of Bechtel, and Secretary of Defense Weinberger was vice president and general counsel of Bechtel. In the ensuing months, the Post and the FBI have been content to ignore the matter, four billion dollar contracts being "small change" in Washington.

Newsweek noted July 12, 1982 that Kenneth Davis, vice president of Bechtel in charge of nuclear plant construction since 1974, had joined Reagan's administration as deputy secretary of Energy involving nuclear production, becoming the fifth member of Bechtel to join Reagan's team. Most reporters would be up in arms if five executives of General Motors joined a White House team.

Like most family concerns, Bechtel has a paternal attitude towards its employees. *Fortune* noted it paid 100% bonuses in good years. *Newsweek* quoted a former employee, March 18, 1968, "They are all robots there. They tend to pigeonhole you for years and years." *Fortune* noted that Stephen Bechtel Sr. had stepped down as head of the firm in 1961 at the age of 60, turning the presidency over to Stephen Jr.

"Steve, Ken, and Jr. own one-half of the shares of the common stock, and most of the preferred. The corporation has first option on stock when one leaves or dies."

Fortune usually writes about Bechtel with reverence, but did mention "occasionally dissatisfied customers" and bravely concluded, "A world like that can hardly do without a company like Bechtel."

In April, 1968, Bechtel dedicated a new bronze 23 story building in San Francisco. The Feb., 1951 *Fortune* had run a full page color portrait of Stephen Bechtel Sr., citing some of the firm's recent achievements, a 506 mile pipeline for Pacific Gas & Electric, a $25 million plant for Lever in Los Angeles, and others. In Nov. 1952, Bechtel proposed a 2500 mile pipeline from the Arctic to Paris, promising to deliver oil at 25 per 1000 cuft, much cheaper than coal. Nothing came of this proposal, but Bechtel, after acquiring Peabody Coal Co. the nation's largest, in a consortium with Newmont Mining for $1.2 billion Bechtel joined with Lehman Bros. Energy Transport System to build 70% of the world's coal slurry lines. Peabody had been founded by Francis Stuyvesant Peabody, of the famed philanthropic family which originated the American foundation network to control the American people.

Bechtel now began frenetic lobbying to build coal slurry lines. An intensive campaign in Virginia failed in 1983, because of the countervailing power of the Norfolk & Western Railroad, 40% of whose revenues come from hauling coal. The legislators were bemused by the amount of money spent on the coal slurry bill, but never knew it was a Bechtel lobbying operation. Steven D. White, president of Bechtel Investments, said in a letter to *Forbes*, April 9, 1984,

> "Bechtel remains strongly committed to the concept of coal slurry pipelines and in particular to the ETSI coal slurry pipeline."

In 1982, Bechtel offered to build a coal slurry line in Russia, but perhaps because of its well-known CIA connection, the offer was ignored. The UPI reported from Houston Aug. 2, 1984 that a $3 billion proposal for a slurry line from Wyoming to the Gulf Coast had been defeated.

Michael Berryhill noted in Harpers, Dec. 1983, that Dallas was planning an $8.3 billion rail network.

> "The Bechtel Corp., the huge and secretive San Francisco firm with strong ties to the Republican Party, prepared the feasibility study, and will probably get the design contract."

Bechtel is also planning a $5 billion convention center in Hoffman Estates, Ill., near Chicago and other huge projects. Bechtel frequently remains behind the scenes in its major projects. The proposed MX missile plan was headline news for weeks, but not a single journalist bothered to find out that the MX proposal had been drawn up by a presidential commission composed of John McCone, Richard Helms, and Nicholas Brady, former Senator from New Jersey and now chairman of Dillon Read — loyal Bechtelites, one and all. Mother Jones pointed out in June 1984 that Stephen Bechtel Sr. was on the advisory committee of the Export Import Bank, which finances many Bechtel projects, and that Bechtel Corp. created a new position for John Moore, president of EXIM Bank, as "executive vice president for financial services", which he had no doubt rendered. Mother Jones continued,

> "Never before has a corporation been so visibly linked to the presidency. It has had close ties with every chief of state since Eisenhower. Bechtel contributed heavily to Reagan's campaign in 1980. Peter Flanigan of Dillon Read played a key role. Shultz and Weinberger endorsed Reagan in the spring of 1980, joined by Walter Wriston of Citibank, who is on the Bechtel board of counselors, and Robert Quenon, president of Peabody Coal Co. Kenneth Davis, a Bechtel vice president, is No. 2 in the Dept. of Energy. Casey (CIA) represented Pertomina, the giant oil company of Indonesia which has been a good customer of Bechtel."

When any business places this many men in a President's office, it is no longer a matter of "influence"; it is a matter of control. A Reagan panel of business leaders, including Stephen Bechtel Jr. recently recommended that the nation must spend $3.5 billion a year to rebuild its "infrastructure", roads, subways, bridges etc. Bechtel could expect to get a large share of this business. The Prime Minister of Canada, John Turner, was director of Canadian Bechtel.

Chapter Eight

The Foundations

The World Order controls the citizens of the United States through the tax exempt foundations. These foundations create and implement government policy through their staff members in key positions in the executive, legislative and judiciary departments. The foundations create educational policy through their staff members in key positions at every level of the educational system. The foundations control religious doctrine through their staff members in key positions in the leading religious denominations.

"Foundation" is a misleading term; Webster calls it an endowment, but a foundation is really a trust, which Roget states is a "syndicate". If, instead of Rockefeller Foundation, we were to say Rockefeller Syndicate, we would be much closer to the truth. Alpheus T. Mason, in his biography of Justice Brandeis, quotes Brandeis as pointing out that "Socialism has been developed largely by the power of individual trusts." What we have then, are criminal syndicates masquerading as philanthropic enterprises while they inflict Socialist world slavery on nations and peoples for the benefit of the World Order.

Norman Dodd, director of research for the Reece Committee in its attempt to investigate tax exempt foundations, was asked by Congressman B. Carroll Reece in January, 1954,

> "Do you accept the premise that the United States is the victim of a conspiracy?" "Yes," said Dodd. "Then," said Congressman Reece, "you must conduct the investigation on that basis." B.E. Hutchinson, chairman of Chrysler Corp., although approving the goals of the investigation, warned

Dodd, "If you proceed as you have outlined, you will be killed."

Dodd stated,

> "The foundation world is a coordinated, well-directed system, the purpose of which is to ensure that the wealth of our country shall be used to divorce it from the ideas which brought it into being. The foundations are the biggest single influence in collectivism."

The 1975 Report of the Rockefeller Foundation showed as $100,000 grant to the Institute for World Order, operated by Prof. Saul Mendlovitz, who states in the Institute publication Transition, Oct. 1974,

> "I am arguing for a new governance or alternative institutions to those now responsible for global concert; people will be demanding a central guidance system; it means a governance is about to come into being in which the policy elites in various nation states who have the authority and capacity to make decisions — will no longer have that as their prerogative. There will be a governance that will say — you can't build an army anymore. You must give a certain amount of your economic income to other areas of the world."

In short, a World Order — no national armies; no private incomes; no individual freedom. Ironically, all this is being financed by those who created wealth by the exercise of individual freedom in the United States.

Mendlovitz does not use the word "government", which might imply a government by the consent of the people, as in the United States. He uses "governance", the imperial form, meaning a dictatorial decree. Every act of the foundation-syndicates, and of their masters in the World Order, is intended to implement a ruthless type of Oriental despotism. As is traditional in this type of despotism, the most efficient palace servants are eunuchs. Eunuchs work for little or no pay, because they do not have the expense of rearing families. In the foundation world, we find the eunuch as the predominant type of official. The eunuchs move in and out of the foundations into prominent posts in government, education and religion. Although they may marry and have children, psychologically they remain eunuchs, those who have forsworn their manhood to become palace servants of the World Order. Columnist Jeffrey Hart recently commented on this type, referring to Mondale's selection of Geraldine Ferraro as his vice presidential nominee, "Mondale should have chosen a man, in order to balance the ticket."

We well may ask, if the World Order is in control, why do we need an "Institute for World Order" Why do we need the foundations as Gauleiters of the Order's control? The answer is that the World Order rules because it conceals its power; it denies that it exists. Although its power is obvious everywhere, in the government, in education, in the religious orders, in the wars and revolutions and famines which are so meticulously planned and executed, the World Order, like the Mafia, refuses to acknowledge its own existence. Its subsidiaries come and go, but the Order remains constant. When too many people discover the Council on Foreign Relations, power is moved into the Bilderbergers, or the Trilateral Commission. The Order's control remains constant.

The *New York Times* noted April 29, 1984 that 1400 officials were attending the annual meeting of the Council on Foundations. There were 21,697 foundations in the U.S., which in 1983 distributed $3.4 billion in grants. These grants are dispensed only to those who implement the program of the World Order, and whose goal is world slavery.

The international banking families, whose origins go back to the Middle Ages, set up the principal American foundations to protect the wealth they had amassed in their dealings in slaves, drugs and gold, and to perpetuate that wealth through means which can only be described as "imperial decrees", government charters, in order to neutralize all potential rivals or opposition by controlling them and directing or misdirecting their opposition.

None of the charters of the foundations indicate their real purpose. They are replete with such phrases as "the wellbeing of mankind" "the elimination of poverty", the "elimination of disease", "the promotion of world brotherhood". Compassion, caring, charity, these are the watchwords of the foundations. There is no hint to the unwary of the despotic instincts which drive these "caring" people to promote world wars and world slavery, nor is there any warning to the menials of the foundations that if they falter at any time in their dedication to the goals of the World Order, the penalty is sudden death.

Few American citizens can grasp the disturbing fact that the governing power in the United States is not a government agency, or laws, or political parties. Rather, it is the power of the Assassins, those behind the scenes figures who have the power to order the assassination of anyone whom they can no longer control. We have seen two Presidents of the United States, Abraham Lincoln and John Fitzgerald Kennedy, assassinated because they ordered the Treasury of the United States to print non-interest-bearing dollar bills, a development which threatened to deprive the international bankers of billions of dollars in unearned profits.

For five thousand years, the code name of the Assassins has been the "Kananites" (See *The Curse of Canaan*, by Eustace Mullins[3].) This was the assassins' own name for themselves, symbolized by the initials KN'N, in Aramaic, which in Greek meant the Kananites. They were also called Zelotes, or Zealots, as fanatics who were willing to commit murder for their cause. To the world, they were known as Assassins, originating in modern times as a Judeo-Shiite sect founded by a Persian, Hassan Sabah, in 1090. He had been initiated into the Grand Lodge of Cairo, and travelled throughout Persia organizing the Assassins as a missionary under the protection of Abu Mansur Sedakah Ibn Yussuf, who, although he was Jewish, had risen to the eminence of Vizier to the Caliph al-Mustansir. In India, the Phansigars, or stranglers, got their name from a Hindustani phansi, a noose. In Northern India, they were called Thugs, or deceivers. In Tamul, they were called Ari Tulucar, or Mussulman noosers; in

---

[3] *The Curse of Canaan*, Omnia Veritas Ltd, www.omnia-veritas.com.

Canarese, Tanti Calleru, or thieves, who use a wire or cat gut noose. We mention the Oriental correspondents of our present day assassins, those who rule by terrorism in the United States, because they have the same origins, the same loyalties, and the same goal, the Rule of the World Order.

Many eunuchs who became a liability to the World Order have been eliminated without mercy. When Hiss, White and others faced Congressional investigation, many of their acquaintances became casualties. A lawyer named Marvin Smith, a close friend of Hiss, fell out of a window. Laurence Duggan, an intimate of both Hiss and White, was slated to testify when he fell out of a twelfth story window. Duggan was an official of the Institute of International Education, of which his father was founder and president, but these family ties offered him no protection. In his haste to get to the window, he tore off one shoe, and left his office in a shambles as he fought his way across it. The verdict was "suicide". The Canadian diplomat, Herbert Norman, and the Harvard Professor F. O. Matthiesen, also went out the window before they could be made to testify about their associations. The phenomena became so common that it gave rise to a new term "defenestration", meaning the avoidance of testimony, and a suitable warning to others who might think of talking.

We have read ad nauseam about men of great wealth who, after careers of astounding ruthlessness while amassing their fortunes, suddenly underwent a profound conversion, like Paul, and became men of goodwill. It is true that the "benefactions" of the Carnegies and the Rockefellers are the most potent influences in American life today.

They collect ever higher taxes, increase the control of government over every aspect of human life, and plan more wars and revolutions to further their goals. From the outset, American foundations have exhibited a twofold image — in front is the; tireless do-gooder who balks at nothing if it serves a good cause. Behind him are the evil conspirators who are intent on preserving and increasing their wealth and power. The foundation in its present form, originated in the concept of a Boston family, the Peabodys. Henry James in his novel *The Bostonians*, ridiculed a family friend, Elizabeth Peabody, for her fifty years of relentless humanitarian zeal, portraying her as the legendary Miss Birdseye. George Peabody, after slave trading operations in Washington and Baltimore, moved to London, where he was set up as a front by the Rothschild family. He amassed a fortune by buying up depressed stock in American panics, and chose a Boston trader, Junius Morgan, to carry on his business. In 1865, Peabody set up the first largescale American foundation, the Peabody Educational Fund, endowing it with $1 million in government bonds. By 1867, this had grown to $2 million; by 1869, $3.6 million. Ostensibly set up to educate Southern Negroes after the Civil War, it was a key operation in the carpetbagger strategy to gain control of Southern lands and to control their state governments. These states had to borrow heavily from Wall Street bankers to rebuild their services, and they remained deeply in debt for the next century.

Because of its international connections, the Peabody Fund attracted a stellar board of directors. Gen. Ulysses Grant served on its board for eighteen years; Grover Cleveland served fourteen years; McKinley two years; Theodore Roosevelt thirteen years. J.P. Morgan served on the board for 28 years and never missed a meeting. His partner, Anthony Drexel, served 12 years. A fund with similar goals was the John F. Slater Fund for the Education of Freedmen, established by John F. Slater (1815-1884) a wealthy Northern textile manufacturer. Set up with $1 million, by 1882, it had grown to $4 million. The three original trustees were President Rutherford B. Hayes, Daniel Coit Gilman, and Morris K. Jesup, treasurer.

When John D. Rockefeller discovered that the foundations offered the road to world power, the Peabody Fund proved to be his model. He and his "Director of Charity", Fredrick T. Gates, set up the Southern Educational Board, which merged with the Peabody and Slater Funds. They later set up the General Education Board which absorbed its three predecessors. Its charter stated that its purpose was "the promotion of education within the USA without distinctions of race, creed or sex". Its goals were racial amalgamation and the abolition of distinctions between the sexes. Its incorporators included its first president,

William H. Baldwin Jr., pres. Long Island Railroad, formerly with Union Pacific, the Harriman-Schiff operation; Frederick T. Gates, Rockefeller's right-hand man; Daniel Coit Gilman, vice pres. Peabody Fund and the Slater Fund, president Univ. of California 1872-75, president John Hopkins Univ. 1875-1901, and first president of the Carnegie Institute. Gilman was an original incorporator of the Russell Sage Foundation and the Carnegie Institute. The fact that one man was an incorporator of the three most influential foundations in America shows how centralized the control of these supposedly autonomous foundations has always been by a few ruthless individuals. Gilman is usually listed as a charter member of the World Order, because he, together with Andrew Dickson White and Timothy Dwight, set up the Russell Trust at Yale in 1856, to finance the Skull and Bones organization, whose members are the leading front men in America. W. Averell Harriman, President George Bush, and propagandist William Buckley of the *National Review* are typical members. Norman Dodd, also a Yale man, said,

> "It was well-known on campus that if you were tapped for Bones you would never have to worry about success in later life."

Of the three founders of this order, Dwight became president of Yale; White, son of a railroad millionaire, was said by the *New York Times* to have inherited enough money to make him free from care for life; he became the first president of Cornell University, and gave the institution $300,000 to set up its School of Government; he became the first president of the American Historical Assn, and was U.S. Ambassador to Russia 1892-94, and Ambassador to Germany 1897-1902. His final legacy was to advise Herbert Hoover to set up the Hoover Institution.

However, it is with the third founder, Daniel Coit Gilman, with whom we are most concerned. Gilman trained John Dewey in collectivist theories of education at Johns Hopkins University. Dewey went on to head the University of Chicago School of Education, and later Teachers College at Columbia University, two of the leading Fabian Socialist schools in the world. Gilman, through his protege, Dewey, has dominated American education throughout the twentieth century. Gilman also trained Richard

Ely at the Johns Hopkins dept. of economics. Ely later taught Woodrow Wilson, whom he describes as "unusual, brilliant". Thus Gilman's influence extended through Ely to Woodrow Wilson, who gave us the Federal Reserve System, the income tax, and the First World War.

Although American, the three founders of this order were educated at the University of Berlin, where they were indoctrinated in the Hegelian philosophy of determinism. This philosophy of education and government teaches that everyone can be controlled and must be controlled in order to achieve predetermined goals. It is the philosophy of Oriental despotism transferred to Europe and adapted to the greater individuality of the European peoples, from whom most Americans are descended. As founder Frederick T. Gates wrote in the General Education Board Occasional Paper No. 1:

> "In our dreams we have limitless resources and the people yield themselves with perfect docility to our moulding hands. The present educational conventions fade from our minds, and, unhampered by tradition, we work our own good will upon a grateful and responsive rural folk."

The members of the World Order regard everyone as a peasant; they have only contempt for those who are too naive to see that they are being robbed, tricked and enslaved.

Other original directors of General Education Board included Morris K. Jesup, a banker who had been treasurer of the Peabody and Slater Funds. He was a director of Western Union, a Kuhn Loeb controlled company, Metropolitan Trust, and Atlantic Mutual Insurance; Robert C. Ogden of John Wanamker Co., who served as president of Southern Educational Board, Tuskegee Institute, Union Theological Seminary, and Hampton Institute; Walter Hines Page, who as Ambassador to Britain helped involve us in World War I; Sir Roderick Jones, chief of Reuters News Agency at its historic address, 24 Old Jewry, London, relates a bit of history in his autobiography, *A Life in Reuters*, a luncheon given by him for Gen. Smuts, Sir Starr Jameson, and Dr. Walter Hines Page (all three of whom had Rothschild connections).

"We dined in a private room at the Windham Club, the one in which twenty years later the terms of the abdication of King Edward VII were settled. We drifted on to the question of the U.S. entering the war, for which Britain and France so patiently waited. Dr. Page then revealed to us, under seal of secrecy, that he had received from the President that afternoon, a personal communication upon the strength of which he could affirm that, at last, the die was cast. Consequently, it was not without emotion that he found himself able to assure us that the U.S. would be at war with the Central Powers inside a week from that date. The Ambassador's assurance was correct to the day. We dined on Friday, March 30, On April 2 President Wilson asked Congress to declare a State of War with Germany. On April 6, the U.S. was at war."

Can anyone fail to make a connection between the director of a "charity" designed to control the education of every citizen of the U.S., and its director who conspired to involve us in a world war?

Another incorporator of General Education Board was George Foster Peabody, a member of the family which had set up the Peabody Fund. He married Katrina Trask, relict of Spencer Trask, a wealthy stockbroker who specialized in railroad issues. Their estate, Yaddo, a magnificent upstate mansion, was left as a foundation to provide writers and artists a place to work. The grantees, one need not add, have been unanimously and relentlessly "liberal" in their philosophy and work, although they have regrettably failed to produce any significant contributions to American art or literature. Spencer Trask had been killed when someone shunted a freight train onto the line carrying his sumptuous private car. George Foster Peabody promptly moved into Yaddo with Katrina, and lived ten years with her before marrying her in 1921. She died shortly thereafter, and Peabody "adopted" a lissome young divorcee, Marjorie White, when he was informed the church would not allow him to marry her. He then appointed her sister, Elizabeth Ames, director of Yaddo, where she remained as virtual dictator for many years. The music room at Yaddo displays a large bronze plaque which reads, "George Foster Peabody, Lover of Men". Peabody was appointed the first director of the Federal Reserve Bank of New York in 1914, serving during the crucial years of World War I, until 1921. He was an enthusiastic supporter of the Bolshevik Revolution in Russia, and later became a director of FDR's Warm Springs Foundation, and the Hampton Institute. Louise Ware writes in her biography of Peabody, "He (Peabody) added that the national crisis (World War I), when every man was needed, should insure the Negro opportunity." Peabody was chairman of Combustion Engineering Corp., president of Broadway Realtors, director of Mexican Lead Co., Mexican Coal & Coke, Mexican National Railways, Tezuitlan Copper Refining and Smelting, and served as treasurer of the Democratic National Party. Despite his "capitalist" background, Peabody was always an avowed Socialist. Ware notes that he wrote to Norman Thomas,

> "I have always been most sympathetic to individual Socialist aspirations. I have particularly observed the Fabian System of England with hopeful anticipations."

This admirer of Fabian Socialism is the man who helped install the General Education Board as the guiding force behind all educational developments in the U.S. since 1910.

The *Springfield Republican* noted, Oct. 1866,

> "For all who know anything of the subject know very well that Peabody and his partners in London gave us no faith and no help in our struggle for national existence. They participated to the full in the common English distrust of our cause and our success, and talked and acted for the South rather than for our nation. No individual contributed so much to flooding our money markets with the evidences of our debt in Europe, and breaking down their prices and weakening financial confidence in our nationality than George Peabody & Co. and none made more money by the operation. All the money that Mr. Peabody is giving away so lavishly among our institutions of learning was gained by the speculations of his house in our misfortunes."

This editorial was also reprinted in the *New York Times* Oct. 31, 1866. The writer did not know that Peabody was a front for the Rothschilds, or that the establishment of the Peabody Fund was intended to give them political and financial control of the impoverished South, or that it would inaugurate the "Era of Foundations" as the controlling factor in American life.

John D. Rockefeller used General Education Board funds through Standard Oil representatives in Russia to provoke the Russian Revolution in 1905. No wonder the Soviet masses cheer when a Rockefeller arrives to visit them. To date, the Rockefellers have "given" more than $5 billion from stock income, meaning that Americans have had to ante up billions of dollars in taxes which would otherwise have been revenue on this income. Congressman Wright Patman, chmn of the House Banking & Currency Committee, proved in 1967 Hearings that 14 Rockefeller foundations held assets of more than $1 billion in Standard Oil stock. Not only did they pay no tax on this stock, but it gave them permanent control over the family owned firm. Rival financiers could not buy control of Standard Oil because its stock was insulated by foundation ownership... As Patman pointed out, the fact that the Rockefellers escaped paying huge sums in taxes gave them an unsurpassed market advantage over other firms which had to pay normal rates of taxation, the agitation for increased "corporate taxation" adds to Rockefeller's advantage. Patman said,

> "The Foundations are the best investments the Rockefeller family could have made."

A family member, Senator Nelson Aldrich, shepherded the General Education Board charter through congress. The Rockefeller Foundation charter proved more difficult. It was a flagrant effort to evade government decrees against the Standard Oil monopoly, but was finally pushed through in 1913 by Sen. Robert F. Wagner of N. Y., setting aside $50 million in Standard Oil of New Jersey stock for "charitable work". The Rockefeller Foundation charter was signed on May 22, 1913. Its incorporators were John D. Rockefeller, John D. Rockefeller Jr.; Henry Pratt Judson, of the Lyman and Pratt families, president of University of Chicago; Simon Flexner, educated at University of Berlin and Univ. of Strasbourg, had served with Rockefeller Institute since 1903 as prof, of medicine; Starr Jameson, "personal counsel to John D. Rockefeller in his benevolences"; Jerome D. Greene, secretary of Harvard Corp. 1910-11, banker with Lee Higginson of London, 1912-18; sec. Reparations commission at Paris Peace Conference; Wickliffe Rose, prof. Peabody College, secretary Peabody Educational Fund, trustee of Slater Fund and General Education Board; and Charles W. Eliot, also of the Lyman family, married Ellen Peabody, educated in Germany, president emeritus of Harvard. An offshoot, the China Medical Board, secured Standard Oil the market for "oil for the lamps of China", and gave the family entree into the highly profitable Asiatic drug trade. The breakthrough was obtained after they financed the rise to power of the Soong family, who created modern China.

The list of officers of the Rockefeller Foundation from 1913-63 reveals a great deal about this organization. The four chairmen of the board have been John D. Rockefeller Jr. 1917, 1939, Walter D. Stewart, 1939-50, John Foster Dulles, 1950-52, and John D. Rockefeller 3rd, 1952-63.

Walter D. Stewart served with Bernard Baruch on the War Industries Board in 1918, was with the Federal Reserve Board from 1922-25, and then joined the law firm of Case, Pomery, a Rockefeller firm. He was economic adviser to the Bank of England 1928-30, Special Adviser to Bank for International Settlements 1931, Presidential Council of Economic Advisors for Eisenhower 1953-56, and later president of the Institute for Advanced Study. In this list of legal and financial posts, one is struck by the conspicuous absence of any "charitable" endeavours.

John Foster Dulles, as senior partner of the law firm of Sullivan and Cromwell, carried on the firm's traditional involvement in promoting wars and revolutions. Few Americans know that Sullivan & Cromwell's intrigues made the Panama Canal possible.

A 736 page volume, *The Story of Panama*, the U.S. House Hearings on Panama in 1913, offers hundreds of pages of documentation proving that William Nelson Cromwell, founder of the firm, and Dulles' mentor, instigated and promoted the Panamanian Revolution for J.P. Morgan and J & W Seligmap. Morgan subsequently received $40 million in gold from the U.S.

Treasury, the largest check it had ever drawn to that time. $35 million of this sum was clear profit. President Theodore Roosevelt sued the *New York World* for libel for printing some of the facts about himself and Cromwell. The case was unanimously thrown out of court by the Supreme Court.

We find in "The Roosevelt Panama Libel Case Against the N.Y. World" the following:

> "On Oct. 3, 1908, the Democratic National Committee was considering the advisability of making public a statement that William Nelson Cromwell in connection with M. Bunau Varilla, A French speculator, had formed a syndicate at the time when it was quite evident that the U.S. would take over the rights of French bondholders in the DE Lesseps Canal, and that this syndicate included among others Charles P. Taft, brother of William Howard Taft, and Douglas Robinson, brother-in-law of President Theodore Roosevelt. These financiers invested their money because of a full knowledge of the intention of the U.S. Government to acquire the French property at a price of about $40 million and thus — because of the alleged information from Government sources — were enabled to reap a rich profit."

On Aug. 29, 1908, the Democratic National Committee issued a statement from its headquarters in Chicago identifying Cromwell as,

> "William Nelson Cromwell of New York, the great Wall Street lawyer, attorney for the Panama Canal combine, Kuhn Loeb Co., the Harriman interests, the sugar trust, the Standard Oil trust et al."

Thus the Democratic leaders identified Cromwell as the lawyer for the seven men who controlled America for the Rothschilds. The Democrats continued:

> "In Sept. 1904, during the absences of Secretary Taft from Washington, Mr. Cromwell, a private citizen practically ran the War Dept. John F. Wallace, Chief Engineer of the Panama Canal, testified before the Senate Committee on Feb. 5, 1905, 'Cromwell appeared to me to be a dangerous man'."

The House Hearings devoted many pages to Cromwell's activities, well worth anyone's reading, including damning testimony from Congressman Rainey:

> "The revolutionists were in the pay of the Panama Railroad & Steamship Co., a New Jersey corporation. The representative of that corporation was William Nelson Cromwell. He was the revolutionist who promoted and made possible the revolution on the Isthmus of Panama. At that time he was a shareholder in the railroad and its general counsel in the United States. William Nelson Cromwell — the most dangerous man this country has produced since the days of Aaron Burr — is a professional revolutionist."

John Foster Dulles, chairman of the board of the Rockefeller Foundation, inherited the mantle of Cromwell as the most dangerous man in America. A member of the Rockefeller family through his marriage to Janet Pomeroy Avery, he was secretary to his uncle, Secretary of State Robert Lansing, at the Paris Peace Conference. Thomas Lamont, partner of J.P. Morgan, wrote of Dulles at that time,

> "All of us placed great reliance upon John Foster Dulles."

Dulles later turned up in Germany with Baron Kurt von Schroder to guarantee Hitler the funds to take over Germany. U.S. Ambassador to Germany William Dodd writes in his Diary, Dec. 4, 1933,

> "John Foster Dulles, legal Counsel for associated American banks, called this afternoon to give an account of claims being urged on behalf of bondholders against German cities and corporations, more than a billion dollars. He seemed very clever and resolute."

Ron Pruessen, in his biography of Dulles, mentions Dulles' "secret discussions with the German Cabinet Dec. 1933 and Jan. 1934 in Berlin." Pruessen lists Dulles' banking clients during the 1920s, "J.P. Morgan, the national City Co., Kuhn, Loeb & Co., Dillon Read, Guaranty Trust, Lee Higginson, and Brown Bros Harriman." Dulles had a legal monopoly on Wall Street.

John Foster Dulles never lost his penchant for starting wars. How many Americans know that it was John Foster Dulles who sent a telegram from Tokyo to President Truman's advisers,

> "If it appears that the South Koreans cannot repulse the attack, then we believe that U.S. force should be used."

Although Dulles never revealed who "we" included, this telegram set off our involvement in the Korean War.

Among the presidents of the Rockefeller Foundation, we find George E. Vincent, who was president of the Chautauqua Institution. He served with Herbert Hoover on the Commission for Relief in Belgium; Max Mason, president of the University of Chicago, to which the Rockefellers gave some $400 million; Raymond Blaine Fosdick, who served as secretary to the League of Nations, 1919-20, later was official biographer of John D. Rockefeller; his brother Harry Emerson Fosdick, who was pastor of Rockefeller's church; Chester I. Barnard, president of AT&T, director of the U.S. Telephone Agency during World War I; Dean Rusk, who served two presidents as Secretary of State; and J. George Harrar, who was Andrew D. White professor at Cornell.

The Secretaries of the Rockefeller Foundation are: Jerome D. Greene, who was secretary to the president of Harvard 1901-05, and on the board of Harvard Overseers 1911-1950, secretary of the Reparations Commission under Bernard Baruch at the Paris Peace Conference 1919, general manager of the Rockefeller Institute of Medical Research 1910-1939, director of Brookings Institution, 1928-1945, and chairman of the notorious Rockefeller financed Institute of Pacific Relations, of which Laurence Rockefeller was secretary, and which had close relations with the Soviet spy Richard Sorge in Japan; Edwin R. Embree, who set up the Julius Rosenwald Foundation in 1917 "for the wellbeing of mankind", seven of whose trustees were identified as members of Communist front organizations.

Vice presidents of the Rockefeller Foundation since 1913 include; Roger S. Greene, the organizer of the Committee to Defend America by Aiding the Allies, whose purpose was to involve us in World War II and who served with the Dept. of

State from 1940-44; and Alan Gregg, who served with the British Expeditionary Force 1917-19.

All of these officers also are listed as directors of the Rockefeller Foundation. Other directors include; The Lord Franks, British Ambassador to the U.S. 1948-52, a key member of the London Connection which operates the United States as a colony of the British Empire; he is a director of the Rhodes Trust, the Schroder Bank, visiting professor at the University of Chicago, chairman of Lloyd's Bank, and presently chancellor of East Anglia University; Charles Evans Hughes, governor of New York, presidential candidate who is believed to have actually defeated Woodrow Wilson in 1916, later Chief Justice of the Supreme Court, appointed to that post by his good friend Herbert Hoover; James R. Angell, chmn National Research Council. 1919-20, president of the Carnegie Corp., president of Yale (his daughter is Mrs. William Rockefeller); he was a director of *New York Life* and NBC; Trevor Arnett, president of the International Board of Education; Harry Pratt Judson, president Univ. of Minnesota, president American University in China, director of Rockefeller's China Medical Board; Vernon Kellogg, Herbert Hoover's assistant in the U.S. Food Administration, during World War I and the American Relief Administration 1919-21, later secretary National Research Council and trustee of Brookings Instn; Starr Murphy, who lists himself in Who's Who as "the personal counsel and representative of John D. Rockefeller in his bevenolences"; Wickliffe Rose, director of public health, Rockefeller Foundation 1913-23; president Peabody College 1892-02, agent Peabody Education Fund 1907-15, Rockefeller Sanitary Commission and Southern Educational Board 1909-15, International Health Board 1913-28, president General Education Board 1913-28, International Education Board 1923-28, director Red Cross and Atlantic Council; A. Barton Hepburn, Supt. Banks N.Y. State 1880-83, chief bank examiner N.Y. 1888-92, Comptroller U.S. Army 1892-93, vice pres. National City Bank 1897-99, president Chase Natl Bank 1899-1922, member Federal Advisory Council, Federal Reserve System, 1918, Director N.Y. Life, Sears, Woolworth, Studebaker, Texas Co.; Julius Rosenwald, set up Rosenwald Foundation to carry on Peabody fund agitation in the South, "total involvement"; he also gave $700,000 to Rockefeller's University of Chicago, was trustee Baron de Hirsch Fund, Zionist settlement program; Martin A. Ryerson, president board of trustees University of Chicago, trustee Carnegie Institution; Karl T. Compton, assigned to American Embassy Paris 1918, he was chmn U.S. Radar Mission to USSR 1943, spec. rep. secretary of War 1943-44, spec, advsr atomic development 1945, achieved immortality as the man who told Pres. Truman to drop the atomic bomb on Japan, the first use of this horror weapon, also director of Ford Foundation, Sloan Kettering Institute, Royal Society of London; John W. Davis, lawyer for Morgan and Rockefeller, Ambassador to Britain 1918-21, Democratic candidate president 1924; John Sloan Dickey, with Dept. State 1940-45, president Dartmouth, served on President's Commission on Civil Rights; Harold W. Dodds, president Princeton, was Herbert Hoover's executive secretary U.S. Food Administration 1917-19, trustee Brookings Institution and Carnegie Foundation, director Prudential Insurance; Lewis W. Douglas, grad. Oxford, married Peggy Zinsser, Director of Budget 1933-34, president American Cynamid, Ambassador to Great Britain 1947, chairman of board Metropolitan Life, director General Motors, Homestake Mining Co.; Orvil Dryfoos, who married Marion Sulzberger and became chairman of *New York Times*, trustee Baron de Hirsch Fund; Lee A. DuBridge, president California Institute of Technology, trustee Rand Corp. member U.S. Atomic Energy Commission, awarded the King's Medal for service to Great Britain 1943; David Leon Edsall, dean Harvard Medical School 1918-35; Charles William Eliot, who married Ellen Peabody, studied European educational methods, president of Harvard for many years, promoted Hegelian school of determinism; Simon Flexner who studied at Univ. of Berlin, Univ. of Strasburg, set up Rockefeller Institute of Medical Research, member Royal Society of London, many medical societies; Douglas Freeman, editor Richmond News Leader, director Woodrow Wilson Foundation, Equitable Life; Herbert S. Gasser, organized Chemical Warfare Service 1918, fellow Royal Society, London and Edinburgh; Frederick T. Gates, lists himself as "business and benevolent representative" of John D. Rockefeller 1893-1912; Walter S. Gifford, organized U.S. Council Natl Defense 1916-18 formed to involve us in World War I, invited by Col. House to serve on U.S. Inter Allied Council 1918, president ATT, chairman of board of Carnegie Institution; Robert F. Goheen, president Princeton 1957-72, Woodrow Wilson Fellowship, Smithsonian Institution, Institute of International Education, Dreyfus Fund, board of overseers Harvard Univ. Carnegie Foundation; Herbert Spencer Hadley, as atty gen. of Missouri prosecuted Standard Oil, they then backed him for Governor, he served from 1909-13; Wallace K. Harrison, architect Rockefeller Center and UN Building; Theodore Hesburgh, president Notre Dame Univ., Woodrow Wilson Fellowship, Carnegie Foundation, Ford Foundation, Rockefeller Bros Fund, Hoover Commission; Ernest M.Hopkins, asst. to Sec. of War 1918, Office of Procurement & Management 1941, president Dartmouth 1916-45; Arthur A. Houghton, chmn Corning Glass, office Price Management 1941-42, adv. com. on arts Federal Reserve System, director *New York Life*, U.S. Trust, J.P. Morgan Library; Clark Kerr, pres. Univ. of California 1952-73; Robert A. Lovett, married Adele Brown, of Brown Bros; he was partner Brown Bros Harriman 1926-61, spec, asst Sec. of War 1940-41, Sec. War for Air 1941-45, Under, Sec. State 1947-49, replaced James A. Forrestal as Secretary of Defense when Forrestal fell from window at Naval Hospital, served as Sec. Defense 195-52, director Royal Globe Insurance of London, *N.Y. Life*, Freeport Sulphur, chairman Union Pacific, director Carnegie Instn; his father, Judge Robert S. Lovett was attorney for UP, advised Harriman and Kahn not to answer, questions about their stock dealings, all records burned in 1911; Benjamin McKelway, editor *Washington Star*; Henry Allen Moe, Rhodes Scholar, ran Guggenheim Foundation for many years, barrister of Inner Temple, London, chmn Museum, of Modern Art set up by Rockefeller family, also Natl Endowment for the Humanities; William Myers, director Federal Reserve Bank of N. Y., pres. Committee on Foreign Aid 1947, director Carnegie Foundation, Arco, Smith Corona, Continental Can, Grand Union, Mutual Life; Thomas. Parkinson, adj Gen. U.S. Army 1918-19, chairman Equitable Life, Chase Natl Bank, ATT, Borden; Thomas Parran, Surgeon General U.S. 1936-48; Alfred N. Richards, staff British Medical Research 1917-18, organized U.S. Chemical Warfare

Service 1918; Dean Rusk, Rhodes Scholar, joined Dept. State 1946, important role with John Foster Dulles in involving U.S. in Korean War, asst. Sec. War 1946-47, UN Affairs Dept. State 1947-49, president Rockefeller Foundation 1950-60, Secretary of State 1961-69; Geoffrey S. Smith, married into Coolidge family, counsel Natl Refugee Commission 1940, OPM 1941, War Production Board 1942, pres. Girard Trust, director Bell Telephone; Robert G. Sproull, pres. Univ. of Calif, his brother Allan was president Federal Reserve Bank of N.Y. for many years, Robert was director of Institute of International Education, Carnegie Foundation, American Group on Allied Reparations 1945, Citizens Committee for the Marshall Plan, Institute of Pacific Relations; Frank Stanton, OWI 1942-45, president of CBS for many years; Robert T. Stevens, chairman of family firm J.T. Stevens, giant textile firm, director Federal Reserve Bank of N.Y., J.P. Morgan, General Electric, General Foods, New York Telephone, Secretary Army 1953-55, involved in McCarthy Hearings; George D. Woods, chairman First Boston, Kaiser Steel, General Staff U.S. Army 1942-45, director *New York Times*; Arthur M. Woods, asst. Sec. War World War I, director of Rockefeller firm Colorado Fuel & Iron, scene of massacre of workers, Ludlow massacre; Owen D. Young, chairman General Electric, director RCA, American Foreign Power, General Motors, NBC, RKO, Federal Reserve Bank of N.Y., agent gen. for reparations payments 1919-24, chosen by Bernard Baruch; Winthrop Aldrich, Rockefeller family member, chairman Chase National Bank, director ATT, International Paper, Metropolitan Life, Westinghouse, Federal Reserve Bank of N.Y., Rockefeller Center, served as Ambassador Great Britain 1953-57; Barry Bingham, editor Louisville Courier Journal, served in Europe 1942-45, special mission to France for ECA 1949-50; Chester Bowles, founded ad agency Benton & Bowles, served with OPA, WPB WWII, ambassador to India 1951-53, Woodrow Wilson Foundation, partner Sen. William Benton; Lloyd D. Brace, pres. First Natl Bank, director ATT. Gillette, John Hancock, Stone & Webster, U.S. Smelting; Richard Bradfield, educated at Univ. of Berlin, married into Stillman family Guggenheim fellow, carried out Far Eastern policy for Rockefeller Foundation as head division of agriculture 1955-57; Dieter Bronk, pres. Rockefeller

Institute Medical Research, Sloan Kettering Institute, received Order of British Empire; William H. Claflin, treas. Harvard; Ralph Bunche, educated at Harvard and London School of Economics, with British section OSS 1941-44, Dept. State 1944-47, Dumbarton Oaks 1944, UN at San Francisco with Alger Hiss 1945, UN London 1945, Und. Sec UN 1947-71, Palestine Mediator 1948 - after Count Bernadotte was assassinated by Begin; C. Douglas Dillon born Switzerland 1909, director U.S. & Foreign Securities 1937-63, chairman Dillon Read 1946-53, Ambassador to France 1953-57, under Sec. State 1958-1960, helped Bechtel obtain Arabian contracts (Bechtel later bought out his family firm, Dillon Read), Secretary of Treasury 1960-65, is trustee Brookings Instn, Hoover Institution, Heritage Foundation, his daughter is Princess Joan of Luxembourg, married into family which is direct descendant of William of Orange who chartered the Bank of England; Edward Robinson, was with Peabody Co., Spencer Trask co. treasurer Rockefeller Foundation & General Education Board 1938-62; Kenneth Wernimont, joined Institute of International Education 1937, Dept. of Agriculture 1938-46 in Latin America, Mexican missions for Rockefeller; Charles W. Cole, pres. Amherst, Ambassador to Chile 1961-64, director Charles E. Merill Trust; Thomas B. Applegate Jr. exec, secretary to John D. Rockefeller 1942-46, chief Far East Division of Dept. of State; Edmund E. day, dean Wharton School of Finance U. Pa 1912-29, Guggenheim fellow, president 1933-39 Natl Bureau of Economic Research set up by Rockefellers.

The 1981 list of Rockefeller Foundation trustees also includes James C. Fletcher, whose "charitable" background is listed in Who's Who as "Naval ordinance 1940", and forty years of subsequent experience in guided missiles and strategic weapons, with Hughes Aircraft 1948-54, guided missiles with Ramo-Wolldridge 1954-58, Aerojet General 1960-71, chmn Minuteman 1961, chmn Naval Warfare panel 1967-73, and board of American Ordinance Assn. Another 1981 trustee is James D. Wolfensohn, who serves as president J. Henry Schroder Banking Corp. N.Y., and its parent company, Schroders Ltd. of London.

Examining the dominant members of the Rockefeller Foundation, we find men whose lives have been devoted to war and revolution, chemical warfare, international, intrigue, and mass murder; we find the chairman of the board was John Foster Dulles, who inherited the title of "most dangerous man in America" from his mentor, William Nelson Cromwell; Dulles obtained crucial financing for Hitler, and sent the key telegram involving the U.S. in the Korean War, while his brother, a director of Schroder Bank, set up the CIA; we find Karl T. Compton, who gave the word to drop the atomic bomb on Japan in 1945 and unleashed the horror of atomic warfare on the entire world (he was also trustee of Ford Foundation); we find Lord Franks, key member of the Rhodes Trust, the Schroder Bank; what we do not find is anyone who has ever engaged in any charitable endeavour. The Rockefeller directors of what is properly the "Rockefeller Syndicate" interlock with the nation's major banks, corporations, universities and government departments. This is the network which illegally rules America, which, by its tax evasion, places a tremendous tax burden on all American taxpayers, and which makes our elections a farce because these men determine all policies which are implemented in the United States.

Through the Sealantic Fund, the Rockefellers control American schools of theology and the religious institutions of America; through the Rockefeller Bros Fund they control government policy. In 1958, the Rockefeller Bros Fund convened American leaders to urge greater military spending; the group included Gen. Lucius Clay of Lehman Bros., former chief of U.S. forces in Europe; Gordon Dean of the U.S. Atomic Energy Commission; Deverux C. Josephs of J.P. Morgan Co.; Henry Luce of Time Mag. Thomas B. McCabe, chmn Federal Reserve Board of Governors; Anna M. Rosenberg, secretary to Bernard Baruch. and Asst. Sec. Defense (she married Julius Rosenberg), was on Social Security Board 1936-43, charter member of New Deal Administration, War Manpower Commission 1942-45, trustee of Ford Foundation and Rockefeller Foundation, later married Paul Hoffman, head of ECA; Dean Rusk of the Rockefeller Foundation; David Sarnoff, founder of RCA; Henry Kissinger; and Roswell Gilpatrick, und. Sec. Air Force 1951-53.

Gilpatric was partner of the Kuhn, Loeb law firm of Cravath de Gersdorff Swaine and Wood 1931-61, Yale Corp. Woodrow Wilson Foundation; his brother Chadbourne was a Rhodes Scholar, OSS Europe World War II, and CIA 1947 to present; another brother, Donald, was on the staff of Natl City Bank, Board of Economic Warfare 1943-43, economic advisor Allied Headquarters during World War II, U.S. Member UNRRA, dir. ECA 1948, now director of Olin Matheson and Winchester Arms.

Every American worker is regularly reminded of one Rockefeller Foundation "boon to mankind" when he receives his mutilated pay check with the "withholding tax" ripped from it. In 1943, at the height of World War II, Congress passed an "emergency" wartime tax bill, the Current Tax Payment act of 1943. Enacted on June 9, 1943, the bill became known as the Withholding Tax. The "emergency" ended some forty years ago, and in the intervening decades the bill has been and it is illegal. It is illegal because it is not "withholding" and because it is not a tax. Since it is not what it claims to be, it cannot be enforced, as it has no legal standing. In legal terms, the withholding tax is a garnishee. Webster defines a garnishee as a legal notice served with a writ of attachment to attach the wages of a debtor on behalf of a creditor. However, the withholding tax is not a legal notice served with a writ of attachment, nor is it issued by any court, and is not collectible under U.S. law. Second, the "debt", or tax, can only be established on the annual return at the end of the taxable year, as provided by law. IRS claims that the withholding tax establishes "the liability at the source". However, no debt has been established at the time of collection.

The withholding tax is also illegal because it was enacted into law as the result of a conspiracy by persons who concealed their motives and their allegiances. Beardsley Ruml, who foisted the plan on Congress, told a *New Yorker* reporter that the withholding tax plan originated at a luncheon of "intellectuals" at the luxurious Plaza Hotel. He refused to identify any of the other conspirators. *Fortune* said of him,

> "Beardsley Ruml of pay-as-you-go fame (characterized by Congressman Wright Patman as protecting the first crop

of war millionaires), is beyond a doubt one of the most mentally agile and popular men in American history. Like many other interesting personalities, the treasurer of Macy's, chairman of the Federal Reserve Bank of New York and eminent fiscal planner is a far from simple character. The former dean of social sciences at the Univ. of Chicago later worked for the Carnegie Corp. In 1922 the Rockefellers made the 28-year old Ruml director of the Laura Spelman Rockefeller Memorial ($80 million). The Memorial had been founded for charitable aid to women, but Mr. Ruml, arguing that the welfare of the individual depends on the welfare of the whole society, threw the organization and $25 million of the funds behind the social sciences."

Ruml's idea of the withholding tax is suggested in his book. *Government Business and Values*, p. 179,

"It is evident that the progress of science, technology and education will force important changes in our personal, social and economic relationships. To meet these changes, government must change and modify the laws, rules and regulations under which we live."

Note that Ruml says "force" changes, by "government" decree. This is the entire foundation program, to impose by force their will on the American electorate, in a criminal syndicalist conspiracy against the wellbeing of every American.

The 1971 list of trustees of the Rockefeller Foundation shows it continues to be the ruling hierarchy of the U.S. It includes W. Michael Blumenthal, and C. Douglas Dillon, both of whom served as Secretaries of the Treasury; Robert F. Goheen, president of Princeton; Vernon Jordan, the token black; Robert V. Roosa, and Cyrus Vance, Secretary of State under Carter. Roosa is a founding member and secretary of the Trilateral commission. While he was on the staff of the Federal Reserve Bank of N.Y., Roosa trained a group known as the "Roosa Bloc", his chief protege being Paul Volcker, who, as chairman of the Federal Reserve Board of Governors, unleashed a ruinous recession in the U.S. with 20% interest rates and 25% inflation. Of course the banks profited handsomely while driving millions of Americans into bankruptcy. The *New York Times* reported that

David Rockefeller and Roosa "suggested" to Carter that he appoint Volcker as chairman of the Federal Reserve Board. Roosa is a partner of Brown Bros. Harriman, director of Texaco, American Express, Owen Corning Fiberglass, director National Bureau of Economic Research, trustee Sloan Kettering Institute, and chairman of Brookings Institution.

Brookings Institution was incorporated in 1927 by Frederic A. Delano, 2244 S. St NW Washington D.C.; Harold G. Moulton, 3700 Oliver St. NW, Washington, a Univ. of Chicago economist; and Leo S. Rowe, who had been asst. Secretary Treasury 1917-19, working closely with Eugene Meyer and the War Finance Corp. chief of Latin American div. Dept. of State 1919-20, director Pan American Union 1920-36.

The Brookings Institution was founded by Robert S. Brookings born 1850, unmarried, a St. Louis merchant and head of the Cupples Co. which revolutionized the distribution of goods from railway stations. In World War I, Brookings was Baruch's assistant at the War Industries Board, which had dictatorial powers over American industrialists, and Chairman of the Price Fixing Committee of WIB. An original trustee of Carnegie Endowment for International Peace, Brookings set up the Brookings Graduate School of Economics, which merged with the Institute of Government Research and the Institute of Economics in 1927 to form the present Brookings Institution. It is listed as "not a membership organization", whose goal is "to set national priorities", in short, to make government policy, which it does. It rode into power with Roosevelt's New Deal, hardly a surprising development, since its incorporator, Frederic A. Delano, was FDR's uncle. The present chairman, Robert V. Roosa, was preceded in that office by C. Douglas Dillon. It has always been the forum of the world's most powerful financiers.

In 1984, Brookings Institution originated a new program for the government, written by a team of economists headed by Alice Rivlin, former director Congressional Budget Office. Rivlin proposed that the income tax be replaced or augmented by a consumption tax laid upon all consumption, bequests and gifts. In short, the traditionally leftwing Brookings Institution hopes to enact into law the illegal IRS technique of "composite net worth", laying an income tax on citizens by estimating what they spend or consume, a "cash flow" tax as inescapable as the Rockefeller-Ruml withholding tax. Their only goal is to grind the working man into hopeless poverty through ruthless extortion by government agents.

In 1978, corporations gave Brookings $95,000; in 1984, this figure had jumped to $1.6 million. Most of their $13 million budget continues to be paid by the major foundations, Ford, Rockefeller, Carnegie, Milbank Memorial Fund. The foundations work together, not only because of their close interlocking, but because they have a common program. That program was published by Karl Marx in 1848 as *The Communist Manifesto*:

> - Abolition of all property in land.
> - Application of all rents of land to public purposes.
> - A heavy progressive or graduated income tax.
> - Abolition of all right of inheritance.
> - Confiscation of property of emigrants and rebels.
> - Centralization of credit in the hands of the state, by means of a national bank, with state capital an exclusive monopoly
> - Extension of factories and instruments of production owned by the state, bringing into cultivation of waste lands, and improvement of the soil generally in accordance with a common plan.
> - Equal obligation of all to work.
> - Establishment of industrial armies, especially for agriculture.
> - Combination of agriculture with manufacturing industries.
> - Gradual abolition of distinction between town and country, by more equitable distribution of population over the country.
> - Free education for all children in public schools.

> Combination of education with industrial production.

> Abolition of child labour in its present form.

The foundations never oppose or contradict a single plank of the Communist Manifesto. The program has given us "vocational training" instead of education, which is a different form of child labour.

Present directors of Brookings include Louis W. Cabot, of Cabot Corp., director of Federal Reserve Bank of Boston, R.R. Donnelley, Owen Corning Fiberglass, chmn of board of Harvard Overseers, and Natl Committee for U.S. China Trade. He served with OPA and WPB during World War II, later with ECA and UN Council FAO; Barton M. Biggs, with E. F. Hutton, Morgan Stanley, Rand McNally, now director of Lehman Institute; Edward W. Carter, chairman Carter Hawley Hale Stores, trustee of the billion dollar James Irvine Foundation in California, Harvard Board of Overseers, Woodrow Wilson Institute, ATT, Delmonte, Lockheed, Southern Cal Edison, Pacific Mutual *Life* Ins.; Frank T. Cary, chairman IBM, director J.P. Morgan, ABC, Morgan Guaranty Trust, Merck, Texaco, Rockefeller Univ. Museum of Modern Art; William T. Coleman Jr, former Sec. transportation; John B Debutts former chairman ATT; Roger W. Heyns, director Kaiser Steel, Levi Strauss, Times Mirror Corp., Norton Simon Museum, James Irvine Fndtn; Carla A. Hills, former Sec. HUD - her husband is chairman SEC, she is on board of IBM, American Airlines, Trilateral Commission, Woodrow Wilson School, Stanford, & Norton Simon Museum; Lane Kirkland, head of the CIO; Bruce K. McLaury, president of Brookings, was with Federal Reserve Bank of N.Y. 1958-69, dep. und. sec. Treasury for monetary affairs 1969-71, president Federal Reserve Bank of Minnesota 1971-77, member Trilateral Commission; Robert S. McNamara, former Secretary of Defense, president of the World Bank; Arjay Miller, also was with Ford Motor, director *Washington Post*, TWA, Andrew Mellon Foundation; Donald S. Perkins; Eugene R. Black, former president World Bank; Wm Mc. Martin Jr. former chairman Federal Reserve Board of Governors; Robert Brookings Smith; Sidney Stein Jr., Chicago banker, Federal Bureau of Budget

1941-45, Presidential Consultant on Budget 1961-67, committee on Foreign Aid; Robert D. Calkins, Stanford Food Research Institute 1925-32. General Education Board 1947-52, president Brookings 1952-67, was with the NRA and agricultural administration 1933-35, director Federal Reserve Bank of N.Y. 1943-49, War Labor Board, 1942-45, OPA and War Dept. 1942; Warren M. Shapleigh, pres. Ralston Purina, director J.P. Morgan, Morgan Guaranty Trust, Brown Group First Natl Bank St. Louis; James D. Robinson III, chairman AMAX, Bristol Myers, Coca Cola, Union Pacific, Trust Co. of Ga., was asst to pres. Morgan Guaranty Trust 1961-68, trustee Rockefeller Univ.

The heavy representation of Morgan and Rockefeller directors on the board of Brookings explains the relentless drive of the "big rich" to increase taxes and government control of the average American citizen. The Business section of the *New York Times* April 15, 1984, long in advance of the election, carried a headline story on the Business page that

> "Whoever Wins in November, There Will Still be a $100 Billion Increase for U.S. Taxpayers."

Another major U.S. foundation, the Russell Sage Foundation, was incorporated in 1907 by Daniel Coit Gilman and Cleveland H. Dodge. A director of National City Bank, Dodge masterminded the Presidential campaign of Woodrow Wilson, after subsidizing his academic career at Princeton with $5000 a year from himself and Moses Pyne, grandson of the founder of National City Bank.

In 1980, the Russell Sage Foundation had assets of $52 million, and expenditures of $2 million. Sage was a Wall Street speculator who made a fortune in railroad stocks. Nicolson's biography of Dwight Morrow notes that,

> "It has always been a tradition that the partners of J.P. Morgan should engage in all forms of public and charitable activity. Morrow was a trustee of Russell Sage Foundation, director Natl Bureau of Economic Research, N.Y. Commission of ReEmployment, and Carnegie Endowment for International Peace. He was a director of General Electric and Bankers Trust."

The present chairman of Russell Sage Foundation is Herma Hill Kaye, leading Women's Rights organizer, trustee of the Rosenberg Foundation; president is Marshall A. Robinson, also is director of Ford Foundation and director of Herbert Hoover's Belgian American Educational Foundation; directors of Russell Sage are Robert McCormick Adams — he was recently named to replace S. Dillon Ripley as head of the Smithsonian (Ripley was an OSS agent 1942-45, Guggenheim fellow, Fulbright fellow, Natl Science Fndtn fellow); Adams' wife Ruth was principal organizer of Eaton's Pugwash Conferences which were run by the KGB. Adams is moving into a new $485,000 mansion voted him by the Smithsonian board - the "new class" likes to live well; William D. Carey, chairman US-USSR Trade & Economic Council, received a Rockefeller public service award 1964; Earl F. Cheit, dean of School of Business Administration, U. Cal at Berkeley - Cheit is also director of Mitre corp., program officer Ford Foundation and council of Carnegie Institution; Carl Kaysen, economist with Natl Bureau of Economic Research, was with OSS 1942, prof. Harvard 1946-66, Institute for Advanced Study 1966-70, lecturer London School of Economics, spl. asst to President Kennedy for national security, Carnegie Commission, Paley lecturer Hebrew University, and director of Polaroid (financed by James Paul Warburg), trustee German Marshall Fund, Fulbright scholar London School of Economics, Guggenheim fellow, Ford Foundation fellow; Frederick Mosteller, spec, economist War Dept. 1942-43, Guggenheim fellow, Myrdal Prize; John S. Reed, chairman Santa Fe Industries, Kraft, Northern Trust, Dart & Kraft, Atchison Topeka Santa Fe RR; Oscar M. Ruebhausen, atty Lend Lease Administration 1942-44, gen. counsel OSRD Washington 1944-46, partner of law firm of Debevoise Plimpton since 1937, director Equitable Life, International Development Bank, chmn UN Day NY, Hudson Institute.

The directors of the major foundations have been particularly active in wartime positions, even though they seem to have little experience in charitable endeavours. Beardsley Ruml was a trustee of Russell Sage Foundation from 1928-33. For many years the most prominent figure on Sage's board was Frederic A. Delano, who was born in Hong Kong, where his father, Captain

Warren Delano, was engaged in the opium trade. An uncle of Franklin D. Roosevelt, Delano was an original member of the Federal Reserve Board of Governors in 1914, and was later named by his nephew as Governor of the Federal Reserve Bank of Richmond. He was an original incorporator of Brookings Institution, Carnegie Institution, and Carnegie Endowment for International Peace, director of the Smithsonian Museum, Commission for Relief in Belgium, and Belgian American Educational Foundation set up by Herbert Hoover in World War I, chmn Natl Planning Board 1934-43. His wife's sister married Ed Burling, who founded the Washington law firm of Covington & Burling, whose partners later included Dean Acheson and Donald Hiss, brother of Alger. Frederic A. Delano married Mathilda Peasley of Chicago; Edward Burling married her sister Louise. They were the daughters of a railroad tycoon, James C. Peasley of the Burlington Railroad, also president of the National State Bank. Judge J. Harry Covington and Edward Burling founded the law firm of Covington and Burling in Washington in 1919. Covington, a Maryland congressman, had been appointed Chief Justice of the Supreme Court of Washington, D.C., by Woodrow Wilson as a reward for voting for the passage of the Federal Reserve Act. In 1918, Wilson appointed

Covington as United States Railroad Commissioner. Covington was a director of Kennecott Copper and Union Trust. Wilson had also appointed Edward Burling chief counsel of the U.S. Shipping Board. He served in this post from 1917-1919, working closely with Herbert Hoover and Prentiss Gray, later of J. Henry Schroder Co. Delano's sister was Mrs. Price Collier of Tuxedo Park, N. Y.; his son-in-law was James L. Houghtaling, who was special attache at the American Embassy in Petrograd during the Bolshevik Revolution in 1917 (he later wrote Diary of the Russian Revolution) Federal Emergency Administration 1933, Commissioner of Naturalization and Immigration 1937-40, War Finance, Dept of the Treasury 1944-46; chairman Fair Employment Board Civil Service Commission 1949-52 - his mother was a Peabody of Boston.

The first board of directors of Russell Sage Foundation consisted of Daniel Coit Gilman, Helen Gould, Margaret Sage and Dwight Morrow.

Although the name of Andrew Carnegie looms large on the roster of American foundations, for many years the five Carnegie foundations have been mere appendages of the Rockefeller Foundation. Carnegie sold his steel interests to J.P. Morgan and the Rothschilds for $1 billion, but was not permitted to walk away with the money; like Cecil Rhodes, Rockefeller, and others, he was directed to put it into foundations which would carry out the program of the World Order. The Carnegie Institution of Washington was incorporated in 1909 by Daniel Coit Gilman, Cleveland H. Dodge, Frederic A. Delano, Andrew Dickson White, and Elihu Root, Darius Ogden Mills and William E. Morrow. Note that the original incorporators include two of the three incorporators of the Russell Trust, Gilman and White. In 1921, the Carnegie Endowment for International Peace was incorporated by Frederic A. Delano, Roberts. Brookings, Elihu Root, who became its first president, John W. Davis, Dwight Morrow, James T. Shotwell. Thus we see that the major foundations were all organized by the same small group of people, bankers and lawyers who function as front men for the World Order.

James T. Shotwell ably represented the goals of the World Order for more than sixty years. Born in Canada in 1874, he joined the staff of Columbia University in 1900 as a prof, of history. In 1916 he was invited by Col. House to set up a study group, the Inquiry, with Walter Lippmann, to "study postwar political economic historical and legal developments", although we were not even in the war! This was the core of the American Commission to Negotiate Peace at Versailles which wrote the Peace Treaty. In 1917, Shotwell became personal adviser to President Woodrow Wilson. He was appointed official historian of the ACNP, and actually wrote the social security clauses of the Versailles Treaty. He wrote a 150-volume history of World War I, published by Columbia. He had become a close friend of Herbert Hoover during the war, and advised him on setting up the Hoover Institution. Shotwell organized the International

Labor Conference, and joined the Carnegie Endowment in 1924. In 1941, Shotwell led a Committee which demanded the release of Communist Party leader Earl Browder. He joined the State Dept. in 1940, serving until 1944. When Franklin D. Roosevelt asked him to join the State Dept. team of Alger Hiss, Henry Wallace and Sumner Welles to organize the United Nations, Shotwell was already Chairman of the Commission to Study the Organization of the Peace, which he had set up in 1939, before the war started, just as he had done in 1916! Shotwell was Honorary Chairman of the San Francisco Conference to Organize the United Nations with Alger Hiss. When Hiss was arrested, Shotwell succeeded him as President of the Carnegie Endowment for International Peace.

The trustees of CEIP in 1948 lists the ruling clique of America; John W. Davis, Frederic A. Delano, John Foster Dulles, Dwight David Eisenhower, Douglas S. Freeman, Francis P. Gaines (president of Washington & Lee University), Alger Hiss, Philip C. Jessup, David Rockefeller, and Eliot Wadsworth. A key member, Philip C. Jessup had such a long record of association with Communist front groups that not a single Senator dared to vote for his confirmation as U.S. Representative to the UN in Oct. 1951. President Truman stubbornly refused to withdraw his name, but sent him as an "alternate" delegate. Jessup had been assistant to Elihu Root at the Hague Court; he was Herbert Lehman's Asst. Sec. General of UNRRA, whose deputy, Laurence Duggan later fell out of the window. Jessup had represented the U.S. at the Bretton Woods Conference, and was Alger Hiss' assistant in Charge of Judicial Organization at the UN San Francisco Conference. Jessup was Chairman of the Pacific Council of the Institute of Pacific Relations, a hotbed of Communist intrigue and espionage. IPR had financed the Soviet spy, Richard Sorge, when he set up his network in Japan. Laurence Rockefeller served as secretary at the IPR meetings. The McCarran Committee reported,

> "The IPR has been considered by the American Communist Party and by Soviet officials as an instrument of Communist policy, propaganda, and military intelligence."

In June, 1945, the FBI raided the offices of IPR's Amerasia Magazine, confiscated 1800 stolen confidential government documents, and arrested several Communist spies. The following year, the Rockefeller Foundation gave IPR $233,000. Jessup was a member of the wealthy Stotesbury family, partners of J.P. Morgan. His brother John Jessup was a wealthy banker, president Equitable Trust Co., director of Coca Cola and Diamond State Telephone Co. CEIP has offices in Washington, and in New York at 30 Rockefeller Plaza. It has a $45 million endowment, and annual expenses of $3 million. Its president is Thomas L. Hughes, who presided over the OSS Group at the Dept. of State after it had been disbanded by President Truman; a Rhodes Scholar, he was legislative counsel for Hubert Humphrey 1955-58, adm. asst Chester Bowles, 1959-60, spl. asst to Secretary of State for Intelligence 1961-69, spec, ambassador, chief of mission, rank of ambassador London 1969-70; he had previously served as judge advocate general USAF 1952-54. Hughes is director of German Marshall Fund, USAF Academy, Ditchley Foundation, School of Foreign Service , Georgetown, Woodrow Wilson School, Princeton, Social Sciences Foundation, Hubert Humphrey Institute Public Affairs; directors of CEIP are Larry Fabian, who directed Bureau of Intelligence State Dept. 1962, resident fellow Brookings Instn 1965-71; Fabian is also director Middle East Institute, Hudson Institute, Institute of Strategic Studies, and Rockefeller Foundation; John Chancellor, vice chmn NBC News, Moscow Correspondent 1960, Voice of America 1966-67; Harding F. Bancroft, a New York attorney who joined OPA 1941, Lend Lease Administration 1943, served as director UN Affairs Dept. of State 1945-53, is exec, vice president *New York Times* from 1953 to present; Thomas W. Braden, nationally syndicated columnist, whose wife Joan has been having an affair with Robert McNamara for three years (the World Order permits a certain degree of intimacy) - a longtime Rockefeller associate who was given one of the well-publicized Nelson Rockefeller "loans", Braden is executive secretary Museum of Modern Art, served with the King's Royal Rifles of Britain 1941-44; Kingman Brewster, Wall Street lawyer with Winthrop Putnam Simpson & Roberts, was president of Yale 1961-67, Ambassador to England 1977-81, chmn English

Speaking Union, National Endowment for Humanities, Kaiser Foundation; Anthony J. A. Bryan, born in Mexico, naturalized 1947, now president of Copperweld, a firm owned by Rothschilds Imetal Corp., and Federal Express, another Rothschild firm - Bryan served with RCAF 1914-5; Richard A. Debs, Fulbright scholar, lawyer for Federal Reserve Bank of N.Y. 1960 to present, president Morgan Stanley 1976, FOMC 1973-76, chair 162 man of Carnegie Hall; Hedley Donovan, Rhodes Scholar, director of Ford Foundation, Trilateral Commission, senior advisor to President of the U.S. 1979-80, director *Washington Post*, *Fortune*, *Time*; C. Clyde Ferguson, dean of law school at Harvard, legal adviser NAACP 1962 to present, personal adviser Gov. Rockefeller, 1959-64, Ambassador to Uganda 1970-72; Lane Kirkland, president of CIO, also on board Wesley Posvar, who recently figured in investigation of Air Force grants to his school; he was with Strategic Planning Group USAF Headquarters, 1954-57, is a director of Rand corp.; Norman Ramsey, physicist, studied at Harvard and Oxford, MIT, was with MIT Radiation Laboratory & Los Alamos laboratory 1942-45 in development of atomic bomb, trustee Brookhaven Lab, physics dept. Harvard, Rockefeller U. NATO; Benno C. Schmidt, managing partner J.H. Whitney Co.; Jean Kennedy Smith; Donald B. Straus, president American Arbitration Assn., Planned Parenthood, Institute of Advanced Study; Leonard Woodcock, UAW, life member NAACP; Charles J. Zwick, director Bureau of Budget 1965-69, director Johns Manville, Southern Bell Telephone, Rand Corp.

The Carnegie Corp. of New York has assets of $346 million, expenditures $13 million in 1980. Chairman is Alan Pifer, educated at Groton, Harvard and Cambridge England. He has been a director of American Ditchley Foundation since 1975, and is on the board of overseers of Harvard, chairman Presidential Task Force on Education, Presidential Committee of White House Fellowships, African American Institute, director Federal Reserve Bank of N.Y. - he was secretary U.S. Educational Com. in London 1948-53, director McGraw Hill; exec, vice pres of Carnegie is David Zav Robinson, served with Office of Naval Research London 1959-60, prof, of physics Princeton 1970-76, atomic research.

THE WORLD ORDER – Our Secret Rulers

The Carnegie Corporation was incorporated in 1911 by Andrew Carnegie and Elihu Root, who had been Secretary of War under McKinley and Secretary of Interior under Theodore Roosevelt, lawyer for J.P. Morgan, who took charge of the Carnegie fortune for the program of the World Order.

Directors of Carnegie Corp. include Richard H. Sullivan, asst. dean Harvard 1941-42, president Reed College 1956-57, director John & Mary Markle Foundation; John C. Taylor III, chairman Paul Weiss Rifkind; Jack G. Clarke, atty with Sullivan & Cromwell, counsel Standard Oil of New Jersey, Middle East representative SO, sr. vice pres EXXON since 1975, American Ditchley Fndtn., Aspen Institute; Thomas R. Donahue, sec. treas. AFL-CIO, Natl Urban League; David A. Hamburg, psychologist U.S. Army med. serv. since 1950, Natl Institute of Mental Health, head dept. psychiatry Stanford Univ 1961-72, Harvard study on aggression; Helene L. Kaplan, lawyer with Webster & Sheffield, director Brandeis, Barnard College, Mitre Corp., John F. Guggenheim Fndtn, American Arbitration Assn - her husband Mark Kaplan, president Drexel Burnham & Lambert, controlled by the Belgian Rothschilds, president Engelhard Chemical, now attorney Skadden Arps Slate Meagher & Flom, director Philbro, Elgin, Grey Advertising, DFS Group Ltd. adv com. Center for Natl Policy Review, Unimax Corp., Marcade Group, Hong Kong; Carl F. Mueller, Bankers Trust, Carl Loeb Rhoades, Cabot Corp., Macmillan, John S. Guggenheim Fndtn; John C. Whitehead, banker with Goldman Sachs since 1947, director Pillsbury, Crompton, HouseHold Finance, Equitable Life, Loctite Corp., Dillard Dept. Stores, is on board Georgetown Center for Strategic Studies, and Republican Natl Finance Committee.

As president of the Carnegie Corp. Alan Pifer interlocks with many leading banking institutions, according to a special chart devoted to him in *Federal Reserve Directors: A Study of Corporate Influence*, an August 1976 staff report of the House Banking & Currency Committee, which shows he interlocks with Rockefeller Center, J.Henry Schroder Banking Corp., J. Henry Schroder Trust Co., J.P. Morgan Co., Equitable Life, Federal Reserve Bank of Boston and the Cabot Corp.

The Carnegie foundations also interlock with the John and Mary Markle Foundation, established 1927 with $50 million. It dispenses largesse to journalists who espouse the goals of the World Order. Markle was the biggest coal operator in the U.S., partners with the Roosevelt and Delano family in Kentania Coal Corp., which obtained millions of acres for a few cents an acre from impoverished residents of Kentucky and Tennessee, and hauled billions of dollars of coal from their holdings. In 1933, Roosevelt called on Markle to help settle the coal strike. The first president of Markle Foundation was Frank C. Vanderlip, member of the Jekyll Island team which wrote the Federal Reserve Act in 1910. Lloyd N. Morrissette is now president; he has been vice pres. Carnegie Corp. since 1967, formerly chairman of the Rand Corp., director American Council on Germany; directors are Daniel Pomeroy Davison, son of F. Trubee Davison and Dorothy Peabody - he is president of U.S. Trust, director J.P. Morgan, Morgan Guaranty Trust, and Scovill; Joel L. Fleishman who is also director of Fleishman Foundation, Ford Foundation, and Alfred P. Sloan Foundation; Barbara Hauptfuhrer, wife of Robert P. (Schoenhut) Hauptfuhrer, he is vice pres. of Sun Oil; F. Warren Hellman, has been with Lehman Bros, since 1959, president of Peabody International Co.; Maximilian Kempner, lawyer, born in Berlin, member of the historic von Mendelsohn banking family, is director of American Council on Germany; Gertrude Michelson, vice pres of Macy's since 1947, director Chubb, Quaker Oats, Harper & Row, Federal Reserve Bank of N.Y., and Spelman College; Richard M. Stewart, president of Anaconda.

The Carnegie and Markle Foundations also interlock with the American Council on Germany, founded in 1952, which exercises control over the "free" nation of West Germany. Its director is David Klein, who has been in the U.S. Foreign Service since 1947, Russian Specialist at State Dept. since 1950, served in Moscow 1952-54, political officer in Bonn 1957-60, U.S. Minister to Berlin 1971-74. Together with the German Marshall Fund, it maintains tight control over German government, academic life, and communications in this militarily occupied country. The $21 million German Marshall Fund, a branch of the CIA, is headquartered in Washington and spends $5 million a

THE WORLD ORDER – Our Secret Rulers

year supervising German affairs. Its president is Frank Loy, born in Nuremberg. His father's name was Loewi, which he anglicized to the present spelling. (Loy) came to the U.S. in 1939, studied at Harvard, joined the influential West Coast law firm of O'Melveny & Myers 1954-65, political director and spec, economist AID 1965-70, pres. Pennsylvania Co. 1978-79, vice pres. of PanAm Airways 1970-73, director of Arvida Corp. (subsidiary Penn Central), Buckeye Pipeline Co., and Edgewater Oil Co. Chairman of the trustees of German Marshall Fund is Eugene B. Skolnikoff, Rhodes Scholar, director of CEIP, Ford Foundation, Rockefeller Foundation 1963-65, chairman Center for International Studies, spec, asst to President of U.S. 1958-63 and 1977-81, president of Federation of Jewish Agencies, Hebrew Union College; Irving Bluestone; Harvey Brooks, prof, physics Harvard since 1950, director of Raytheon; Marion Edleman, head of legal div. NAACP, adv. council Martin Luther King Fndtn, Eleanor Roosevelt Institute, Yale Univ. Corp., received Whitney Young award. Her husband Peter Edleman was law clerk for Supreme Court Justice Arthur Goldberg, Judge Henry Friendly, spec. legal asst. Robert F. Kennedy 1964-68, would have been named Atty . Gen. in an RFK administration, is director of RFK Memorial, directed Edward Kennedy's presidential campaign, was Ford Foundation fellow; Robert Ellsworth, partner Lazard Freres, asst. to President of the U.S. 1969, Ambassador to NATO, 1969-70, deputy Sec. Defense 1976-77, Institute of Strategic Studies, Atlantic Institute, Atlantic Council; Guido Goldman; Carl Kaplan; John E. Kilgore Jr. banker with J.H. Whitney Co., Paine Webber, now chmn Cambridge Royalty Co. of Houston (whose directors are Frederic A. Bush, H. Haslam, Francis J. Rheinhardt Jr.). Other directors of German Marshall Fund are Joyce Dannen Miller, dir. Amalgamated Clothing Workers Union since 1962, Planned Parenthood, ACLU, A. Philip Randolph Institute, Sidney Hillman Foundation, AFL-CIO, NAACP, Jewish Labor Committee, American Jewish Committee; Steven Muller, born in Hamburg, naturalized 1949, Rhodes Scholar, pres Johns Hopkins Univ., Center for International Studies, CSX Corp., vice chairman Federal Reserve Bank of Richmond; John L. Siegenthaler, publisher Nashville Tennessean; Richard C.

Steadman, partner J.H. Whitney Co., intelligence analyst U.S. Govt. 1957-59, American Ditchley Foundation, Russell C. Train, judge U.S. Tax Court 1957-65, chief counsel House Ways & Means Committee 1953-54, EPA 1973-77, president World Wildlife Fund, director Union Carbide, Trilateral Commission, U.S. Commission for UNESCO.

These German associated groups had their origin in the Morgenthau Plan, which resolved to lay Germany waste after World War II. They maintain ironclad censorship in Germany, in order to protect the borders of the Soviet Union (a primary concern), with ruthless economic exploitation of the German people at the hands of the World Order, and extort huge reparations payments from the German workers, who have already paid more than $30 billion.

The most tragic victims of the World Order's network of foundations and universities are the nation's youth. Filled with hope and ambition, they attend colleges to prepare for careers, where their chief advisers are the foundation eunuchs. They are carefully scrutinized to see if they can be useful to the World Order, in which case they may be given grants or fellowships, but the cruel fact is that unless they are fortunate enough to be born into a family connection with members of the World Order, or become protege of a eunuch, most doors will forever remain closed to them. Despite their talents or ability, they will be relegated to joining the hewers of wood and the drawers of water for the rest of their lives. At no time during their education will they be apprised of the fact that they are the victims of a cruel hoax, that success in business, drama, art or literature will be denied them because they do not have the required connection with the World Order. The art scene is dominated by the New York art dealers, who in turn are dominated by the Museum of Modern Art, founded and controlled by the Rockefeller family. The founders were Nelson Rockefeller, Abby Aldrich Rockefeller (wife of John D. Jr.), Blanchette Hooker, wife of John D. 3rd, and Lizzie Bliss. Such is their power that they can declare empty beer cans or piles of rope or rocks to be Great Art, worth many thousands of dollars. They achieve a dual purpose of destroying the creative life of the people while promoting the work of their favorite propagandists. The new treasurer of the Smithsonian Museum, Ann Leven, was formerly treasurer of Museum of Modern Art, also senior vice president of corporate planning at Chase Manhattan Bank.

Nov. 1955 *Fortune* featured an article by William H. Whyte, "Where the Foundations Fall Down", which pointed out that the foundations only grant funds to "big team" projects in institutions which are under their control. Whyte says 76% of all foundation grants are made to these "team" projects, citing huge sums given to the Russian Research Center at Harvard by Carnegie, and Ford grants to the Center for Advanced Study in Behavioural Science at Stanford. Foundation grants are rarely given to individuals, and most can be traced to some underlying propaganda drive, such as the $200,000 which the Rockefeller Foundation gave to establish the National Bureau of Economic Research, whose "studies" effectively dominate the world of American business today.

The involvement of the major foundations in military and espionage work is shown by the makeup of two powerful "think tanks", the Rand corp. and the Mitre Corp. Chairman of the $180 million Mitre corp. is Robert Charpie, president of Cabot Corp., director First Natl of Boston, Champion and Honeywell. President of Mitre is Robert Everett, who serves on the USAF Science Advisory Board, and Northern Energy Corp.; directors are William T. Golden of Altschul's firm, General American Investors, Block Drug, Verde Exploration Ltd.; he is also secretary of the Carnegie Instn. Washington; William J. McCune Jr. chairman of Polaroid; Teddy F. Walkowicz, chairman Natl Aviation & Technology Corp.; and Robert C. Sprague, vice pres. of his family firm, Sprague Electric, which interlocks with the defense firm GK Technologies, of which former President Ford is director.

The chairman of Rand Corp. ($50 million research budget annually) is Donald Rumsfeld, President Nixon's right-hand man in Washington for many years; president is Donald B. Rice, Jr., served in office of Secretary of Defense 1967-70, OMB 1969-72, director of Wells Fargo; directors are Harold Brown, former Secretary of Defense director of AMAX, CBS, IBM, Uniroyal, and Trilateral Commission, Frank Carlucci, a State Dept. official since 1950, has served in Office of Economic Opportunity 1969-71, OMB 1971-72, under Sec. HEW 1974-75, Ambassador to Portugal 1975-78, dep. dir CIA 1978-81, dep. Secretary Defense 1981-84, now chairman Sears World Trade Corp.; Carla Hills, former Secretary HUD; Walter J. Humann, exec, vice pres. Hunt Oil Co. since 1976, president Hunt Investment Corp., president White House Fellows Institute; Walter E. Massey, physicist, spec, in atomic weaponry, Argonne Natl Lab, Natl Science Fndtn, Natl Urban League; Newton Minow, Adlai Stevenson's law partner, chmn FCC 1961-63, director Mayo Fndtn, Wm. Benton Fndtn, chairman of board Jewish Theological Seminary, received George F. Peabody award; Paul G. Rogers, Congressman from Florida, now partner the influential Washington law firm Hogan & Hartson; Dennis Stanfill, Rhodes Scholar, chairman 20th century fund, was with Lehman Bros., now treasurer Times Mirror Corp. Los Angeles, served as political officer Chief of Naval Opns 1956-59; Solomon J. Buchsbaum, physicist who came to U.S. 1953, naturalised 1957, pres. Science Advisory Committee, Bell Labs, chmn Energy Research Board naval research MIT, Argonne Lab, IBM fellow; William T. Coleman Jr.; Edwin E. Huddleson Jr. law clerk to Judge Hand, Justice Frank Murphy, and the State Dept.; general counsel Atomic Energy Commission, president Harvard Law Review; Charles F. Knight, chairman of Emerson Electric, defense contractor controlled by the Symington family, director Standard Oil of Ohio, McDonnell Douglas; Michael E. May, born in France, physicist at Livermore Nuclear Lab, National Security Council 1974; Lloyd B. Morrissette, now president of Markle Fndtn, vice pres. Carnegie Corp., director of American Council on Germany; Don W. Seldin, who was chief of medical services at Parkland Hospital Dallas when the body of Kennedy was brought in; and George W. Weyerhauser, director of SoCal, Boeing, Federal Reserve Bank of San Francisco, member of the lumber family.

Because of growing Congressional outcry against the vast expenditures of the major foundations on behalf of Communist revolutionary causes, the World Order decided to give the American people some "anti-Communist" foundations, based in the Hoover Institution on War, Peace and Revolution. The Hoover group is generally thought to be conservative, but on examining their personnel and directors, we find the same old international crowd of Bolsheviks and financiers.

The Hoover Institution was founded at Stanford University, Palo Alto, Calif, in 1919 with a donation of $50,000 from Herbert Hoover. He had been a member of the first graduating class at Stanford, founded with a bequest from Leland Stanford, the Southern Pacific railroad tycoon. His only son, Leland Stanford Jr. died in a hotel room in Florence, Italy at the age of fifteen. His grieving mother became the prey of a number of spiritualists, one of whom persuaded her to start a spiritualist university, founded on such mystical Eastern teachings, as

> "The balance between night and day is the balance of the world", and "The mainspring of the movement of the world". "Life and death is the great secret of immortality."

Because of the difficulty of organizing these doctrines into a coherent academic curriculum, Mrs. Stanford was dissuaded from the idea of a "spiritualist" university, and the present Stanford University then came into being. Reputedly "conservative", it has in fact been dominated by Harvard Liberals for many years.

Herbert Hoover founded the Hoover Institution at the suggestion of three men, Andrew Dickson White, Daniel Coit Gilman, and Ray Lyman Wilbur, president of Stanford. *Newsweek* June 7, 1954 noted that Hoover said,

> "In 1915 while head of the Committee on Relief in Belgium, I happened to read some remarks by President Andrew White of Cornell made at a conference on the disappearance of contemporaneous documents and fugitive literature."

Hoover says he resolved to institute a search of Europe after the war to obtain documents and preserve them in an academic setting. Gilman and Wilbur aided him in planning this program. Both White and Gilman were original incorporators of the Russell Trust, which has dominated American education for a century. Wilbur requested that Hoover install this collection at

Stanford. Wilbur served as director of the Rockefeller Foundation 1923-40, and General Education Board, 1930-40. His nephew and successor as president at Stanford, Richard Lyman, is now president of the Rockefeller Foundation. Wilbur also served as Secretary of the Interior in Hoover's Cabinet 1929-33. During this period, he signed the contracts for Hoover Dam, having thought up that name. The dam was not completed until after FDR took office; he maliciously ordered his Secretary of Interior, Harold Ickes, to change the name to Boulder Dam. Hoover points out in his Memoirs that,

> "two-thirds of the work had been done during the Hoover Administration, all contracts were let as Hoover Dam, as was customary with many presidents with works named after them when these works were done during their administrations; on May 8, 1933, Secretary Ickes, on orders from Roosevelt changed the name to Boulder Dam."

Roosevelt dedicated the dam Sept. 30, 1933 without mentioning Hoover or the fact that most of the work had been done during the Hoover Administration. On March 10, 1947, the House unanimously voted to change the name back to Hoover Dam. Hoover wrote to Congressman Jack Z. Anderson, who had sponsored the bill,

> "When a President of the U.S. tears one's name down that is a public defamation and an insult. I am grateful to you for removing it."

Because of the importance of the Hoover Institution in the Reagan Administration, it is important to recap the career of the man who founded it. As a mining stock promoter in London, Hoover had been barred from dealing on the London Stock Exchange, and his associate, who apparently took the rap, went to prison for several years. The incident brought Hoover to the favorable attention of the Rothschilds, who made him a director of their firm, Rio Tinto. Chairman was Lord Milner, who founded the Round Tables, which later became the Royal Institute of International Affairs and its subsidiary, the Council on Foreign Relations.

In 1916, the promotors of World War I were dismayed when Germany insisted she could not continue in the war, because of shortages of food and money. The Czar's physician, Gleb Botkin, revealed in 1931 that the Kaiser's chief military adviser, and chief of his armies on the Russian border, Grand Duke of Hesse-Darmstadt, risked his life on a secret mission to Russia to Czarskoe Selo, the Imperial Palace, where he asked his sister, Empress Alexandra, to let him talk to the Czar about making a separate peace with Germany. The Empress, fearful of criticism, refused to receive him, and after spending the night at the palace, he was escorted back to the German lines.

To keep Germany in the war, Paul Warburg, head of the Federal Reserve System, hastily arranged for credits to be routed to his brother, Max Warburg, through Stockholm to M.M. Warburg Co. Hamburg. Food presented a more difficult problem. It was finally decided to ship it directly to Belgium as "relief for the starving Belgians". The supplies could then be shipped over Rothschild railway lines into Germany. As director for this "relief operation", the Rothschilds chose Herbert Hoover. His partner in the Relief Commission was Emilie Francqui, chosen by Baron Lambert, head of the Belgian Rothschild family. The plan was so successful that it kept World War I going for an additional two years, allowing the U.S. to get into the "war to end wars". John Hamill, author of *The Strange Career of Herbert Hoover* states that Emile Francqui, director of Societe Generale, a Jesuit bank, opened an office in his bank as the National Relief and Food Committee, with a letter of authorization from the German Gov. Gen. von der Goltz. Francqui then went to London with this letter, accompanied by Baron Lambert, head of the Belgian Rothschilds, and Hugh Gibson, secretary of the American Legation in Brussels.

The Report of the National Committee states that

> "The National Committee and its subsidiary organizations were not subject to control of the Belgian Public Administration and neither was it accountable to the Public as a public authority. The National Committee existed by itself according to the will of its founders and those who had given it their support. That is why it was sovereign in the

decisions it made and excluded all control of its actions by the Public."

Hamill says,

> "From its commencement, the Food Division had been organized and conducted on a commercial basis. The Commission for Relief in Belgium raised its sale prices to the National Committee by an amount equivalent to the profit that had formerly been taken by it. Hoover referred to this as 'benevolence'."

Francqui had previously been a partner of Hoover in the Kaipeng coal mine swindle in China, which set off the Boxer Rebellion, the Chinese vowing to kill all "white devils" in China; and the Congo atrocities, where Francqui was remembered by the sobriquet, "the Butcher of the Congo". He was an ideal choice to be partner in a benevolent enterprise.

The National Committee report published in 1919 showed that as of Dec. 31, 1918 the Committee had spent $260 million. In 1921, trying to make the accounts balance, this figure was revised upward to $442 million showed as spent during the same period. However, $182 million was unaccounted for. In Dec. 1918, Francqui showed expenditure for relief of $40 million, four times as much as for any previous month, although the war was now over. On Jan. 13, 1932, the *New York Times* reported widespread attacks on Hoover in the Belgian press,

> "that President Hoover, during his Belgian Relief days, had manifestly been party to a scheme to make money out of Belgium."

Hoover was then appointed U.S. Food Administrator in Washington. Although the operation was principally run by Lewis L. Strauss of Kuhn, Loeb Co., Hoover still depended heavily on his longtime associate, Edgar Rickard. On Nov. 13, 1918, Hoover sent a letter to President Wilson requesting authority for Edgar Rickard "to act in my stead" while he was in Europe. Wilson signed the letter Nov. 16, 1918,

> "Whereas by virtue of exec, order Nov. 16, 1918, Edgar Rickard now exercise all powers heretofore delegated to Herbert Hoover as U.S. Food Administrator."

Rickard assumed the title of "Acting Food Administrator in Washington" according to a letter from Herbert Hoover Jan. 17, 1919, "since my departure to come to conference in Paris."

The U.S. Food Administration was then split into four divisions, Sugar Equalization Board, Belgian Relief, U.S. Grain Corp. and U.S. Shipping Board. On Dec. 16, 1918, Wilson sent a letter to the State Dept. an executive order, "Please pay at once to the U.S. Food Administration Grain Corp. $5 million from my fund for National Security and Defense." The order was referred to the Secretary of Treasury for payment and approved.

Justice Brandeis biography by Mason notes,

> "Norman Hapgood wrote Brandeis from London Jan. 10, 1917, 'Herbert Hoover is the most interesting man I know. You will enjoy his experience in diplomacy, finance etc. in England, France, Belgium and Germany!"

In early February he talked with Justice Brandeis, who arranged for him to see Senator McAdoo, Wilson's son-in-law, leading to Hoover's appointment as U.S. Food Administrator.

On Jan. 21, 1919, the *New York Times* noted the Senate debate in which Hoover was assailed for his proposed $100 million request for aid to Europe. The plan was criticized by Sen. Penrose and Sen. Gore as one that would unload the surplus of American meat packers in Europe. Sen. Penrose asked Sen. Martin, the Democratic floor leader if Hoover "is an American citizen and has ever voted in an American election?" Martin retorted, "I do not propose to be drawn into such an irrelevantism as that". Penrose then declared, "I do not believe he is a citizen of the U.S., who has taken no oath of office, and whose allegiance is in doubt." The criticism so piqued Hoover that he signed a letter of resignation reciting his "four years of public service without remuneration." It was never submitted and turned up many years later in the personal papers of his assistant, Lewis L. Strauss.

The *New York Times* noted Sept. 4, 1919 that Edgar Rickard had made a speech at Stanford Univ. vigorously promoting the League of Nations. Hoover and Col. House were also working together to obtain Senate approval and public approval for Wilson's League of Nations plan.

The members of the Commission for Relief in Belgium team have subsequently played a very prominent role in the history of the U.S. Hoover became Secretary of Commerce and later President of the U.S. A team from Hoover Institution moved into Washington in 1980 as the vanguard of a "conservative" administration. Prentiss Gray, Hoover's assistant in U.S. Food Administration, became president of J.Henry Schroder Banking Corp. in 1922. Julius H. Barnes, another Hoover associate, became Chairman of J.Henry Schroder Bank. Perhaps a surplus of "relief funds" subsequently purchased a number of American corporations. Barnes became president of Pitney Bowes, Pejepscot Paper, General Bronze, Barnes-Ames Corp., Northwest Bancorporation, and Erie & St. Lawrence Corp. Edgar Rickard, Hoover's partner since they launched a magazine in 1909 to promote their mining stocks, had been honorary secretary of Commission for Relief in Belgium; he now became president of Androscoggin Water Power Co., president Belgo-American Trading Co; vice pres. of Erie & St. Lawrence Corp.; president of Hazard Wire Rope Co., president of Hazeltine Corp.; vice pres. of Intercontinental Development Corp., president of Latour Corp., president of Pejepscot Paper Co., and vice president of Pitney Bowes Co., chairman of Wood Fibre Board Corp. Robert Grant of the U.S. Food Administration became director of the U.S. Mint in Washington. Prentiss Gray became vice pres. of British American Continental Corp., Electric Shareholdings Corp., Hydroelectric Securities Corp., Manati Sugar Corp., St. Regis Paper, Swiss American Electric Prudential Investors, International Holdings and Investment Corp., the last two being companies controlled by Societe Generale and Francqui. These investment firms were organized by Belgian capitalist Capt. Alfred Loewenstein, who mysteriously vanished from his plane while flying over the English Channel.

While his closest advisers pursued their multi-million dollar careers, Herbert Hoover remained dedicated to his ideals of public service. He became Secretary of Commerce, and chose as his secretary Christian A. Herter, who had been his secretary at the Belgian Relief Commission, 1920-21, and had also been secretary of the American Commission to Negotiate Peace. He was secretary to Hoover 1919-24 at Commerce; he married into the Pratt family of Standard Oil, who gave their Manhattan mansion as headquarters for the CFR, and he was later appointed Secretary of State.

Charles Michelson wrote of Hoover's career at the Dept. of Commerce, in *The Ghost Talks*, 1944,

> "Officially, Mr. Hoover was ever a promoter. When he took over the Dept. of Commerce, it was a reasonably modern organization. He took the Bureau of Mines from interior. He dipped into the State Dept. when he realized his idea of commercial agents abroad, and left the old commercial attaches of our legations jobless. It was not by accident that he builded for his department the hugest and perhaps the most lavishly furnished palace that housed a branch of the government."

One of Hoover's most notable deeds, as Secretary of Commerce, was his award of the Hazeltine radio patents to his partner since 1909, Edgar Rickard, a gift conservatively estimated to be worth at that time one million dollars. When Hoover organized his campaign for the presidency, he gave as his personal address Suite 2000. 42 Broadway N.Y. Suite 2000 was also listed as the office of Edgar Rickard. It was also the address of Hoover's erstwhile accomplice in the U.S. Food Administration, Julius H. Barnes, chairman of the Schroder Bank, which was to soon win notoriety as Hitler's personal bank.

Although "Wild Bill" Donovan had served Hoover faithfully for four years while he sought the nomination to the Presidency, Hoover did not hesitate to cast him aside when he became a political liability because of his Catholic religion. The *New York Times* noted June 17, 1928.

> "W. A. Bechtel of San Francisco sent a congratulatory telegram to the nominee, in behalf of the construction industry we congratulate the Republican Party on its selection of a candidate for chief Engineer of the greatest business in the world for the next four years, one of our fellow Californians who has shown yourself deserving of this great honor."

Hoover was soon preparing contracts for the largest public work of that time, the Hoover Dam, of which Bechtel was to become the chief contractor.

Despite his charitable preoccupations, Hoover still engaged in free enterprise. On Dec. 7, 1919, he and his partner Julius H. Barnes had bought the *Washington Herald*; it was later acquired by the Patterson McCormick family, and still later, by Eugene Meyer, who promptly closed it down. Barnes also bought the Penobscot Paper Co. for $750,000 in 1919; he happened to have some extra cash on hand. The *New York Times* Jan. 28, 1920 reported that Col. House was busily developing a boom at Austin, Texas for Hoover as President, with the aid of some British friends. The *Times* further noted Jan. 28, 1920 that the British Government denied that Lord Grey was taking part in the Hoover boom.

At a dinner at the Hotel Commodore, April 23, 1920, Julius Barnes and Herbert Hoover were the guests of honor. The keynote speaker announced that the name of Herbert Hoover was "known throughout the civilized world".

From the time that White, Gilman and Wilbur persuaded Hoover to gather documents for the Hoover Library, much support was made available from official sources. Even then, no one was sure just how World War I had gotten started. It was to someone's interest to see to it that as many pertinent and secret documents from the warring powers should be gathered in one place, gone over and, if necessary, secluded from prying eyes. Hoover was able to call upon Gen. Pershing to provide hundreds of Army officers to aid him in his quest. In his Foreword to The Special Collection of the Hoover Library, Hoover says that he recruited 1500 officers from the American Army, and the Supreme Economic Council, and sent them to all parts of Europe. The *New York Times* Feb. 5, 1921 says that Hoover had as many as 4000 agents in Europe, going from country to country to gather these documents. Even in those pre-inflationary times, the cost of maintaining 4000 agents in Europe must have been prohibitive. No one has ever found out who was paying them. Also, many of the documents were purchased outright. The only expenditure Hoover ever made public was the original $50,000 he had given in 1919 to establish the library. Who spent millions of dollars to put this collection together? It is most unlikely that Hoover would have parted with such sums, but no one has ever admitted putting any money into this project.

The *Times* noted in the Hotel Commodore story that Hoover, a member of the first graduating class at Stanford, had presented the school with a collection of 375,000 volumes. It included the most valuable collection of secret Bolshevik records in existence, among them, the lists of the original district Soviets, which had been bought from a doorkeeper for $200. The *Times* noted that the Soviet Government had no copies of these rare archives! *Time*, June 30, 1941, noted that the Bolsheviks had allowed Hoover to remove 25 carloads of material, at a time when Russian refugees were permitted to leave only with the clothes on their backs. The solicitude for Hoover's collection may have been influenced by the fact that he had saved the infant Bolshevik regime from extinction by rushing large quantities of food to them.

Hoover's collection also included the complete secret files of the German War Council during World War I, a gift from President Ebert; Mata Hari's diary, and sixty rare volumes from the Czar's personal library. Many of the collections were permanently sealed. *Time* noted that the Hoover Institution contained 300 sealed collections, which no one has ever been allowed to examine.

One can only speculate whether interested parties, perhaps the Rothschilds, Hoover's employers, determined at the close of World War I, to remove the secret documents of Europe's warring nations to some far-off place, such as the West Coast of America, to lessen their political liability, damaging evidence of various acts of collusion. The initial organization of the material was done by a Stanford professor of history, Ephraim D. Adams (1865-1930). Adams and his wife were installed in an office in Paris May 22, 1919, to receive the first shipments of documents. Other offices were opened in Berlin, London, and New York. Aiding Adams were Dr. Alonzo Engelbert Tyler, who had been educated at the University of Berlin, served on War Trade Board 1917-19, and staff member of Stanford Food Research Institute;

Dr. Carl Baruch Alsberg, also educated at University of Berlin, worked for the Dept. of Agriculture; and Dr. Joseph Stancliffe Davis, a Harvard professor of economics.

The advisory committee of the original Hoover Library consisted of Dr. James R. Angell, president of Yale, and president of Carnegie Corp.; Dr. J.C. Merriam, educated at the University of Munich, chmn Natl Research Council, and Carnegie Institution; Herbert Hoover; and Julius H. Barnes.

Prof. Adams was Director of the Hoover Library 1920-25. He was succeeded by Ralph H. Lutz, who headed the library from 1925-44. Lutz had served on the Supreme Economic Council, Paris under Bernard Baruch 1918-19. In 1910 he received a Ph.D. from the University of Heidelberg. He had taken his undergraduate degree from Stanford 1906. He had served as vice chmn Hoover Library under Adams 1920-25. Harold H. Fisher was director Hoover Library 1944-52. He had been deputy director of American Relief Administration and its chief historian under Hoover 1920-24. He was professor of history at Stanford Univ. from 1933 on, becoming emeritus in 1955 , director of Hoover's Belgian American Educational Foundation 1943-64, and chairman of the Pacific Council of IPR 1953-61 during the period when the FBI arrested a number of IPR executives and charged them with espionage. While chairman of IPR, Fisher continued to give his mailing address as Hoover Institution, Stanford University. The *New York Times* noted Oct. 29, 1929, that Hoover, as President of the U.S., had sent greetings to the IPR meeting, "My best greetings and wishes".

The next director of the Hoover Institution was C. Easton Rothwell, 1952-60; he had been chairman of research at the Hoover Institution 1947-52. From 1941-46, he served as chief of spec, research and political affairs, Dept./State; he was exec. sec. UN Conference at San Francisco 1945 under Alger Hiss; was on the staff of Brookings Institution 1946-7, staff of the Natl War College 1951, delegate to Fulbright Conference, Cambridge England 1954.

In 1960, the library, now known as the Hoover Institution on War, Revolution and Peace, was headed by Wesley Glenn

Campbell, who is still its director. Born in Ontario, Campbell took his degree from Harvard in 1946, PH.D. 1948, and taught there in the Economics Dept. five years. He became economist for the Chamber of Commerce 1951-54, American Enterprise Institute, 1954-60, when he became head of Hoover Institution. He is director of Hoover's Belgian American Education Foundation, and the super-secret Mont Pelerin Society, which publishes no information about its meetings. Campbell married Rita Ricardo, who continues to use her maiden name. She is a direct descendant of the famed economist, David Ricardo, whose theory of rent was appropriated by Karl Marx. Ricardo also originated "the law of wages", which states that workers must be limited to a bare subsistence wage, the amount controlled by "taxation". Ricardo also regarded workers as mere producers of "labour-time", a theory which Marx adopted as basic to his concept of labour. It embodies the classic parasitic view that the host exists only to produce sustenance for the parasite, and has no right to the products and gains of his own labour. An article in "CHANGE", Oct. 1981 states that Rita Ricardo "helped shape Reagan's thinking on social security and national health insurance", both of which are applied as taxation on the worker's income.

In 1964, Campbell and other Hoover personnel were the chief advisers of the Goldwater campaign; within two decades they had become the most influential policy-makers at the White House.

The *New York Times* Index for the period of Hoover's presidency, 1929-33, contains no references to either Stanford or the Hoover Library. On June 23, 1933, the *Times* noted that the ex-President would maintain an office at Stanford. Instead, he took a suite at New York's Waldorf Astoria, and spent the remainder of his life there. Although he was rarely seen at the Hoover Institution, he presided over the annual gatherings of the West Coast powerhouse, Bohemian Grove, and was viewed as its reigning figure.

The *New York Times* March 24, 1935 referred to "Hoover's Palo Alto Brain Trust", although the Brain Trust did not take power in Washington until 1980. On June 30, 1941, a new 14 story, 210 ft. building, costing $1.2 million, was dedicated for the Hoover Institution at Stanford by President Seymour of Yale, a Romanesque tower housing some 5 million documents, many of them sealed. The *Saturday Evening Post*, Mar. 11, 1950, noted that Edgar Rickard, director of Hoover Institution, had raised $600,000 in 1937 towards the cost of this new building.

Hoover stated that the purpose of the library was "to expose through research the inequities of Communism", although he had originally written it as "to demonstrate the evils of the doctrine of Karl Marx." A later president of Stanford, Wallace Sterling, re-edited this in 1960 to read "to expand human knowledge, that human welfare may thus be enhanced", a classic example of Orwell's "Doublethink". Sterling explained this act of censorship by claiming, "We cannot have research with predetermined conclusion". Sterling, also born in Ontario, had been a member of the Hoover research staff from 1932-37, was awarded the Hoover Medal. He was with the Ditchley Foundation 1962-76, and has served on the staff of HEW and the Natl War College.

On July 21, 1957, the Hoover Library officially changed its name to Hoover Institution on War, Peace and Revolution. It receives funding from Lilly, Pew, and Volker Funds, and the Sarah Mellon Scaife Foundation. Ford Foundation gave it $255,000 in 1953. On July 6, 1943, the Lilly Fund had financed a three day conference at the institution for Bertram Wolfe, New York, Raymond Aron, France, and Richard Lowenstein of Berlin. All of these beneficiaries were old line liberals.

In 1927, because of Wilbur's directorship there, the Rockefeller Foundation gave the Hoover Library $200,000 for Slavic Studies. The Carnegie Corp. also gave $180,000. On Jan. 7, 1975, President Ford signed a $30 million scholarship bill; tacked onto it was a $7 million grant to the Hoover Institution. The Dept. of Justice gave the Hoover $600,000 to study crime.

Stanford University's campus is world headquarters for Hewlett-Packard and the multi-billion electronics industry. The 8800 acres of Stanford's campus was originally Leland Stanford's Palo Alto Stock Farm, which he endowed with some $20 million. The campus houses a $105 million Atomic Energy

Commission laboratory built through the influence of L.L. Strauss, chairman of AEC and director of Hoover Institution. Two thousand acres have been set aside for rental units. A shopping center on the campus pays $500,000 rent annually. The 300 acres Stanford Research Park houses the world headquarters of Hewlett-Packard. In 1912, Lee de Forest invented the vacuum tube in Palo Alto, launching the radio industry. Prof. Louis Term an of Stanford invented the Stanford-Binet IQ test; his son Fred became professor of electric engineering at Stanford, and persuaded two of his students, Bill Hewlett and Dave Packard, to start an electronics concern. Hewlett-Packard now has $4.4 billion annual sales, 68,000 employees. Fortune says Bill Hewlett is worth $1,045 billion, Dave Packard is worth $2.115 billion.

Prof. William Shockley invented the transistor here, launching the Silicon Valley complex. His invention was later taken over by Fairchild Semiconductor, which is now owned by Schlumberger Inc. Shockley received little or nothing for his discovery.

Stanford received $3 million from the Ford Foundation for a medical center, and in Sept. 1959, the Ford Foundation gave Stanford $25 million, its largest gift to any educational institution. The *New York Times* noted on Oct. 10, 1977, that Stanford "known as the Harvard of the West", had completed a $300 million fund-raising campaign headed by Arjay Miller, former president of Ford Motor Co. The Harvard influence has always been strong at Stanford and the Hoover Institution. Donald Kennedy, who became president of Stanford in 1980, married Jeanne Dewey, took his AB., MA., and PH.D. from Harvard, and served on the Harvard Board of Overseers from 1970-76. He was Commissioner of Food & Drugs under President Carter 1977-79, before becoming president of Stanford.

Stanford has other important real estate holdings. *Time*, Jan. 14, 1966 noted that Stanford has a German castle at Beutelsbach, a villa in Florence, a hotel in Tours, and occupies Harlaxton Manor, a 365 room stone mansion in Lincolnshire leased to Stanford by the Jesuits.

The Guide to the Hoover Institution, published in 1980, notes that Rita Campbell is Archivist; Robert Hessen is Deputy Archivist. The collection is composed of 24% North America, 26% Russia and Eastern Europe; 27% Western Europe, and 1.8% Latin America. Page 5 of the Guide notes that the collection was inspired by two historians, Andrew D. White, president of Cornell, and Ephraim Adams of Stanford. No. 2358 in the collection is the Paris files of the Czarist Secret Police; No. 2373, the files of the Imperial Russian Okhrana (secret police); No. 2382, a list of the atrocities committed by Soviet political agents in Kiev.

On June 25, 1962, Alfred Kohlberg (known as the head of the China Lobby) died; he left 15 cabinets of papers which are restricted until 1991. The Max. E. Fleischmann Foundation spent $250,000 for Boris Nikolaevsky's 40-year collection of Russian documents, which were then presented to Hoover Institution. The Hoover collection also includes the personal diaries of Joseph Goebbels and Heinrich Himmler, the files of Basil Malakoff, Soviet Ambassador in Washington 1919-26, the files of the Bank for International Settlements, and the official Japanese records of the attack on Pearl Harbor.

In 1966, Alan H. Belmont joined the Hoover as exec. asst. to the director. He had formerly been with the FBI 1936-65, serving as personal assistant to J. Edgar Hoover. Also at the Hoover was Stefan Possony, educated at the University of Vienna, came to the U.S. in 1940, was advisor to the War Dept. 1943-46, and was appointed director of international political studies at the Hoover in 1961.

In 1963, the directors of the Hoover Institution included Richard Amberg, publisher of the St. Louis Post-Dispatch; Clarence Bamberger, mining engineer; William J. Baroody, who had founded the American Enterprise Institute, and was chairman of the Woodrow Wilson International Center for Scholars; Karl R. Bendetsen, chairman of Champion Paper, was special War Dept. representative to Gen. MacArthur 1941, spec, adviser to Secretary of the Army, asst. Secretary of Defense 1948-52, chairman of the Panama Canal Co., and Ambassador to West Germany and the Philippine Islands; James B. Black Jr. of

Lehman Bros; Arthur Curtice, chmn General Motors; Paul L. Davies Jr. who directed the evacuation of the Japanese from the West Coast to concentration camps in 1941, heads leading West Coast law firm of Pillsbury Madison & Sutro, partner Lehman Bros., director of IBM, Southern Pacific and Caterpillar; Northcutt Ely Washington lawyer who represented Sec. Wilbur in negotiating the contracts for Hoover Dam 1930-33; Richard E. Guggenheim, president of Rosenberg Foundation; Harold H. Helm, chmn Chemical Bank, director of Westinghouse, Uniroyal, Colgate, Wool worth, Bethlehem Steel, Equitable, McDonnell Douglas, and Cummins Engine; John A. McCone of Bechtel-McCone 1937-45, Und. Sec. AF 1950-51, Chmn AEC 1958-60, director CIA 1961-65; N. Loyall McLaren, president of the billion dollar James Irvine Foundation, was treasurer of the UN Conference at San Francisco 1945 under Alger Hiss, was also appointed to Allied Commission on Reparations 1945; Jeremiah Milbank, New York financier, head of the Milbank Foundation and director Chase Manhattan Bank; George C. Montgomery, chairman of Kern County Land Co.; William I. Nichols, publisher of THIS WEEK, served with War Production Board 1942-45; David Packard, chmn Hewlett-Packard - his personal fortune increased by $1 billion in 1983; Richard M. Scaife, vice pres. Mellon Natl Bank; Adm. L.L. Strauss, of Kuhn, Loeb Co., chmn AEC 1946-50, lists himself in Who's Who as "financial adviser to Messrs. Rockefeller"; R. Douglas Stewart, Ford, Rockefeller, & Guggenheim; Thomas Gale Moore was Reagan's expert on energy policy; Paul Craig Roberts became asst. Sec. Treasury; Richard V. Allen, who had been on the staff of the Hoover Institution since 1966, served on National Security Council 1969, dep. asst. to the President 1969-70, now became Reagan's asst. for national security affairs; Martin Anderson, senior fellow at Hoover Institution 1971-81, became Reagan's asst for policy development; he thought up the ridiculous boondoggle of "Urban Enterprise Zones".

One of the "Hoover Hotshots" on Reagan's team was described in *Omni March* 1984 Continuum:

> "Honegger Hotline: Pres. aide Barbara Honegger was hired by Martin Anderson at Hoover Institution while writing a book on the draft; she wore a scarab necklace and was the

first graduate in experimental psychology at John F. Kennedy University, Olinda, Calif.; she had advised Reagan to decide against underground shells of MX missiles because psychics would target them; she had him put 5500 additional warheads on our 33 nuclear submarines because psychic brainwaves are absorbed by the churning sea. Despite Anderson's protests, she was finally ushered out of the White House."

So much for "the Extreme Right" in scarab necklaces and dodging psychic brain waves.

Campbell's Presidential Transition Team spent $1 million from donors plus $2 million provided by Congress, but could not get a single "rightwinger" installed on Reagan's staff. The largest payment went to longtime liberal Joseph Califano, who was paid $86,047.93 for representing Alexander Haig at his Senate confirmation hearings as Secretary of State. "Rightwinger" Haig said Califano was an old-time friend. The deputy director of the Transition Team, Verne Orr, served as comptroller of the Reagan campaign, and is now Secretary of the Air Force.

Seymour Martin Lipset, who voted for John Anderson in 1980, took a survey of the 25 Hoover fellows in 1984; he found 11 Democrats, 10 Republicans, 3 independent, and one who was not a citizen. The Three Honorary Fellows of Hoover Institution are Ronald Reagan, Alexander Solzhenitsyn, and Frederick von Hayek. Reagan is in Washington, Solzhenitsyn lives in Vermont; von Hayek is retired in Salzburg. None of them has any connection with the administration of the Hoover Institution. Reagan has already donated his papers to the Hoover Institution.

In June, 1981, Hoover Institution held a gala reception at the Sheraton Carlton in Washington, with many White House officials present. They effectively short-circuited all of Reagan's campaign promises for lower taxes, decreased government spending, and the goal of "getting the government off of our backs".

The present star of the Hoover Institution is Milton Friedman, who is credited with bringing economic disaster to Chile, Israel, the United States, and other countries in which his "monetarist" theories have been introduced. Friedman's "monetarism" is the same old bankers' swindle of endless creation of more interest bearing debt money, requiring ever increasing taxes merely to meet the interest payments. He and Jack Kemp are now pushing for a "flat tax" to lock Americans into a tax corral from which they can never hope to escape. Friedman came to the Hoover in 1977 as senior research fellow, simultaneously accepting a post as economic consultant to the Federal Reserve Bank of San Francisco. He and his consort, Murray Rothbard, dominate a closely interlocked network of "hard money" "conservative" groups, which includes the Heritage Foundation, Mont Pelerin Society, Cato Institute, Ludwig von Mises Institute, and American Enterprise Institute, which hold banquet meetings, always with no visible result. Their mentor is the late Ludwig von Mises, born in Austria, and founder of "the Austrian School of Economics", who taught at New York University from 1946 until his death. The Institute is now run by his widow, Margit Herzfeld, to whom President Reagan said, at a testimonial dinner for her husband, "You don't know how often I consult the books of your husband before making a decision." She still doesn't know.

At the age of 16, Milton Friedman became the protege of Arthur Burns at Rutgers and Columbia. Their economic principles stemmed from the "Viennese School" founded by Karl Menger and Eugen Böhm von Bawerk president of Quaker Oats; Gardner Simonds, chmn Tenneco, Kern County Land Co.; Robert C. Tyson, chmn U.S. Steel, director of Chemical Bank, Uniroyal; Thos. J. Watson Jr. chmn of IBM, director of Rockefeller Foundation; Stephen Duggan chmn. emeritus Institute of International Education - father of late Laurence Duggan who died mysteriously, member of World Peace Foundation, League of Nations Association; John Foster Dulles; Anson Phelps Stokes, of the Institute of International Education, director General Education Board; Harold H. Swift, chmn Swift Packing Co. chmn War Finance Committee Dept. of Treasury 1941-44; Augustus Trowbidge intelligence director of American Exped. Force under Pershing in World War I.

In 1980, the directors of Hoover Institution included Bendetsen, Black, Philip Habib, of Bechtel, and Reagan's

Special Ambassador to the Middle East; Henry T. Bodman, chairman Natl Bank of Detroit, director and vice chmn American Enterprise Institute - his son Richard served with the Treasury Dept., was Asst. Sec. Interior, now president of COMSAT; David Tennant Bryan, married into the Harkness family, chmn Media General; Willard C. Butcher, former chmn Chase Manhattan, now director American Enterprise Institute; Joseph Coors, director Heritage Foundation; Charles A. Dana Jr., director Manufacturers Hanover Trust, Dana Foundation; Shelby Cullon Davis, was with CBS 1932-34, economic adviser to Dewey in his Presidential campaigns, Ambassador to Switzerland 1969-75, trustee of Princeton, Heritage Foundation; Maurice Greenberg, president American International Group; Alan Greenspan, president Economics Advisers since 1981, consultant to U.S. Treasury and Federal Reserve Board 1971-74, director of *Time*, General Foods, J.P. Morgan, Morgan Guaranty Trust; Bryce Harlow, asst. to President of U.S. 1959-61, and 1969-70, now Washington lobbyist for Proctor & Gamble; A. Carol Kotchian, president Lockheed; J. Claybum La Force, dean of Graduate School of Management Univ. of California, Fulbright scholar, director Natl Bureau of Economic Research, Mont Pelerin Society; William B. Macomber Jr., president Metropolitan Museum, was with CIA 1951-53, spec. asst. for intelligence at State Dept. 1953-54, spec. asst. to Und Sec. State Herbert Hoover Jr. and Sec. of State John Foster Dulles 1955-57, Ambassador to Teheran and Jordan;

Emil Mosbacher Jr. known as "Kingmaker", was chief of protocol State Dept. 1969-72, director Chubb, Chemial Bank, Avon, AM AX - his brother Robert was nat. chmn Bush for President, chmn Gerald Ford's unsuccessful election campaign, co chmn Republican Natl Committee; David Packard, of Hewlett Packard, American Enterprise Institute; Donald Rumsfeld, pres. Rand Corp., pres. G.D. Searle, asst to Pres. Nixon 1969-73, perm. rep. to NATO 1973-74, director of Sears, and Institute of Strategic Studies, London.

Although the "butcher paper weeklies" such as The Nation issue grim warnings that the Hoover Institution is deeply engaged in the practice of "cold war anti-Communism", the *New York*

Times has noted that the Hoover is surprisingly liberal. Its longtime senior fellow is Sidney Hook, old-line Socialist who keeps a portrait of George Meany on his office wall; Seymour Martin Lipset, longtime liberal closely identified with the offices of Democratic Senators Henry Jackson and Daniel Moynihan, taught at Harvard, Univ. of Calif., received the Gunnar Myrdal Prize 1970, nat. chmn B'Nai B'Rith Hillel and United Jewish Appeal; John Bunzel, Democratic liberal now associated with the Libertarian Party; Stanley Fischer, liberal from MIT; Joseph Pechman, the Hoover Institution resident tax expert - he had been tax expert at Brookings Institution Washington for many years before coming to Hoover; other resident liberals are Dennis J. Dollin, Theodore Draper and Peter Duignan. Lipset was quoted in an interview in the *New York Times* as follows:

> "Over half the senior fellows here are not rightwingers, not even conservatives; they are leftwing Democrats and Socialists."

These are the architects of Reagan's "rightwing" administration, the usual flimflam in which the same tired old Marxists are trotted out as the inspired libertarians of a world run by the "Hard Right"! The head of Reagan's Presidential Transition Team on cabinet appointments in 1980 was. W. Glenn Campbell, Harvard graduate and head of Hoover Institution; Reagan's adviser on social security was his wife, Rita Ricardo Campbell. More than half of the Hoover staff went to Washington with Reagan. Richard Starr and Peter Duignan were his advisers on foreign policy; Duignan had received fellowships from Bauwerk. Mengertaught von Hayek, Eric Voegelin and Fritz Machluys. At that time, Vienna was dominated by the House of Rothschild, which had controlled the national debt of Austria since the Congress of Vienna in 1815. Austria's Tyrol silver mines were owned by the Rothschilds, as were her railways. Empress Elizabeth's closest friend was Julie de Rothschild, sister of Baron Albert, head of the Austrian House. Count Richard Coudenhove-Kalergi, who founded the Pan

European Union[4], was named after Richard Wagner, one of whose students was Gustav Mahler. Mahler's studies with Wagner were funded by Baron Albert de Rothschild. Coudenhove Kalergi's father was a close friend of Theodor Herzl, founder of Zionism. Coudenhove-Kalergi writes in his Memoirs,

> "At the beginning of 1924, we received a call from Baron Louis de Rothschild; one of his friends, Max Warburg from Hamburg, had read my book and wanted to get to know us. To my great surprise, Warburg spontaneously offered us 60,000 gold marks, to tide the movement over for its first three years. Max Warburg, who was one of the most distinguished and wisest men that I have ever come into contact with, had a principle of financing these movements. He remained sincerely interested in Pan-Europe for his entire life. Max Warburg arranged his 1925 trip to the United States to introduce me to Paul Warburg and financier Bernard Baruch."

In Chicago, Jane Adams of Hull House had been for five years a protege of Beatrice Webb, founder of the Fabian Society. In 1892, the University of Chicago was organized as the center of the Fabian Socialist program in America, with J. Laurence Laughlin, spokesman for the Cobden Club's "free trade" program in England; Laughlin later became Paul Warburg's chief propagandist to stump for the passing of the Federal Reserve Act. John Dewey became head of the sociology dept. at the Univ. of Chicago; Wesley Clair Mitchell was head of the economics dept. In 1913, they moved to Columbia University. They were later hired by Baruch at the War Industries Board, and prepared all the statistics for American representatives at the Versailles Peace Conference. In Feb. 1920, Mitchell met with the rest of the staff of Baruch's War Industries Board in New York with a Round Table group financed by Kuhn Loeb & Co. and Lazard Freres, to

---

[4] See Practical Idealism, the Kalergi Plan to destroy European peoples, Omnia Veritas Ltd, www.omnia-veritas.com.

found the Natl Bureau of Economic Research, of which Mitchell became director. His protege was Arthur Burns, later chmn of the Natl Buro, chmn Federal Reserve Governors, partner of Lazard Freres, and U.S. Ambassador to West Germany.

Burns then brought in his protege, Milton Friedman, who has proposed that we legalize the sale of dope to raise $100 billion a year for the GNP.

Wesley Clair Mitchell's career was devoted to uniting the Austrian and British schools of economics in a single force to direct the American economy. He achieved success through the careers of his protégés, Burns and Friedman, who offer us the "flat rate" tax to pay interest on their bank-created debt money. It is the ancient European system introduced by the House of Rothschild to loot national economies by the rentier system of national debt.

A keystone of the Friedman-Burns network is the Mont Pelerin Society, a secretive group of economists which meets every two years, but issues no findings or recommendations. These supposedly conservative hard money economists first met at Mont Pelerin, Switzerland in 1947 to oppose the leftwing statist economists who had dominated the field for fifty years. They were led by Frederick von Hayek, a graduate of the Viennese school of economics, who became a British citizen in 1938. He was Tooke prof, of economics, Univ. of London 1931-50, prof, of social and moral science at the Univ. of Chicago 1950-62, and prof, of economics Univ. of Freiburg 1926-69, when he retired to Salzburg. He was a disciple of Ludwig von Mises, who taught Henry Hazlitt, another founder of Mont Pelerin. Hazlitt reported the founding meeting in *Newsweek*, Sept. 25, 1961, listing among those present Jacques Rueff, economic director of France, Pedro Beltran, president of Peru, Sen. Luigi Einaudi, prof, economics at Turin 1901-35, Governor of the Bank of Italy 1945-48, president of Italy 1948-55; Dr. Ludwig Erhard, Economic Minister of Germany, director of World Bank; Wilhelm Roepke, Erhard's economic adviser; Trygve Hoff, Norway; Muller-Armack and William Rappard of Germany; Ludwig von Mises; Frank Knight; Milton Friedman and Henry Hazlitt.

In 1962, the Mont Pelerin Society met at Knokke, Belgium, announcing that

> "The Mont Pelerin Society takes no formal action, passes no resolutions, and seeks no publicity."

In 1970, the Society met in Munich, where Milton Friedman was elected president. Present were Wesley Campbell and Martin Anderson from the Hoover Institution. In 1974, 300 members of the Society met at Brussels, where they were addressed by Milton Friedman and his protege Murray Rothbard. Rothbard was sponsored by the Cato Institute, a "conservative" group whose director, Earl C. Ravenel, is also director of the Institute for Policy Studies, the leftwing policy-making organization founded by James Paul Warburg. Cato is funded by Charles Koch of Kansas, head of Koch Industries, who amassed a fortune of $700 million. He also funds the Libertarian Party, which calls for opening U.S. borders to all illegal immigrants, legalizing of drugs, and other alarming recommendations. Koch funds these groups through his bank, Morgan Guaranty Trust of N.Y. Cato gave a two year grant to Rothbard to write a book, *For a New Liberty*, which says,

> "Before World War II, so devoted was Stalin to peace that he failed to make adequate provision against Nazi attack."

Rothbard should have said,

> "So devoted was Stalin to murder that he killed most of his Army officers, leaving him vulnerable to Nazi attack."

Rothbard asserts that the U.S. is imperialist and warmongering, while the Soviet Union is peace-loving, rational and misunderstood! The Cato Institute magazine *Inquiry* lists 9 staff writers, among them Natl Hentoff of the Village Voice, Marcus Raskin, head of the Institute for Policy Studies, and Penny Lernoux, correspondent of the *Nation*, all of whom would be hurt if they were not described as extreme liberals.

In 1975, George Roche III, who had become a member of the Society in 1971, hosted the meeting at Hillsdale College, of which he is president. William Buckley, also a member, addressed the group with a routine encomium for von Hayek.

In 1980, the Mont Pelerin Society met at the Hoover Institution, with 600 members and guests present. Ralph Harris was guest speaker. As Margaret Thatcher's director of economics, he had been made Baron Harris of High Cross in 1979. Count Max Thurn, permanent secretary of the Society, also addressed the meeting. He is a member of the wealthy Thurn und Taxis family, closely related to the British royal family.

The Encyclopaedia of Associations lists the Mont Pelerin Society c/o Edwin Feulner, treasurer, Box 7031, Alexandria, Va; secretary Dr. Max Thurn, Elizabethstrasse 4, Vienna. Feulner is president of the Heritage Foundation, served as confidential asst. to Secretary of Defense 1969-70; adm asst. Phil Crane 1940-44, public affairs fellow Hoover Institution 1965-67, chmn Institute European Strategy and Defense Studies London since 1979.

Heritage Foundation, part of the network of "conservative" groups, sponsored Reagan's posthumous award of the Medal of Freedom to Whittaker Chambers in March 1984. Its directors are Shelby Cullom Davis, director of Hoover; Joseph Coors, director of Hoover; Midge Decter, exec, director Committee for a Free World; her husband is "neoconservative" Norman Podhoretz, editor of Commentary magazine; Robert Dee, chmn Smith Kline drug firm, director United Technologies with William Simon; William Simon, director Citibank, former Secretary of the Treasury; Lewis E. Lehman, head of the Lehman Institute; John D. Wrather, heir to an oil fortune, head of the entertainment conglomerate Wrather Inc. and director of Hoover.

Feulner claims that Heritage cooperates with more than 400 groups in the U.S. and 100 overseas. Honorary chairman is Frank Shakespeare. Chairman of the editorial board is David Meiselman of the Mont Pelerin Society. Richard Reeves mentions in the *N.Y. Times* Magazine, July 15, 1984,

> "Edwin J. Feulner is president of the Heritage Foundation, one of the right's most productive idea factories."

He failed to cite a single "idea" produced by this factory. The star of Heritage and its closely affiliated American Enterprise Institute is Jeane Kirkpatrick, U.S. Ambassador to the UN. She is routinely mentioned in terms of fulsome praise such as the

Communist Party used to reserve for Stalin; *National Review* gushes over her, and also raves about "the ever gallant, charming, freedom-loving Friedmans" whose "energy, lucidity and patience" awes Buckley's propagandists.

Jeane Kirkpatrick has been prof, at Georgetown Univ. since 1967, chief of research American Enterprise Institute since 1977, director of Center for Strategic and International Studies at Georgetown. She is the wife of veteran intelligence operative Evron Kirkpatrick, OSS 1945, intelligence specialist Dept. of State 1946-54 as chief psychological intelligence research staff specializing in behavioural science (people control). He has been head of the American Political Science Association since 1954, and is president of the American Peace Society which publishes a quarterly called World Affairs.

Jeane Kirkpatrick is known as "the Queen of the American Right". During her service as American Ambassador to the United Nations, she defended Israel so furiously that she was given a $100,000 gift from Raymond and Miriam Klein as a reward for her "personal commitment to Israel". We are not aware of any rewards given to her for her commitment to the United States. Because of her loyalty to Israel, she is routinely paid $25,000 to speak before pro-Zionist groups. For years, she had been apolitical advisor to the Democratic National committee, but in 1985 she suddenly became a Republican. She serves on the board of a Trotskyite group known as the League for Industrial Democracy, which is funded by the Rockefellers and is the last gasp of the old Socialist Workers Party. Multi-faceted political personalities such as Kirkpatrick puzzle many observers, who do not understand that she is of that strange breed known as "neoconservatives". They are distinguished from real American conservatives by a number of warning signs, but let Peter Steinfels, in his definitive work, *The Neoconservatives*, explain it.

> "The leading neoconservatives who were socialists in those years (the 1930s) were virtually all anti-Stalinists (Trotskyites). Well-drilled in Marxist texts and socialist history, blooded in the tribal wars between Communists, democratic socialists, and fifty-seven varieties of Trotskyists,

they were already trained and in motion when the Cold War put their skills at a premium."

Steinfels goes on to point out (p. 50) that

"Neoconservatives have been strong supporters of Israel."

Jeane Kirkpatrick periodically writes columns which could easily be written by the Mossad, such as her column of Jan. 20, 1992, *Washington Post*, in which she sobs that Israel is being undermined in Washington, and that the Bush administration is anti-Israel. "Is this part of the new world order?" she moans, tormented by the vision of another Holocaust. Steinfels quotes a leading neocon, Irving Kristol that "Neoconservatism is not at all hostile to the idea of the welfare state." In fact, the neocons are all statists, which makes them ideal servants of the World Order. They have a number of think-tank publications, such as Commentary, financed by the American Jewish Committee, Partisan Review, the New Leader, and the Public Interest, many of which are funded with CIA funds.

Another neoconservative front is the Unification Church of Rev. Sun Moon, funded by the Korean CIA with our own CIA funds. It spends billions of dollars on "conservative" publications such as the *Washington Times*, which is edited by Arnold de Borchgrave, a relative of the Rothschilds. At the FBI, J. Edgar Hoover also got into the "neoconservative" act by hiring Roy Godson, a self-styled "social democrat", to educate FBI agents on Marxist ideology. He was the son of Joseph Godson, who helped Jay Lovestone found the communist Party of America. Roy Godson is now consultant to the National Security Council, hired at the behest of Henry Kissinger. J. Edgar Hoover was fascinated by Communists; he hired Jay Lovestone, founder of the American Communist Party, to ghostwrite his best-selling *Masters of Deceit*. It was indeed a masterpiece of deceit, as no one knew it had been written by a Communist.

A major force in CIA propaganda, Israeli promotions and "neoconservative" agitprop is the *National Review*. It was incorporated for William Buckely in 1955 by William Casey, later director of the CIA, and became part of the network of fake "rightwing" organizations in the United States promoting the

Trotskyite movement in Communism, such as the Heritage Foundation, run by a British Fabian Socialist with Coors' beer profits, the American Enterprise Institute, and many other like deceits of the World Order. Because the neocons always prate of "democracy" while noisily slopping at the public through, their masterstroke has been a boondoggle called Project Democracy. The neocons convinced Congress that they should fund a project which would promote democracy in every country in the world. It was the brainchild of Lane Kirkpatrick, veteran socialist, with Jay Lovestone, Jesuit Father Edmund Walsh of Georgetown University and the stern Sen. Orrin Hatch, a bishop of the Mormon Church. Hatch maneuvered the National Endowment for Democracy Act through Congress in 1983. Carl Gershman, a staff director of the Anti-Defamation League, was chosen as its president. It has funded a number of pet neoconservative groups, all of which have proven to be disasters. In 1990 and 1991, the National Endowment for Democracy passed out bribes to Russian officials to "encourage democracy" and enormous sums, which cannot be traced, to various Russian groups, none of which played any role in the downfall of the Communist system.

The Godfather of the neoconservatives is Henry Kissinger. A German national, Kissinger returned to his birthplace as a sergeant in the U.S. Army, soon identified as a recruit to the KGB with the code name of "Bor". He became a student at Harvard University, and was soon hired by the Rockefellers as the protege of an even more mysterious personage, one Helmut Sonnenfeldt, who remains a Washington insider. He campaigned for Nelson Rockefeller's presidential bid, and when Nixon won out, Kissinger publicly sneered at him as a know-nothing. A few days later, Nixon, acting under orders, named him Secretary of State. Israeli Ambassador to the U.S. Abba Eban quoted terrorist Menachem Begin,

> "The appointment of Dr. Kissinger as secretary of state has as much significance as the United Nations vote to create the State of Israel."

Kissinger later appeared as speaker at more than twenty-five Anti-Defamation League events during his term of office. He placed top Zionists in many government agencies, developed

ADL support in key evangelical groups such as Jerry Falwell and Pat Robertson, and persuaded Sheldon Cohen, Former Commissioner of the Internal Revenue Service, to rewrite IRS regulations which ensured that the ADL and hundreds of other Zionist organizations would have permanent tax exempt status. He conceived of the Project Democracy boondoggle, and guided it through Congress, as a Trotskyite project. However, his main commitment was to the British Secret Service, as he boasted in a speech at Chatham House, home of the Royal Institute of International Affairs, in London, May 10, 1982,

> "In my White House incarnation then, I kept the British Foreign Office better informed and more closely engaged than I did the American State Department."

Why did Kissinger, the Zionist, work so closely with the British Foreign Office? The answer is in the origin of the Anti-Defamation League, which is generally thought of as a strictly Jewish operation. It is actually an SIS branch, which was founded by Henry Lord Palmerston, British Foreign Minister, who also created the entire Zionist movement as a weapon of British espionage from 1843 to 1860. The ADL began as B'Nai B'Rith, and was modelled on Ptolemaic Egypt's death cult of Isis. Palmerston formulated it as an arm of British intelligence which had the specific mission of subverting and destroying the American Republic. This is still its mission today. Palmerston was aided in the development of B'Nai B'Rith as a worldwide power by Baruch Rothschild. It subsequently directed the abolitionist movement in the northern U.S., the Southern Secession, and the Civil War, which it capped by the assassination of President Abraham Lincoln. The ADL's favorite weapon to discredit its opponents is the charge of antisemitism, which it recently levelled at columnist Pat Buchanan because of his Presidential bid. It is ludicrous for an arm of British intelligence to denounce anyone as "antisemitic".

B'Nai B'Rith launched its goal of permanently destabilizing the Middle East with a letter from Secretary Balfour to Lord Rothschild on Nov. 2, 1917, during the First World War:

> "Dear Lord Rothschild: I have much pleasure in conveying to you, on behalf of His Majesty's Government,

the following declaration of sympathy with Jewish Zionist aspirations, which have been submitted to, and approved by, the Cabinet. His Majesty's Government views with favor the establishment in Palestine of a national home for the Jewish people, and will use their best endeavors to facilitate this object, it being clearly understood that nothing shall be done to prejudice the existing civil and religious rights of existing non-Jewish communities in Palestine or the rights and political status enjoyed by Jews in any other country."

As agent for these interests, Kissinger is the author of Bush's new world order program, claiming that it is the heir of Lord Castlereagh's "Balance of power" policy which he originated at the Congress of Vienna in 1815. However, Pat Buchanan notes that the balance of power got England into World War I and II (which was, after all, the program), and that this world order is now coming to an end. After leaving office, Kissinger installed his protégés in key positions in Washington. He formed a firm called Kissinger Associates with a Rothschild relative, Lord Carrington, and signed up America's leading corporations to promote their international interests. As president he named Lawrence Eagleburger, who is now Bush's Acting Secretary of State, and as chairman, Gen. Brent Scowcroft, who is Bush's director of the National Security Council, Other Kissinger protégés in Washington are Col. Oliver North and Gen. Alexander Haig. Kissinger is engaged in extensive business interests in Communist China, with a group called China Ventures. He and Bush valiantly defended the Chinese massacre of unarmed students in Beijing's Tiananmen Square, and pleaded that it not interfere with such business ventures as Prescott Bush's bid to build luxury real estate in China. He is the brother of the President. Deng Ziaoping, Chinese dictator, explained the student massacres,

> "The recent rioting gave us a great deal of enlightenment and refreshed our minds. Without the socialist road, China has no future, and without it there would not be the great China U.S. Russia triangle of world power. I tell Americans, China's greatest asset is its stability."

Perhaps the Trilateral goal is the triangle of what would become the three great Communist powers of the world.

The American Enterprise Institute was founded by William J. Baroody and Milton Friedman in 1943; Baroody left in 1978 to take over the $7 million a year Center for Strategic and International Studies at Georgetown. His son, William Jr. former adviser to President Nixon, took over AEI and its staff. Jr. was adm. asst Congressman Melvin Laird 1961-68, who then became Secretary of Defense; Baroody was spec, adviser at Defense 1969-73, spec, adviser to the President of the U.S.I 1973-74, and is chairman of Woodrow Wilson International Center for scholars. Directors of American Enterprise Institute include Edward Bernstein; James S. Duesenberg, Presidential Council of Economic Advisers 1966-68, prof. at Harvard, director of Federal Reserve Bank of Boston, Fulbright fellow Cambridge England 1954-55; Frederick A. Praeger, emigre N.Y. publisher who published a number of propaganda works for the CIA; Herbert Stein, A. Willis Robertson prof of economics, Univ. of Va., editor of AEI publication The Economist since 1977, served on War Production Board 1941-44, Brookings Institution fellow 1967-69, Council of Economic Advisers 1969, chairman 1972-74; Robert H. Bork, prof, law at Yale, former Solicitor General and Acting Atty. Gen. of U.S. 1973-77; Kenneth W. Daum, former partner Cravath Swaine & Moore, Wall Street law firm, now prof, of law, Univ. of Chicago; D. Gale Johnson, prof, economics at Univ. of Chicago since 1944, economist with OPA 1942, State Dept. 1946, U.S. Army econ. 1948, adviser to Congress 1974-76, consultant to TVA, Rand Corp. and AID, director William Benton Fndtn; Robert Nisbet, John Dewey lecturer at John Dewey Society, Rockefeller Foundation grant 1975-78, scholar at AEL since 1978; James D. Wilson, Shattuck prof, at Harvard; Richard B. Madden, chmn exec. committee AEI, chairman Socony Mobil since 1956, director Pacific Gas & Electric, Del Monte and Weyerhauser; Willard. Butcher, former chmn Chase Manhattan Bank; Charles T. Fisher III, president of Natl Bank of Detroit, director of General Motors, Detroit Edison; Richard D. Wood, president of Eli Lilly drugs since 1961, director of Standard Oil of Indiana, and Chemical Bank.

Thus the well-funded "Hard Right" American Enterprise Institute's board of directors reads much like that of the Rockefeller Foundation or the Hoover Institution, the usual New

York banks, Standard Oil, General Motors crowd. The World Order maintains control.

Lewis Lehman, director of Heritage Foundation, and founder of the store Rite Aid drug chain, setup his own foundation in 1978. After agonizing over a trenchant attention-getting name, he chose the obvious, "Lewis Lehman Institute". Its president is Robert W. Tucker, member of the Council on Foreign Relations, professor at John Hopkins School of International Studies, which was made famous by the tenure of Owen Lattimore, denounced by Sen. McCarthy as a leading Soviet agent. Director of Lehman Institute is Barton Biggs of Brookings Institution. Lehman spent $13.9 million campaigning to be elected Governor of New York, but was easily beaten by Mario Cuomo, who only spent $4.8 million. The *New Republic* Dec. 5, 1983 featured an article by Sidney Blumenthal, "How Lewis Lehman Plans to Take Over America."

After examining the lavishly funded network of pseudo-rightwing foundations, it is almost a relief to go back to the forthright Marxist bias of the foundation movement, as exemplified by the Ford Foundation. The Special Committee to Investigate Tax Exempt Foundation reported in 1954,

> "The Ford Foundation affords a good example of the use of a foundation to solve the death tax problem, and, at the same time, the problem of how to retain control of a great enterprise in the hands of a family. Ninety per cent of the ownership of the Ford Motor Co. was transferred to the Ford Foundation, created for the purpose. Had it not been it was almost certain that the family would have lost control."

The Ford family paid a terrible price to save the company. To prevent it from being split up, they had to turn it over to the most leftwing elements in the U.S. Norman Dodd states that while investigating tax exempt foundations, he interviewed H. Rowan Gaither, president of the Ford Foundation. Gaither complained about the "bad press" the Ford Foundation was receiving, and explained to Dodd,

> "Most of us here were, at one time or another, active in either the OSS or the State Dept., or the European Economic

Administration. During those times, and without exception, we operated under directives issued by the White House, the substance of which was to the effect that we should make every effort to alter life in the U.S. as to make possible a comfortable merger with the Soviet Union."

This is still the goal of the foundation movement.

In 1953, the Ford Foundation set up the $15 million Fund for the Republic, with Paul Hoffman, former head of ECA, married to Baruch's secretary, Anna Rosenberg. Directors of the Fund were former Zionist and labor leader Arthur Goldberg, and Henry Luce, of whom H.L. Mencken said, "I know why Henry hires so many Communists on his magazines. It's because they work cheap."

The Fund for the Republic hired Earl Browder, head of the Communist Party "to study the influence of Communism in contemporary America". In 1968, the Fund granted $215,000 to "promote in the U.S. the knowledge of contemporary Cuba. The funds will support the expenses of persons invited by the Castro government to do research in Cuba." The National Guardian Jan. 13, 1968 pointed out that "The Ford Foundation plays a key part in financing and influencing almost all major civil rights groups including Congress of Racial Equality, Southern Christian Leadership, National Urban League, and NAACP."

The Ford Foundation has spent many millions to promote racial agitation and possible civil war in America, completely polarizing the races. In this effort, it is simply carrying on the plan inaugurated by the Rothschilds in 1865 with the Peabody Fund, the Slater Fund, and later the General Education Board, which is now the Rockefeller Foundation. It takes money to promote a civil war. Ford Foundation entered the Hispanic field by giving $600,000 to the openly revolutionary Southwest Council of La Raza in 1968, and an additional $545,717 in 1969. Congressman Henry Gonzalez, himself a Hispanic, denounced La Raza as fomenting "blind, stupid hatred".

Ford money has backed many revolutionary groups in the U.S. engaged in dynamiting and burning buildings, inciting riots, kidnaping and assassination. All of these are criminal offenses but no one is ever arrested. The Ford Motor Co. also built the huge Kama River truck factory in Soviet Russia, which provided the trucks for the Red Army to attack Afghanistan. They rolled into the almost defenseless country on a modern highway, which had been built by AID with American taxpayers' money.

The Ford Foundation has many capitalist and CIA connections. Stephen Bechtel and Chase lawyer John J. McCloy have been board members for years, also Frank Abrams, chmn Standard Oil Co. of New Jersey. The president of the Ford Foundation is Franklin Thomas, a token black; he is also director of the $348 million John Hay Whitney Foundation. Whitney was Ambassador to England 1956-61, Order of the British Empire, chairman Freeport Sulphur, publisher of the *N.Y. Tribune*; he married Betsy Cushing Roosevelt. His daughter Kate married William Haddad of the *New York Post*, who set up the Peace Corps for Kennedy in 1961, is governor of American Jewish Congress, Yale Corp. and Museum of Modern Art; other directors of J.H. Whitney Foundation include Harold Howe, also director of Ford Foundation, Vernon Jordan, director of Rockefeller Foundation, and James F. Brownlee, partner of J.H. Whitney Co., and director of Chase Manhattan Bank, R.H. Macy Co. & chmn Minute Maid Corp.

Other directors of Ford Foundation include its European director, Ralf Dahrendorf, admirer of Marx's "Utopian" policies. In his work, *Marx in Perspective*, he claimed that Marx is the greatest factor in the emergence of modern society. Dahrendorf was fellow of Center of Advanced Study 1957-58, prof, sociology Hamburg, 1958-60, Columbia Univ. 1960, Univ. of Tubingen 1960-64, Secretary of State Foreign Office Germany 1969-70. As a professor of sociology, he created the concept of a "new man", whom he dubbed "homo sociologicus", man transformed by socialism, in which all distinctions of race, and presumably, all other distinctions, have disappeared. Dahrendorf denies there are any differences in the races of mankind, and denounces any idea of "superiority" or differing skills as "ideological distortion". "Homo Sociologicus" is the creature of the social sciences, the socialized man who can be completely controlled by the forces of society.

The Ford Foundation introduced "behaviourism" or people control into the curricula at Harvard Business School through the director, Donald K. David, in 1956. David received a $2 million grant from Ford Foundation for this program, while he was a director of the foundation. In 1970, Ford Foundation established the Police Foundation, headed by Pat Murphy, to train police in behaviourism and "human relations".

Other directors of Ford Foundation are Harriet S. Rabb, asst. dean Columbia U. Law School, director of the NAACP Legal Fund since 1978. Her husband Bruce Rabb is partner of the Wall Street law firm, Stroock Stroock & Lavan, organized the Lehrman Institute and has been secretary of it since 1978; his father, Maxwell Rabb is also partner of this law firm - he was adm. asst. of Sen. Henry Cabot Lodge 1937-43, Secretary of the Cabinet 1953-58 under Eisenhower, joined Stroock Stroock & Lavan in 1958, now Ambassador to Italy, chmn of U.S. delegation to UNESCO; other partners of this firm are William J. van den Heuvel, former law partner of Gen. Donovan, and his assistant when he was Ambassador to Thailand, campaign manager of Jimmy Carter 1976; Rita Hauser, director of Brookings Institution; and Robert B. Anderson former Secretary of Navy and Secretary of Treasury. Stroock Stroock & Lavan specializes in handling the family finances of wealthy old line Jewish families, and is trustee of all three Warburg foundations.

Chairman of the Ford Foundation is Alex Heard, who was with the War Dept. 1939-43, spec, adviser President of the U.S. 1970, director of *Time* since 1968; other directors are Hedley Donovan, editor in chief of *Time*, director of Trilateral Commission; Walter A. Haas, president of Levi Strauss, director of Bank of America, NAACP Legal Fund, chmn of United Jewish Appeal, and Alliance Israelite Universelle; Donald S. Perkins, of J.P. Morgan; Irving S. Shapiro, former chairman of DuPont, director of Citicorp and Citibank, IBM, director USUSSR Trade & Economic Council; Glen E. Watt, of AFL-CIO, member Club of Rome, Trilateral Commission and Aspen Institute.

The purpose of the Pan-European Union, founded by Count Coudenhove-Kalergi, and funded by the Rothschilds and

Warburgs, was to restore the oligarchic control over Europe. To accomplish this goal, it was necessary to emasculate and defeat the powerful republican currents which had their origin in the 14th century Renaissance, which, with its emphasis on the freedom of the human spirit, produced the greatest cultural outpouring in the history of mankind. This individualism was immediately expressed in nationalism; its republican spirit was dedicated to ending hereditary and arbitrary control and dictatorship over the lives of the people, reaching its greatest expression in the Constitution of the United States, which was the result of rebellion.

Because the ruling families of Europe are the direct descendants of William of Orange, who chartered the Bank of England in 1694, the movement to destroy nationalism and individualism has been directed from England, but expressed in the Communist movement. The World Order has planned and executed two World Wars to restore world rule by the oligarchy, a world rule variously called Bolshevism, the League of Nations, or the United Nations, but never the World Order.

The English control of this world movement is demonstrated by the ideology of American foundations, which is created by the Tavistock Institute of Human Relations in London. In 1921, the Duke of Bedford, Marquess of Tavistock, the 11th Duke, gave a building to the Institute to study the effect of shellshock on British soldiers who survived World War I. Its purpose was to establish the "breaking point" of men under stress, under the direction of the British Army Bureau of Psychological Warfare, commanded by Sir John Rawlings-Reese.

Tavistock Institute is headquartered in London, because its prophet, Sigmund Freud, settled here in Maresfield Gardens when he moved to England. He was given a mansion by Princesse Bonaparte. Tavistock's pioneer work in behavioural science along Freudian lines of "controlling" humans established it as the world center of foundation ideology. Its network now extends from the University of Sussex to the U.S. through the Stanford Research Institute, Esalen, MIT, Hudson Institute, Hudson Institute, Heritage Foundation, Center of Strategic and International Studies at Georgetown, where State Dept.

personnel are trained, US Air Force Intelligence, and the Rand and Mitre corporations. The personnel of the foundations are required to undergo indoctrination at one or more of these Tavistock controlled institutions. A network of secret groups, the Mont Pelerin Society, Trilateral Commission, Ditchley Foundation, and Club of Rome is conduit for instructions to the Tavistock network.

Tavistock Institute developed the mass brain-washing techniques which were first used experimentally on American prisoners of war in Korea. Its experiments in crowd control methods have been widely used on the American public, a surreptitious but nevertheless outrageous assault on human freedom by modifying individual behaviour through topical psychology. A German refugee, Kurt Lewin, became director of Tavistock in 1932. He came to the U.S. in 1933 as a "refugee", the first of many infiltrators, and set up the Harvard Psychology Clinic, which originated the propaganda campaign to turn the American public against Germany and involve us in World War II. In 1938, Roosevelt executed a secret agreement with Churchill which in effect ceded U.S. sovereignty to England, because it agreed to let Special Operations Executive control U.S. polices. To implement this agreement, Roosevelt sent Gen. Donovan to London for indoctrination before setting up OSS (now the CIA) under the aegis of SOE-SIS. The entire OSS program, as well as the CIA has always worked on guidelines set up by the Tavistock Institute.

Tavistock Institute originated the mass civilian bombing raids carried out by Roosevelt and Churchill purely as a clinical experiment in mass terror, keeping records of the results as they watched the "guinea pigs" reacting under "controlled laboratory conditions". All Tavistock and American foundation techniques have a single goal — to breakdown the psychological strength of the individual and render him helpless to oppose the dictators of the World Order. Any technique which helps to break down the family unit, and family inculcated principles of religion, honor, patriotism and sexual behaviour, is used by the Tavistock scientists as weapons of crowd control. The methods of Freudian psychotherapy induce permanent mental illness in those who undergo this treatment by destabilizing their character. The victim is then advised to "establish new rituals of personal interaction", that is, to indulge in brief sexual encounters which actually set the participants adrift with no stable personal relationships in their lives, destroying their ability to establish or maintain a family.

Tavistock Institute has developed such power in the U.S. that no one achieves prominence in any field unless he has been trained in behavioural science at Tavistock or one of its subsidiaries. Henry Kissinger, whose meteoric rise to power is otherwise inexplicable, was a German refugee and student of Sir John Rawlings Reese at SHAEF. Dr. Peter Bourne, a Tavistock Institute psychologist, picked Carter for President of the U.S. solely because Carter had undergone an intensive brainwashing program administered by Admiral Hyman Rickover at Annapolis. Paul Mellon's Old Dominion Foundation gave Tavistock $97,000 in 1956, and $12,000 during each of the three following years. Old Dominion also gave the Anna Freud Foundation $8000 a year. Tavistock maintains two schools at Frankfort, birthplace of the Rothschilds, the Frankfurt School, and the Sigmund Freud Institute.

The "experiment" in compulsory racial integration in the U.S. was organized by Ronald Lippert, of the OSS and the American Jewish Congress, and director of child training at the Commission on Community Relations. The program was designed to break down the individual's sense of personal knowledge in his identity, his racial heritage. Through the Stanford Research Institute, Tavistock controls the National Education Association. The Institute of Social Research at the Natl Training Lab brain washes the leading executives of business and government. Such is the power of Tavistock that our entire space program was scrapped for nine years so that the Soviets could catch up. The hiatus was demanded in an article written by Dr. Anatol Rapport, and was promptly granted by the government, to the complete mystification of everyone connected with NASA. Another prominent Tavistock operation is the Wharton School of Finance.

A single common denominator identifies the common Tavistock strategy — the use of drugs. The infamous MK Ultra program of the CIA, directed by Dr. Sidney Gottlieb, in which unsuspecting CIA officials were given LSD, and their reaction studied like guinea pigs, resulted in several deaths. The U.S. Government had to pay millions in damages to the families of the victims, but the culprits were never indicted. The program originated when Sandoz AG, a Swiss drug firm, owned by S.G. Warburg Co. of London, developed Lysergic acid. Roosevelt's advisor, James Paul Warburg, son of Paul Warburg who wrote the Federal Reserve Act, and nephew of Max Warburg who had financed Hitler, set up the Institute for Policy Studies to promote the drug. The result was the LSD "counter-culture" of the 1960s, the "student revolution", which was financed by $25 million from the CIA.

One part of MK Ultra was the Human Ecology Fund; the CIA also paid Dr. Herbert Kelman of Harvard to carry out further experiments on mind control. In the 1950s, the CIA financed extensive LSD experiments in Canada. Dr. D. Ewen Cameron, president of the Canadian Psychological Assn., and director of Royal Victorian Hospital, Montreal, received large payments from the CIA to give 53 patients large doses of LSD and record their reactions; the patients were drugged into weeks of sleep, and then given electric shock treatments. One victim, the wife of a member of the Canadian Parliament, is now suing the U.S. companies who provided the drug for the CIA. In his biography of Helms, Powers states that in his last days of office, Helms ordered Dr. Sidney Gottlieb, head of MK Ultra, to destroy all records of the CIA's drug-testing program, and that by Jan. 14, 1973, Helms had destroyed five thousand pages of notes taken in his office during his six and a half years as director of the CIA!

Because all efforts of the Tavistock Institute are directed toward producing cyclical collapse, the effect of the CIA programs are tragically apparent. R. Emmett Tyrell Jr., writing in the *Washington Post* Aug. 20, 1984, cites the "squalid consequences of the 60s radicals in SDS" as resulting in "the growing rate of illegitimacy, petty lawlessness, drug addiction, welfare, VD, and mental illness". This is the legacy of the

Warburgs and the CIA. Their principal agency, the Institute for Policy Studies, was funded by James Paul Warburg; its cofounder was Marcus Raskin, protege of McGeorge Bundy, president of the Ford Foundalion. Bundy had Raskin appointed to the post of President Kennedy's personal representative on the National Security Council, and in 1963 funded Students for Democratic Society, through which the CIA operated the drug culture.

Today, the Tavistock Institute operates a $6 billion a year network of foundations in the U.S., all of it funded by U.S. taxpayers' money. Ten major institutions are under its direct control, with 400 subsidiaries, and 3000 other study groups and think tanks which originate many types of programs to increase the control of the World Order over the American people. Typical is the Hudson Institute, a $5 million a year 193 operation with 120 employees, founded in 1965 by Herman Kahn of the Rand Corp. and the Stanford Research Institute; its directors include Alexander Haig, president of United Technologies; Frank Carlucci, deputy secretary of Defense, and now chairman of Sears World Trade Corp.; Daniel C. Searle, chmn of G.D. Searle Drug Co.; and Gov. Pierre DuPont of Delaware. The principal architect of Hudson was Frank Altschul, director of Ford Foundation, partner of Lazard Freres, who married into the Lehman family, president General American Investors, director of U.S. Leather, International Bank of Amsterdam, American Eagle Fire Insurance, the Yale Corp., Institute of International Studies, China Institute in America, whose *Times* obituary in 1981called him "a Renaissance Man" who endowed the Yale Library and the Overbrook Press. Other Hudson associates are Leo Cherne of the Foreign Advisory Intelligence Board, and Sidney Hook of the Hoover Institution.

Stanford Research Institute, adjoining the Hoover Institution, is a $150 million a year operation with 3300 employees. It carries on program surveillance for Bechtel, Kaiser, and 400 other companies, and extensive intelligence operations for the CIA. It is the largest institution on the West Coast promoting mind control and the behavioural sciences.

One of the key agencies as a conduit for secret instructions from Tavistock is the Ditchley Foundation, founded in 1957 by Sir Philip Adams. A long time Foreign Service officer, Adams was Minister to Khartoum in 1954, Ambassador to Jordan during 1966-70, and Egypt in 1973-75; he married the daughter of Baron Trevethin (the Lawrence family, which includes several lord chief justices of Britain.)

The Ditchley Foundation is headquartered at Ditchley Park, near Oxford, in a castle built for the Earl of Lichfield in the 16th century; the present Earl of Lichfield is a cousin of Queen Elizabeth, and is known as a photographer of beautiful women. Ditchley Park was given to the foundation by Ronald and Marietta Tree. Ronald Tree, a godson of Marshall Field, was for many years a high official in British intelligence. He was appointed Parliamentary Private Secretary to the Minister of Pensions, the Minister of Information, and the Minister of Planning. He was first married to Nancy Moncure Perkins, of an old Virginia family. They divorced, and he married Marietta Peabody, granddaughter of Endicott Peabody, headmaster of Groton, where the American elite was trained. Her career gave rise to the term "beautiful people", the glittering international set devoted to leftwing causes. She began her career as a beautiful young "hostess" for Nelson Rockefeller in 1942, became a shop steward for the Newspaper Guild at *Life* Magazine, Fair Housing Practices Committee for New York, 1958 Volunteer for Stevenson, Commission on Human Rights at the UN 1959-61, Human Rights Commission UN 1961-64, Ambassador to the UN 1961-64. Magazine articles gave glowing reports of a "beautiful person's" life in New York, her townhouse at 123 E. 79th St. filled with antique furnishings and art treasures from Ditchley Park, the house run faultlessly by an English butler, as well as their summer home at Barbados, where they entertained Winston Churchill in 1960. The American branch of the Ditchley Foundation is run by Cyrus Vance, former Secretary of State, and director of the Rockefeller Foundation; Alan Pifer, president of the Carnegie Foundation, and Winston Lord, president of the Council on Foreign Relations. Lord was political and military officer at the Dept. of State 1961-64, international security officer Defense Dept. 1969-73, spec. asst. to the President of the

U.S. 1970-73, director of policy planning at Dept. of State 1973-77, member of Atlantic Council and Atlantic Institute. Other Ditchley members have been Wallace Sterling, president of Stanford University, Richard Steadman of the German Marshall Fund, and Donald Perkins of Brookings Institution. Perkins is a director of *Time*, Thyssen Bornemitza, ATT, Corning, Cummins Engine, Freeport Moran, G.D. Searle, and Morgan Guaranty Trust Bank, and chairman of Jewel Tea Co.

One of the principal but little known operations of the Rockefeller Foundation has been its techniques for controlling world agriculture. Its director, Kenneth Wernimont, set up Rockefeller controlled agricultural programs throughout Mexico and Latin America. The independent farmer is a great threat to the World Order, because he produces for himself, and because his produce can be converted into capital, which gives him independence. In Soviet Russia, the Bolsheviks believed they had attained total control over the people; they were dismayed to find their plans threatened by the stubborn independence of the small farmers, the kulaks. Stalin ordered the OGPU to seize all food and animals of the kulaks, and to starve them out. The *Chicago American* Feb. 25, 1935 carried a front page headline, SIX MILLION PERISH IN SOVIET FAMINE: Peasants' Crops Seized, They and their Animals Starve. To draw attention from this atrocity, it was later alleged that the Germans, not the Soviets, had killed six million people, the number taken from the Chicago American headline by a Chicago publicist.

The Communist Party, the Party of the Peasants and Workers, exterminated the peasants and enslaved the workers. Many totalitarian regimes have found the small farmer to be their biggest stumbling block. The French Reign of Terror was directed, not against the aristocrats, many of whom were sympathetic to it, but against the small farmers who refused to turn over their grain to the revolutionary tribunals in exchange for the worthless assignats. In the United States, the foundations are presently engaged in the same type of war of extermination against the American farmer. The traditional formula of land plus labor for the farmer has been altered due to the farmer's need for purchasing power, to buy industrial goods needed in his farming operations. Because of this need for capital, the farmer is especially vulnerable to the World Order's manipulation of interest rates, which is bankrupting him. Just as in the Soviet Union, in the early 1930s, when Stalin ordered the kulaks to give up their small plots of land to live and work on the collective farms, the American small farmer faces the same type of extermination, being forced to give up his small plot of land to become a hired hand for the big agricultural Soviets or trusts. The Brookings Institution and other foundations originated the monetary programs implemented by the Federal Reserve System to destroy the American farmer, a replay of the Soviet tragedy in Russia, with the one proviso that the farmer will be allowed to survive if he becomes a slave worker of the giant trusts.

Once the citizen becomes aware of the true role of the foundations, he can understand the high interest rates, high taxes, the destruction of the family, the degradation of the churches into forums for revolution, the subversion of the universities into CIA cesspools of drug addiction, and the halls of government into sewers of international espionage and intrigue. The American citizen can now understand why every agent of the federal government is against him; the alphabet agencies, the FBI, IRS, CIA, and BATF must make war on the citizen in order to carry out the programs of the foundations.

We have seen the close interlocking of the foundations with international banks and corporations, all stemming from the Peabody Fund of 1865, and the War Industries Board of Bernard Baruch in World War I. The foundations are in direct violation of their charters, which commit them to do "charitable" work, because they make no grants which are not part of a political goal. The charge has been made, and never denied, that the Heritage AEI network has at least two KGB moles on its staff. The employment of professional intelligence operatives as "charitable" workers, as was done in the Red Cross Mission to Russia in 1917, exposes the sinister political, economic and social goals which the World Order requires the foundations to achieve through their "bequests".

Not only is this tax fraud, because the foundations are granted tax exemption solely to do charitable work, but it is criminal syndicalism, conspiracy to commit offenses against the United States of America, Constitutional Law 213, Corpus Juris Secundum 16. For the first time, the close interlocking of the foundation "syndicate" has been revealed by the names of its principal incorporators — Daniel Coit Gilman, who incorporated the Peabody Fund and the John Slater Fund, and became an incorporator of the General Education Board (now the Rockefeller Foundation); Gilman, who also incorporated the Russell Trust in 1856, later became an incorporator of the Carnegie Institution with Andrew Dickson White (Russell Trust) and Frederic A. Delano. Delano also was an original incorporator of the Brookings Institution and the Carnegie Endowment for International Peace. Daniel Coit Gilman incorporated the Russell Sage Foundation with Cleveland H. Dodge of the National City Bank. These foundations incorporators have been closely linked with the Federal Reserve System, the War Industries Board of World War I, the OSS of World War II and the CIA. They have also been closely linked with the American International Corporation, which was formed to instigate the Bolshevik Revolution in Russia. Delano, an uncle of Franklin Delano Roosevelt, was on the original Board of Governors of the Federal Reserve System in 1914. His brother-in-law founded the influential Washington law firm of Covington and Burling. The Delanos and other ruling families of the World Order trace their lineage directly back to William of Orange and the regime which granted the charter of the Bank of England. Her Majesty Queen Elizabeth the Queen Mother, Lady Elizabeth Bowes-Lyon, is the daughter of the 14th Earl of Strathmore. When William of Orange invaded England in 1688, the Scottish lords, who had been loyal to James II, were the last to capitulate. Patrick Lyon took the oath of fealty to William in 1690, and became the first Earl of Strathmore. The family resides at Glamis Castle, which was made famous by Shakespeare's play, *Macbeth*. The present Lord Glamis is Michael Fergus Bowes-Lyon, heir of the 17th Earl of Strathmore, who holds additional titles of Earl of Kinghorne, Viscount Lyon, Farnedyce, Sydlaw, and Strathdichtie.

APPENDIX I

After gaining control of the national government, the Rockefeller Foundation moved to seize control of the state legislatures. The move began in Colorado, where the Rockefellers had perpetrated the infamous "Ludlow Massacre" of workers at their Colorado Fuel & Iron plant. State Senator Henry Wolcott Toll, a Denver lawyer and graduate of Harvard Law School, spearheaded the organization of the American Legislators Association in 1925.

Time, April 27, 1936, noted that Toll in 1930 got financial aid from the Spelman Rockefeller Fund and moved the organization to the campus of Rockefeller's University of Chicago. *Time* noted,

> "Today the Capitol of the U.S. is still in Washington, but so far as the states individually have any point of contact, it is Mr. Toll's office building in Chicago. Presently Rockefeller money is to erect a $500,000 building on Chicago's Midway to house these secretariats, a sort of League of Nations Palace for the local governments of the 48 states."

This became the Council of State Governments at 1313 60th St. Chicago, from which address the Rockefeller Foundation controlled the state legislatures and ramrodded their programs through mostly unsuspecting state bodies.

Time also noted that Toll's plans were approved by a principal character in this story, Frederick A. Delano.

> "His sentiments were echoed with approval by Franklin Roosevelt's uncle, Frederick A. Delano, who, as chairman of the President's Committee on National Resources, was there to lend his advice."

Thus we have the founder of the Brookings Institution guiding foundation control of the state legislatures. The Council of State Governments has now moved to Lexington, Kentucky, where it presently comprises the Conference of Chief Justices, Conference of State Court Administrators, and the National Associations of Attorney Generals, Secretaries of State and State Auditors, State Purchasing Offices, Lieutenant Governors, and State Legislators. The governors of the 50 states comprise the membership of the Council of State Governments.

Chapter Nine

The Rule of the Order

> *"And behold at evening tide trouble; and before the morning he is not. This is the portion of them that spoil us and the lot of them that rob us."*— Isaiah 17; 14.

Five men rule the world. This Council of Five consists of Baron Guy de Rothschild, Evelyn de Rothschild, George Pratt Shultz, Robert Roosa (from Bush's family firm of Brown Brothers Harriman) and one vacancy, at this writing. In the past several years, members of the Council who have died include Averill Harriman, Lord Victor Rothschild, and Prince Thurn und Taxis of Regensburg, Germany. None of them holds public office, but they choose who shall hold office in the nations. These five men comprise the apex of the pyramid of power, the World Order. We may ask, Why should there be a World Order? Is it not sufficient to hold absolute power in a single nation, or in a group of nations? The answer is No, because of the nature of international travel, international trade, and international finance. International travel requires that a person may travel in peace from one nation to another, without being molested. Excepting cases of anarchy, revolution or war, this requirement can usually be met. International trade requires that traders of one nation can go to another nation, transact their business, and return with their goods or their profits. This requirement too is usually met. If not, the offended nation can exercise military force, as Great Britain did in its Opium Wars.

It is the third requirement, international finance, which called into being the World Order. In earlier days, when international trade consisted of barter, payment in gold or silver or piracy, the seizure of goods by force, there was no need for a world arbiter to determine the value of instruments of trade. The development of paper money, stocks, bonds, acceptances and other negotiable instruments necessitated a power, able to exercise influence anywhere in the world, to declare that a piece of paper represented one billion dollars in real wealth, or even one dollar in real wealth. An entry on a computer, flashed from London to New York, states that someone owes five billion dollars to someone else. Without genuine power backing, no such sum could ever be collected, regardless of the factuality or morality of the debt. As anyone in the Mafia can tell you, you don't collect unless you are willing to break legs. The World Order is always prepared to break legs, and break them they do, by the millions.

What would have happened to the earliest settlers in America if they had gone to the Indians and said,

> "Give us your goods and the deeds to your homes and lands. In return, we will give you this beautifully printed piece of paper."

The Indians would, and did, attack them. If the settlers arrived with an army led by a Pizaro or a Cortez, they took the lands without a piece of paper.

The World Order rules with its pieces of paper, but behind every paper is a force which can be employed anywhere in the world. The force may be disguised by various subterfuges as international agreements, associations or other camouflage, but its base is always force.

The World Order rules through a simple technique, Divide and Conquer (*Divide et impera*). Every natural or unnatural division among people, every occasion for hatred or greed, is exploited and exacerbated to the limit. The polarization of racial and ethnic groups in the U.S. is accelerated by a flood of government decrees, originating in foundation "studies", which are designed solely to set American against American. Only in this way can the World Order maintain its iron grip on the daily lives of the people. The World Order also rules by the principle of *1984* — no groups of two or more people are allowed to gather unless the World Order has a representative present. If you start a club of dandelion fanciers, the Order will send someone who will be quietly helpful, avoid taking the front position, and who will offer to pay the rent of a meeting place or the printing of the minutes. In more radical groups, the Order's representative will be the first to suggest dynamiting a building, assassinating an official, or other violent action.

The international terrorism of the Communist Party originated in a small club of German and French workingmen in Paris, dedicated to quiet reading and discussion, until Karl Marx joined. It was then converted into a revolutionary group. This one example explains the Order's determination to allow no group, however insignificant, to remain unmonitored. The World Order adopted the Hegelian dialectic, the dialectic of materialism, which regards the World as Power, and the World as Reality. It denies all other powers and all other realities. It functions on the principle of thesis, antithesis and a synthesis which results when the thesis and antithesis are thrown against each other for a predetermined outcome. Thus the World Order organizes and finances Jewish groups; it then organizes and finances anti-Jewish groups; it organizes Communist groups; it then organizes and finances anti-Communist groups. It is not necessary for the Order to throw these groups against each other; they seek each other out like heat-seeking missiles, and try to destroy each other. By controlling the size and resources of each group, the World Order can always predetermine the outcome.

In this technique, members of the World Order are often identified with one side or the other. John Foster Dulles arranged financing for Hitler, but he was never a Nazi. David Rockefeller may be cheered in Moscow, but he is not a Communist. However, the Order always turns up on the winning side. A distinguishing trait of a member of the World Order, although it may not be admitted, is that he does not believe in anything but the World Order. Another distinguishing trait is his absolute contempt for anyone who actually believes in the tenets of Communism, Zionism, Christianity, or any national, religious or fraternal group, although the Order has members in controlling positions in all of these groups. If you are a sincere Christian, Zionist or Moslem, the World Order regards you as a moron unworthy of respect. You can and will be used, but you will never be respected.

It has taken centuries of patient effort for the World Order to attain the power it exercises today. Its origins as an international force go back to the Phoenician slave-traders, continues through the Phanariot families of the Byzantine Empire, then the Venetian and Genoese traders and bankers of the Middle Ages, who moved into Spain and Portugal, and later into England and Scotland. By the 14th century, the Genoese controlled the Scottish landlords. The Imperial Family of the Byzantine Empire, the Paleologues (meaning 'the Word') were attacked by the Gnostic faction, whose materialistic Aristotelian philosophy was the forerunner of Hegelian dialectic and Marxism. The Paleologues devoutly believed in the Christian faith, as expressed by the Orthodox Rite. The materialistic Venetian and Genoese armies, with the aid of the Turkish "infidels", looted and conquered Constantinople, the legendary "City of God". The Byzantine survivors recreated their culture in Russia, with Moscow as "the third Rome". The plan to destroy the Orthodox Church and its Romanov (new Rome) leader was the hidden goal of the First World War. The victors came away with one billion dollars of the Romanov fortune, after achieving the defeat of their hated enemy, the Orthodox Church.

During the Middle Ages, European power centers coalesced into two camps, the Ghibellines, those who supported the Emperor's Hohenstaufen family, (an Italian adaptation of Weinblingen, the name of the Hohenstaufen estate), and the Guelphs, from Welf, the German prince who competed with Frederick for control of the Holy Roman Empire. The Pope then allied himself with the Guelphs against the Ghibellines resulting in their victory. All of modern history stems directly from the struggle between these two powers. The Guelphs, also called the Neri, or Black Guelphs, and Black Nobility, were the Normans who conquered England in the 11th century; the Genoese who backed Robert Bruce in his conquest of Scotland, and who supported William of Orange in his seizure of the throne of England. William's victory resulted in the formation of the Bank of England and the East India Company, which have ruled the world since the 17th century. Every subsequent coup d'état, revolution and war has centered in the battle of the Guelphs to hold and enhance their power, which is now the World Order.

The power of the Guelphs grew through their control of banking and international trade. It was extended through the Italian centers to the north of Florence, in Lombardy, which became great financial centers. All Italian bankers, including the Genoese, the Venetians, and Milanese, were referred to as "Lombards"; Lombard, in German, means "deposit bank"; the Lombards were bankers to the entire Medieval world. Modern history begins with the transfer of their operations north to Hamburg, Amsterdam, and finally to London.

The great American fortunes originated with the Guelph slave trade to the colonies. Many of the slave traders doubled in piracy. Trinity Church, whose leading vestryman later was J.P. Morgan, was originally known as "the church of the pirates". Capt. William Kidd provided the material to build it in 1697, and a pew was reserved for him. He was arrested the next year, and hanged in chains at Newgate. In 1711, a slave market was set up on Wall Street near the church, and functioned there for many years.

Two of the most powerful influences in the world today are the international drug trade, which began with the East India Co., and international espionage, which began with the Bank of England. The East India Co. was granted a charter in 1600 in the closing days of Queen Elizabeth's reign. In 1622, under James I, it became a joint stock company. In 1661, in an attempt to retain his throne, Charles II granted the East India Co. the power to make war. From 1700 to 1830, the East India Co. gained control of all India, and wrested the historic monopoly of opium from the Great Moguls.

The Crown periodically tried to maintain control of the monster it had unleashed. State Papers (Domestic) Interregnum, xvi, No. 97 (1649-51) states,

"Whereas several warrants have been obtained by the East India Company, for the transporting of several great quantities of Gold and Silver the Ilksom tymes is granted to severall merchants and others upon their petition and suggestions, and whereas under culer of this warrants to divers other great sums of money, both English Gold and Silver is transported out of the nation, which might be prevented by the state would appoint a sworn controlled one skilled in this affaire, to take a view and search of all badge and cases of treasure, that are transported out of the nation, and to see to the packing and making up of said treasure, and that there be sent no more, then, what the stat gives license for, both for quantity and quality, and registered, and returned yearly to the council of state, and that the controller for his view and search and sealing and marking it up shall demand and have tow shillings upon every hundred pounds sterling by tayl, or the value of every hundred pounds sterling, if that the Gold or Silver should be in bares or ingots, for all Gold and Silver that shall be exported by license, either the East India Company or any other person whomsoever, and that it shall not be lawful for any man to transport Gold or Silver before it be viewed and examined by Tho. Violet or his sufficient debity, and registered."

Government supervision of control of international movements of gold and silver has been a national problem since Cicero inveighed against it in the Roman Forum. Sir Walter Raleigh pointed out, in his *Select Observations of the Incomparable Sir Walter Raleigh*, MDCXCVI p.6,

"1. That Nation Can only be in a prosperous Estate that hath a proportionable quantity of Silver or Gold to ballance the Strength and trade of its neighboring Nations.

2. That whilst the Current Cash of this Kingdom can be converted into Bullion, and so made a trading Commodity (as hath been practis'd this hundred Years) 'twill either be conveyed to be best Market, or wrought in Plate at home, notwithstanding the utmost rigour and vigiliancy, to the great and daily Consumption of the Coin, and Detriment of the Nation. That raising the value of our Coin, is the only certain means to keep it in the Nation to make us a rich and thriving State, to recover our lost Trade, and the best Bulwark and

Defence against all the Attacks of our Enemies. That contrary to the Policy of Nations, our standard Coin is of greater value in all places than at home (Spain only excepted) for which reason we bring Spanish Money hither, and for the same Reason our Money is transported to other places, to the great Impoverishment of the Nation."

Sir Walter Raleigh, a patriot, saw that the machinations of the international money dealers were bringing ruin to many Englishmen, and tried to stop it. They in turn conspired against him, and had him beheaded. The Order invariably enlists "the law" against its enemies.

The East India Co. originated as the London Staplers, was later known as the London Mercers Co., merchant guilds which held monopolies over certain avenues of commerce. It was a direct offshoot of the commercial banking establishments of northern Italy, Venice and Genoa. Related firms were the German Hansa, and the Hanse of the Low Countries, which was headquartered in Bruges. It was also allied with the Levant Co. and the Anglo-Muscovy Co. Sebastian Cabot, whose descendants are prominent in the American banking and intelligence, raised the seed money for Anglo-Muscovy in Italy and London. The company operated northern overland trade routes from the Baltic to India and China. Other related firms were the London Company, chartered in 1606 to establish The Virginian Plantation on a communistic basis, and the Plymouth Company, whose descendants control the New England business world.

The "City" banks, which dominate American finance and politics (code name for banks for the "City", financial district of London), descend directly from East India and Bank of England operations. The Rockefeller Empire is the most prominent scion of this dynasty.

To aid their control of finance and politics, the Guelphs perpetuated a host of cults deriving from the Manicheans, which in turn derived from the cults of Babylonia and Ira, from the Atys cultus of the Caucasian area, and from Hindu pantheism. Their offshoots include the Bogomils of the Balkans, the Paulicans of Asia Minor, the anabaptists, communists and antinomians, centering in the (Catharists, the Albigensians of southern France, the patarenes of northern Italy, and the English Savoyards). These gnostic faiths developed into the Rosicrucians, Swedenborgians, Unitarians, the Fabian Society, and the World Council of Churches. The English Savoyards became active in the London Staplers and the rise of oceanic commerce, by using the Venetian-Flanders galley, which brought the lateen sail into Europe from Southeast Asia. The Savoyards formed an extreme leftwing party, led by John Ball, which called for the nationalisation of all land. The Wycliffe-Lollards-Savoyards-Staplers formed the King's Party against the landed nobility (republicanism) and parliament. Then as now, the leftwing sought ownership of all land through an absolute ruler and a totalitarian centralized government.

This leftwing alliance culminated in the University of London. The University of London, which received a $2 million grant in 1924 from Beardsley Ruml as head of the Laura Spelman Rockefeller Fund, and many other grants from American foundations houses Gresham College and the London School of Economics, where Harold Laski taught John F. Kennedy and David Rockefeller the principles of the World Order. The University of London was originally financed by Jeremy Bentham of the East India Co., and John Stuart Mill, whose friend, investment banker George Grote, gave the University of London 6000 pounds to study mental health, the origin of the present worldwide "mental health" movement. Grote also contributed 500 pounds to finance the July Revolution in France in 1830, which put Louis Philippe on the throne.

It was Bentham who first coined the slogan later taken up by Karl Marx, "the greatest good for the greatest number", which has been so useful in inflaming the masses, the Marxist flim flam that you can best serve your interests by serving others. Bentham's business partner was manufacturer Robert Owen, an atheist who taught free love. Like most do-gooders, Owen's cotton mills in Asia, associated with the East India Co., caused bankruptcies and great misery in India. In 1824, Owen bought Father Rapp's anabaptist commune in America, Harmonie on the Wabash, renaming it New Harmony. Owen's associate at New

Harmony was Frances (Fanny) Wright, who initiated the practice of free love in America. She also started the Women's Equal Rights Movement, which was intended to break up families by inciting war between husband and wife. She travelled through the South, preaching the amalgamation of the races, and founded a commune in Tennessee for Negro freedmen. In 1829, she helped found the Workingmen's Party in New York City, which later became the Communist Party. Her grandson, Rev. Wm. Norman Guthrie, who married Anne Norton Stuart, became known as the Red Vicar at his church, St. Marks in the Bowerie, which welcomed Luciferians to its services.

A principal offspring of the East India Co. was the Fabian Society, founded by Sidney and Beatrice Potter Webb, (whose father, Richard Potter, was a close friend of John Stuart Mill). Beatrice's sister Georgina married Daniel Meinertzhagen, chairman of Lazard Bros. London; another sister, Theresa, married Sir Alfred Cripps. John Stuart Mill's father, James, who was with the East India Co., named his son after John Stuart, head of East India Co. John Stuart Mill was secretary of the East India Co. from 1856 until its dissolution. One of Mill's most famous disciples, David Ricardo, originated the Theory of Rents, later expounded by the Marxists, and the "bare subsistence" law of wages, His descendant, Rita Ricardo, married to Wesley Campbell, head of the Hoover Institution, now advises President Reagan on social security.

Robert Owen, promoter of the New Harmony commune, was a principal backer of John Quincy Adams' Presidential campaign. Adams had withheld support from Madison during the War of 1812, and had threatened secession from the Union. As Secretary of State, Adams had drafted the Monroe Doctrine, which gave the British East India Co. control of all Latin American markets, while keeping out all of its competitors! T.D. Allman, in *The Doctrine That Never Was, Harper's*, Jan. 1984, revealed that Monroe actually pledged not to interfere with any European power, unless they set up "new" colonies. The agreement, which was not even called the "Monroe Doctrine" until many years later, guaranteed the East India Company its markets in this hemisphere. When Britain violated the agreement in 1833 by seizing the Malvinas, the U.S. did nothing.

The New England banking and shipping interests controlled by Adams' group created the Second Bank of the United States by repeated stock speculation campaigns, marked by typical bouts of hyperinflation and sudden deflation, which gave them control of millions of acres of farm lands throughout the Mississippi Valley from the Great Lakes to the Gulf of Mexico. This gave them enormous political influence in this entire region, allowing them to seed the southern Mississippi Valley with fanatical Secessionists and Abolitionists, whose revolutionary acts made the Civil War inevitable. Owen also coined the term Socialism; he was a business partner of a cotton manufacturer named Engels, whose son later became his political disciple, and still later became the partner of Karl Marx in founding the world Communist movement.

The trail of the conspirators has been evident throughout the history of Europe since the Middle Ages. In 1547, the Republic of Venice had learned of an anti-Christian conspiracy, and strangled its leaders, Julian Trevisano and Francis de Rugo. The surviving conspirators, Ochinus, Laelius Socinus, Peruta, Gentilis, Jacques Chiari, Francis Lenoir, Darius Socinus, Alicas, and the Abbe Leonard, now spread their poisonous doctrines of hatred throughout Europe. Their message of anarchy, atheism and immorality, levelling and revolution brought bloodshed in every subsequent upheaval on the Continent. In Germany, Adam Weishaupt, Prof, of Canon Law at the University of Munich, and later at Coburg-Gotha, became the Nominal head of the Illuminati; its corresponding branch in Italy was the Alta Vendita, whose first leader was an Italian Nobleman, B. Nubius. His principal agent was Piccolo Tigre, a Jewish banker and jeweler who travelled for the Alta Vendita throughout Europe. In 1822, his instructions to the chapters were confiscated and published, from which we excerpt:

> "We do not cease to recommend to you, to affiliate persons of every class and every manner of association, no matter what kind, only provided that mystery and secrecy shall be the dominant characteristic. Under a pretext most

> futile, but never political or religious, created by yourselves, or better yet, cause to be created by others, associations, having in common music, the fine arts for object. Then infiltrate the poison into those chosen arts; infiltrate it in little doses. A prince who has not a kingdom to expect, is a good fortune for us. There are many of them in that plight. These poor princes will serve our ends, while thinking to labour only for their own. They form a magnificent signboard, and there are always fools enough to be found who are ready to compromise themselves in the service of a conspiracy, of which some prince or other seems to be the ring leader. There is little morality even among the most moral of the world, and one goes fast in the way of that progress. A good hatred, thoroughly cold, thoroughly calculated, is of more worth than all these artificial fires and all these declarations on the platform. Presently, we shall have a printing establishment at Malta placed at our disposal. We shall then be able with impunity, with a sure stroke, and under the British flag, to scatter from one end of Italy to the other, books, pamphlets, etc. which the Alta Vendita shall judge proper to put into circulation."

Karl Rothschild, son of Mayer Amschel, then became head of the Alta Vendita.

On May 1, 1776, Adam Weishaupt issued further instructions to the Illuminati in Bavaria,

> "We labour first of all to draw into our Association all good and learned writers. This we imagine will be the easier obtained, as they must derive an evident advantage from it. Next to such men we seek to gain the masters and secretaries of the Post-Offices, in order to facilitate our correspondence."

The Tasso family of Bologna, later Thurn und Taxis, gained control of post offices and intelligence work in Europe and held that power for five centuries. Although these groups surfaced as charitable or fine arts organizations, their goals of anarchy were concealed in all their efforts. In the twentieth century, they culminated in the League of Nations, the United Nations, the communist Party, the Royal Institute of International affairs, the Council on Foreign Relations, the foundations, and a host of lesser groups. Count Coudenhove-kalergi's Pan Europe

Movement, with its powerful backing by aristocrats and international financiers, was represented in the U.S. by its American branch, founded by Herbert Hoover and Col. House, who were also stumping the U.S. for ratification of the League of Nations. Coundenhove-Kalergi mentioned in his autobiography that he had been financed by the Rothschilds and Warburgs, and in the U.S., by Paul Warburg and Bernard Baruch. He was connected with the Thurn und Taxis family. His grandfather, Count Francis Coudenhove-Kalergi, Austrian Ambassador in Paris, had married Marie Kalergi in 1850. She was one of the wealthiest heiresses in Europe, descended from the Byzantine Emperor Nikophor Phikas; in 1300, when Venice was the dominant power in the Mediterranean, Alexios Kalergis had signed the treaty which made Crete a dominion of Venice. A recent premier of Greece, Emmanuel Tsouderos, was a Kalergi.

Melchior Palyi, in *The Twilight of Gold*, reveals the power plays of the World Order in international finance, when he quotes from the Diary of Governor Emile Moreau of the Bank of France. Palyi says,

> "In October, 1926, Governor Emile Moreau of the Bank of France sent his closest collaborator to London to explore the intentions of Montagu Norman, Governor of the Bank of England. Pierre Quesnay, then general manager of the Bank of France 1926-30, and Bank for International Settlements 1930-37, brought back a report which was recorded by Moreau: 'Quesnay also gives me interesting views about the ambitions of Montagu Norman and the group of financiers who surround him: Sir Otto Niemeyer, Sir Arthur Salter, Sir Henry Strakosch, Sir Robert Kindersley they are striving to make London the great international financial centre. But those close to Norman state this is not his objective he wants more than anything else to witness the setting up of links between the various banks of Issue. The economic and financial organization of the world appears to the Governor of the Bank of England to be the major task of the Twentieth Century. In his view politicians and political institutions are in no fit state to direct with the necessary competence and continuity this task of organization which he would like to see undertaken by central banks , independent at once of

governments and of private finance. Hence his campaign in favour of completely autonomous central banks, dominating their own financial markets and deriving their power from common agreement among themselves. They would succeed in taking out of the political realm those problems which are essential for the development and prosperity of the national financial security, distribution of credit, movement of prices. They would thus prevent internal political struggles from harming the wealth and the economic advancement of nations."

In short, Norman wished to see the imposition of the World Order over the financial affairs of the nations. It was this agreement among the central banks, rather than the front organization, the League of Nations, which became their final instrument of power. Crucial to these arrangements was the monetarist school, the Austrian School of Economics, an outgrowth of the Pan-Europe movement. Margit Herzfeld notes in her biography of Ludwig von Mises that he participated in Count Coudenhove-Kalergi's Pan Europe movement in 1943, He had been brought to the U.S. in 1940 by a grant from the Rockefeller Foundation of $2500 a year to work at the Natl Bureau of Economic Research, which grant was renewed in 1943. Von Mises' pupils, Arthur B urns and Milton Friedman now expound the monetarist theory through a network of super secret "conservative" think tanks led by the Mont Pelerin Society. Herzfeld says that von Mises' most famous protege was the Soviet apologist Murray Rothbard.

One of the most influential conspirators was Walter Rathenau of Germany. He greeted the First World War ecstatically as the golden opportunity to establish world socialism. He wrote on July 31, 1916,

> "For years I had foreseen the twilight of the nations that I had heralded in my speeches and writings. (*A People's State*, by Rathenau). The notion became established that the state is no longer to be regarded as the importunate poor relation and fobbed off grudgingly with a tithe, but that it is entitled to dispose of the capital and income of all its members at its own free will."

Rathenau's dictum was enacted into law by the far-reaching and multi-billion entitlement programs of Lyndon B. Johnson's Great Society, when he persuaded Congress to levy against all of the capital and income of the American people placing it at his disposal to achieve World Order political goals, and finally forcing the nation to the verge of bankruptcy.

Rathenau wrote *In Days to Come*, 1921,

> "No part of the world is now closed to us. No Material tasks are beyond our powers. All the treasures of earth are within our grasp. No thought remains hidden. Every undertaking can be put to the task and realized. The fertilizing distribution of the possessions of the world is our task. We must discover the force that will effect an up and down movement of the masses."

In *The New Society*, 1921, Rathenau wrote,

> "A far reaching policy of socialization is necessary and urgent... The goal of the world revolution upon which we have entered means in its material aspect the melting of all society into one."

This was the "levelling" effect which was a key goal of the conspirators, the Illuminati and the Alta Vendita, resulting in anarchy and the breaking down of national and class borders. Before he could realize his dream of World Socialism, Rathenau was murdered.

Ortega noted the phenomenon of levelling in *The Revolt of the Masses*,

> "A hurricane of farcicality, everywhere and in every form, is presently raging over the lands of Europe. Almost all the positions taken up and proclaimed are false ones. We are living in comic fashion, all the more comic the more apparently tragic is the mask adopted put on. The comic exists wherever life has no basis of inevitableness on which a stand is taken without reserves. Never as now have we these lives without substance or art — deracines from their own destiny — who let themselves float on the lightest current."

Ortega was commenting on the most striking phenomenon of the twentieth century, the hegemony of parasitism which was attained through the World Order. It was the Congress of 1815 at Vienna which unleashed the rats from their nests, nor is it accidental that the Viennese School of Economics has become the principal vehicle through which the World Order maintains its political and financial power. After crushing Napoleon, the emerging oligarchy, which owed no allegiance to any nation or to any philosophy of life, attained power because it knew how to defeat its foes, the republicans and individualists of Europe; but its foes had no idea how to combat, or even to identify, its cleverly camouflaged enemy, because these people were a biological throwback in the continuing development of humanity. They were persons who were unable to become productive members of any society, and who could exist only by maintaining a parasitic attachment upon a host. Incredibly, they seized upon this striking difference as a sign that they had been chosen to rule all of mankind! Initially no more than a harmless illusion, this self-deception was transformed into an evidence of "superiority". Their biological uniqueness, their committal to a parasitic mode of life, became their principal advantage in attaining their goals. They set up techniques of immediately recognizing each other in any part of the world. They resolved to act always cohesively as well-trained and determined phalanx against their unwitting opposition. They made full use of their qualities of non-allegiance and nonalignment, which was actually enmity, undying hatred towards all nations, races and creeds of the host peoples who tolerated their presence. This freedom from all loyalties and moral codes of the kinds which governed all other groups gave them an enormous tactical advantage over those whom they planned to enslave and destroy.

The conspirators knew that their parasitic way of life would not be long endured by any host. They had to set up a program to subdue and overcome all governments, all religious creeds, all group loyalties, and replace them with their own World Order, which would allow any type of perversion, as long as the host peoples tolerated the presence of the parasite. The old morality had been based upon the duties and responsibilities of the citizen to raise a family, attend church, and support his nation. The "new morality", the "liberation theology", swept away all duties of the citizen. He now only had a single duty, to obey the World Order. In return, he was relieved of duties, and was free to gratify his "needs", his sexual desires, perverted gratifications with children and animals, abandonment of monogamous life. The new morality reduced the citizen to a mere animal, which was what the World Order required in order to perpetuate its parasitic way of life.

Society was now replaced by a mere facade of society. Only one crime would be severely punished — any resistance to the World Order. Murder, rape, arson, armed robbery, incest, child molestation, alcoholism, drug addition, homosexuality — all would be excused as minor aberrations, as long as the World Order was allowed to function without hindrance. One former crime, treason, now vanished, because national loyalties no longer existed. No one was expected to be "loyal" to the World Order, except its own members. The host peoples, the slaves, would never be asked for loyalty — only for obedience.

Despite this new "tolerance", which was in itself a revolution against the innate moral codes of all peoples, many citizens continued to resist enslavement by the World Order. Famines, riots, revolutions and wars were instigated to get rid of the troublemakers, but a more universal restraint was required. This was found in drugs. In Asia, for centuries assassins had been sent to carry out their duties after being given quantities of drugs (assassin comes from the word for hasheesh). The World Order realized that drugs would provide the means of "behavioural psychology" or people control, which they had been seeking. The opium clippers began to sail from England to the Far East. By pushing drugs among the Asian masses, they stupefied and controlled them, reaping not only a substantial cash flow, but the raw materials needed for their Industrial Revolution. In the twentieth century, the foundations began to stupefy the European and American population with drugs, the final step in the enthronement of the World Order. They had eradicated the last serious resistance to their program.

All conspiratorial societies for the past thousand years have sought a single goal — hegemony of parasitism. Bharati Darma holds that the world is an order or Cosmos — that it is not chaos — it is not thrown together. Parasitism's existential philosophy holds that man is thrown into the world without plan or program. This is the basic concept of parasitism, which finds itself in the world with only one mission; to find a host or perish. Many physicists now claim that the universe is the result of an accidental explosion which threw its components hither and yon, with no plan or order, an atheistic concept which denies that there is either a Logician or Logic to the universe. Dar Darma states that it is the desire for the life of form which produces the universe, that there is a World Order by which the universe is upheld.

The parasite denies that there is a world order of the universe, or any desire for form in the universe, or that any form exists. Therefore, the parasite is free to impose his own World Order, which has no organic relationship to the universe or to form. The hegemony of parasitism is dedicated solely to maintaining its position on the host from which it draws all of its sustenance. The host is the entire universe of the parasite; he knows nothing beyond it, and desires to know nothing beyond it. Geoffrey LaPage writes in *Parasitic Animals*,

> "Some species of parasitic animals are among the most powerful enemies of man and his civilization."

He posits a Law of Nature — that the parasite is always smaller and weaker than its host, and that the parasite always disguises itself and its aim in order to carry out its parasitic mission. LaPage says,

> "The struggle between host and parasite went on according to the laws of evolution, and this battle is constantly being waged today."

LaPage notes that the parasite can cause biological change, citing particular species which cause changes in the host's reproductive glands. The parasite sometimes castrates the host in order to weaken it, such as the parasitic crustacean Sacculina, which destroys the reproductive organs of its host, the short-tailed spider crab, Inacus Mautitanicus. We see the identical process today in which the hegemony of parasitism seeks to alter the reproductive process of the host by converting the younger generation to unisex and homosexuality, and to render ineffective distinctive sexual characteristics of male and female. This is a classic instance of castration by the parasite.

The natural World Order, which is based upon the irrevocable laws of the universe, has been temporarily replaced on Earth by the unnatural World Order of the parasite. All of the programs and energies of the parasite are devoted to a single goal, maintaining his feeding position upon the host. Freudian psychology was developed by the parasitic order to neutralize the incessant efforts of the host to throw off or dislodge the parasite. Any move to dislodge the parasite is denounced as "reactionary". It is defined and outlawed as an act of aggression, hostility, and alienation. In fact, the host is merely trying to survive by throwing off the parasite. Another law of nature is that the parasite, not only by sucking off the life sustenance of the host, but also by altering its life cycle, will inevitably kill the host. This process is called "the decline and fall of civilization".

LaPage notes that a parasite is not a particular species, but one which has adopted a certain way of life, the way of the parasite. Whether or not it is a virus, the parasite has a viral effect on the host, slowly poisoning and destroying it. Viruses are classic parasites. The spirochete, virus of syphilis, is a classic parasitic organism. In biological parlance, a collection of spirochetes is known as a "Congress".

The U.S. Congress has specifically chartered many parasitic functions in the philanthropic foundations. These groups now dominate educational and governmental institutions, laying down financial and social goals which are designed solely to maintain the hegemony of parasitism through its World Order. The American foundations are not even run by Americans; their policies are formulated in London by the financiers and transmitted to this country through the British Army Bureau of Psychological Warfare front Tavistock Institute. This is a typical disguised parasitic operation.

Censorship and observance of its biological taboos are the basis of the tribal rule of parasitism. The most stringent taboo, one which has never been violated, is the taboo against any mention of parasitism as a force or power in society. No newspaper, magazine, radio or television program, or school or university course has ever been allowed to mention the societal impact of parasitism! It is the greatest and most universal taboo in the world today. Michael Voslensky's *NOMENKLATURA, The Soviet Elite* identifies the Communist "new class" as a parasitic group. In reviewing this work in *Fortune* Oct 15 , 1984, Daniel Seligman notes,

> "Voslensky's portrait leaves us thinking that the Nomenklatura is an entirely parasitic operation. Its interests are clearly not those of most Soviet citizens."

The same observation can be made of the World Order's ruling group in any nation today, and particularly in the United States.

Despite its present hegemony, the World Order of parasitism realizes that it is always subject to being dislodged, which, in effect, would mean its destruction. Therefore, it is necessary to control not only the channels of communication of the host, but his very thought processes as well; to maintain constant vigilance that the host does not develop any concept of the danger of his situation, or any power to throw off the parasite. Therefore, the parasite carefully instructs the host that he exists only because of the "benign" presence of the parasite — that he owes everything to the presence of the parasite, his religion, his social order, his monetary system, and his educational system. The parasite deliberately inculcates in the host the fear that if the parasite happens to be dislodged, the host will lose all these things, and be left with nothing.

Although the World Order has control of the legal system and the courts, it remains vulnerable to any enforcement of the pre-existing body of law which the host had formulated to protect his society. This body of law forbids everything that the parasite is doing, and forces the parasite to maintain a precarious existence outside of the law. If the law were to be enforced at any time, the parasite would be dislodged. The existing body of law clearly forbids the operation of criminal syndicates, which is precisely what the hegemony of parasitism and its World Order is.

Criminal syndicalism denies the equal protection of the law to citizens. Only by acting against criminal syndicalism can the state protect its citizens.

Corpus Juris Secundum 16: Constitutional Law 213 (10) states:

> "The Constitutional guaranty of freedom of speech does not include the right to advocate, or conspire to effect, the violent destruction or overthrow of the government or the criminal destruction of property.
> 214: The Constitutional guaranty of the right of assembly was never intended as a license for illegality or invitation for fraud — the right of freedom of assembly may be abused by using assembly to incite violence and crime, and the people through their legislatures may protect themselves against the abuse."

The assembly of any World Order organization, such as the Council on Foreign Relations or any foundation, is subject to the laws against fraud (their charters claim they are engaged in philanthropy), and enforcement of the laws against criminal syndicalism would end the institutions through which the World Order illegally rules the people of the United States, the illegal conspiracies and the introduction of alien laws into our system by the foundations instructions to Congress.

We have already shown that the Rockefeller Foundation and other key organizations of the World Order are "Syndicates", which are engaged in the practice of criminal syndicalism. But what is a "syndicate"? The Oxford English Dictionary notes that the word stems from "syndic". A syndic is defined as "an officer of government, a chief magistrate, a deputy"'. In 1601 R. Johnson wrote in King and common "especiall men, called Syndiques, who haue the managing of the whole commonwealth." Thus the Rockefeller Foundation and its associated groups are carrying out their delegated function of managing the entire commonwealth, but not for the benefit of the people, or of any government except the secret super-government, the World Order, which they serve. The OED further defines a syndic as "a censor of the actions of another. To accuse." Here too, the syndicate functions according to its definition — the syndicate censors all thought and media, primarily to protect its own power. It also brings accusations — as many American citizens have found to their sorrow. Not even Sir Walter Raleigh was immune. When he interfered with the international money trade, he was accused of "treason" and beheaded.

The OED defines a "syndicate" as follows:

> "3. A combination of capitalists and financiers entered into for the purpose of prosecuting a scheme requiring large sources of capital, especially one having the object of obtaining control of the market in a particular commodity. To control, manage or effect by a syndicate."

Note the key words in this definition — a combination — prosecuting — obtaining control. The scheme does not require "large capital" — it requires "large sources of capital", the bank of England or the Federal Reserve System.

Corpus Juris Secundum 22 A says of Criminal Syndicalism,

> "In a prosecution for being a member of an organization which teaches and abets criminal syndicalism, evidences of crimes committed by past or present members of the organization in their capacity as members is admissible to show its character."

People v. LaRue 216 P 627 C.A. 276. Thus testimony about John Foster Dulles financing the Nazi Government of Germany, his telegram starting the Korean War, and other evidence can be used to indict any member of the Rockefeller Foundation in any state or locality in which the Rockefeller Foundation has ever been active in any way. Since these organizations are all closely interlocked, and there is so much available evidence of their illegal operations, it will be relatively simple to obtain criminal convictions against them for their criminal syndicalist operations.

Corpus Juris Secundum 22, Criminal Law 185 (10); Conspiracy and Monopolies:

> "Where the statute makes mere membership in an organization formed to promote syndicalism a crime, without

an overt act, this offense is indictable in any county into which a member may go during the continuance of his membership, and this is true although such member comes into a county involuntarily. People v. Johansen, 226 P 634, 66 C.A.343."

Corpus Juris Secundum 22, Criminal Law sec. 182 (3) states,

"A prosecution for conspiracy to commit an offense against the U.S. may also be tried in any district wherein any overt act in furtherance of the conspiracy is performed. U.S. v. Cohen C. A.N.J. 197 F 2d 26."

Thus a publication by the Council on Foreign Relations promoting the stripping of sovereignty of the United States of America, mailed into any county of the U.S.; the county authorities can bring the Council on Foreign Relations, or any member therein, to trial in that county, and any action by any member of the Council on Foreign Relations in the past is admissible as evidence, such as starting World War II, subsidizing the Nazi Government, or subsidizing the USSR.

Criminal syndicalism can also be prosecuted according to Corpus Juris Secundum 46, Insurrection and Sedition: sec. 461c.

"Sabotage and syndicalism aiming to abolish the present political and social system, including direct action or sabotage."

Thus any program of a foundation which seeks to abolish the present political or social system of the United States can be prosecuted. Of course every foundation program seeks to accomplish just that, and is indictable.

Not only individuals, but any corporation supporting criminal syndicalism can be prosecuted, according to Corpus Juris Secundum 46 462b. Criminal Syndicalism.

"Statutes against criminal syndicalism apply to corporations as well as to individuals organizing or belonging to criminal syndicalist society; evidence of the character and activities of other organizations with which the organization in which the accused is a member is affiliated is admissible."

Not only can the members of the World Order be arrested and tried anywhere, since they function worldwide in their conspiratorial activities to undermine and overthrow all governments and nations, but because their organizations are so tightly interlocked, any evidence about any one of them can be introduced in prosecuting any member of other organizations in any part of the U.S. or the world. Their attempts to undermine the political and social orders of all peoples make them subject to legal retribution. The People of the U.S. must begin at once to enforce the statutes outlawing criminal syndicalist activities, and bring the criminals to justice.

Being well aware of their danger, the World Order is working frantically to achieve even greater dictatorial powers over the nations of the world. They constantly intensify all problems through the foundations, so that political and economic crises prevent the peoples of the world from organizing against them. The World Order must paralyze its opponents. They terrorize the world with propaganda about approaching international nuclear war, although atomic bombs have been used only once, in 1945, when the Rockefeller Foundation director Karl T. Compton ordered Truman to drop the atomic bomb on Japan.

Because of the billions of lives which have been blighted and destroyed by the conspiracies of the World Order through its hegemony of parasitism, vengeance for these atrocities demands the most thorough going and relentless retribution against the criminal syndicalists. Their record is clear.

In 1984, as these words are written, we are observing the Year of *1984*. George Orwell's book, written in 1949, was thought to be only a warning against what was to come. It was not a warning. *1984* is the Program! Orwell, a lifelong Socialist, fought for many days in the front lines for the Communists in Spain. He was wounded, but this did not lessen his dedication to the goals of World Socialism. The most practical way to achieve these goals was to formulate the program, as Col. House had done in *Philip Dru, Administrator*. Orwell laid down the dictum that slogans must be in Newspeak, "War is Peace, Freedom is Slavery, Ignorance is Strength". This is the program of the hegemony of parasitism through the World Order. Orwell posited three superstates, Eurasia, Oceania, and Eastasia, "permanently at war in one combination or another". He continues,

> "War, however, is no longer the desperate annihilating struggle that it was in the early decades of the 21st century. It is a warfare of limited aims, between combatants who are unable to destroy one another, have no material cause for fighting, and are not divided by any genuine ideological difference... There is no longer in a material sense anything to fight about, the balance of power will always remain roughly even, and the territory which forms the heartland of each superstate always remains inviolate (NOTE: The present writer has pointed out that the CIA does not commit sabotage in Russia, and the KGB does not commit sabotage in the U.S.)... The primary aim of modern warfare (in accordance with the principle of doublethink, the aim is simultaneously recognized and not recognized by the directing brains of the Party) is to use up the products of the machine without raising the general standard of living... the essential act of war is destruction, not necessarily of human lives, but of the products of human labor. The two aims of the party are to conquer the whole surface of the earth and to extinguish once and for all the possibility of independent thought."

Orwell concludes *1984* with a denial that the victims of the World Order have any hope. He claims the World Order will always triumph, which is a great propaganda achievement for the hegemony of parasitism. He writes,

> "If you want a picture of the future, imagine a boot stamping on a human face — forever."

He disposes of his "hero", a citizen who had vainly tried to oppose the Party, by ending the book with the "hero" whimpering that "He loved Big Brother".

The peoples of the world not only will never love Big Brother, but they will soon dispose of him forever.

The program of the World Order remains the same; Divide and Conquer.

"And I will set the Egyptians against the Egyptians: and they shall fight everyone against his brother, and every one against his neighbor: city shall fight against city, and kingdom against kingdom." Isaiah XIX: 2.

At the same time that government officials are stealthily promoting discord in every region of the land, they are also setting up government programs which will step in to set up total dictatorship over the warring factions. The Federal Emergency Management Agency, FEMA, now controls the FBI, state and local police departments, and have extensive plans for national concentration camps throughout the United States. George Bush and Col. North in 1984 ran Rex 84 Readiness Exercise in 1984 as a shakedown run for a national dictatorship. Houston researcher William Pabst released a pamphlet in 1983, *Concentration Camp Plans for U.S. Citizens*, formulated under an operations plan named GARDEN PLOT and Cable Splicer, calling for martial law. Bush now has a secret hideout, Mt. Weather, near Berryville, Va. which is three hundred feet underground, as headquarters for the New World Order. It already has 240 workers. The Federal Reserve System bunker at Culpeper, Va. was built twenty-two years ago as a Communications and Record Center. It formerly contained enormous quantities of cash, which have quietly been removed.

These are the physical manifestations of preparations for a worldwide dictatorship, which the Trilateral Commission Report, drafted at a Commission meeting in Washington, April 22, 1990, calls Beyond Interdependence, the Meshing of the World's Economy and the earth's ecology. David Rockefeller, in his Preface to this report, states,

> "The authors demonstrate that the world has now moved beyond economic interdependence to ecological interdependence - an intermeshing of the two. Jim McNeill (author of the report) is now advising me on the road to Rio. Rio will be the largest summit conference ever held, and it will have the political capacity to produce the basic changes needed in our national and international economic agendas and in our institutions of governance to ensure a secure and sustainable future for the world community. By the year

2012, these changes must be fully integrated into our economic and political life."

What Rockefeller demands is that we change our institutions of government by 2012 to encompass all the goals of the World Order. The Trilateral Commission: Questions and Answers (1990. obtainable from the North American office, 345 E.46th st. NY 10017, tel. 2 12 66 11180) asks:

> "What are the goals of the Trilateral Commission? Growing interdependence is a fact of life in the contemporary world. It transcends and influences national systems. It requires new and more intensive forms of international cooperation to realize its benefits and to counteract economic and political nationalism."
>
> Also proposed is a new Constitution for the United States. Art. VIII Sec 12. No person shall bear arms or possess lethal weapons except police, members of the armed forces, or those licensed under law.

This has been the law in all Communist countries for many years. The would be dictators hope to confiscate the 200,000,000 weapons now in private hands in the United States. Section 8 of the new Constitution provides,

> "The use of public lands, the air, or waters shall be a privilege granted only in the national interest and with restrictions imposed by authorized agencies."

Art II, The Electoral Board, provides for an Overseer to supervise all political parties and candidates. This is the same overseer which had absolute power on the pre-Civil War plantations. History does repeat itself.

Unfortunately for the megalomaniac plans of the minions of the World Order, they are fighting a losing battle. Time is running out for them. Their world order, which they tried to revive by hastily terming it "a new world order", is slowly collapsing, speeded in its demise by the rapid increase in communications, the computer, television, and other factors of modern life. The World Order, which has always been based upon naked force, worked best in the pre-Industrial Age. Because it depends on planning and total control of the economy, World order programs are too inflexible to survive in the fast moving world of today. Within the next several years, if not, indeed, in the next few months, we shall see an exasperated and aroused public complete what has already taken place in the Communist satellites and in Soviet Russia, the final dismantling of the Communist system of the World Order in the United States itself. This is not romanticism or optimism; it is the result of many years of studying present developments, and of a realistic assessment of the prospect before us. It will be a very rewarding one, except for the parasites whose curse on humanity will at last be removed. This is the twenty-first century as I see it.

Other titles

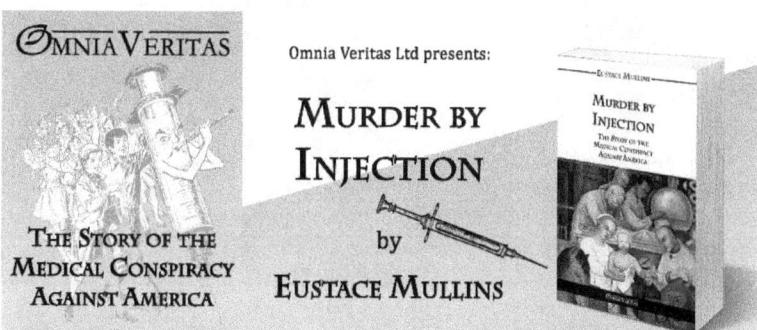

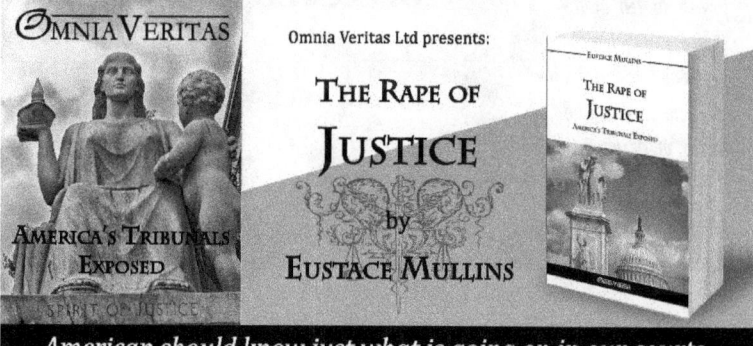

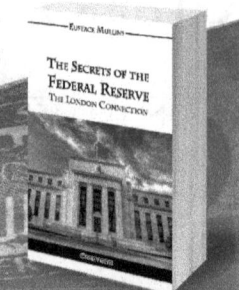

OMNIA VERITAS

Omnia Veritas Ltd presents:

THE SECRETS OF THE FEDERAL RESERVE
by
EUSTACE MULLINS

HERE ARE THE SIMPLE FACTS OF THE GREAT BETRAYAL

Will we continue to be enslaved by the Babylonian debt money system?

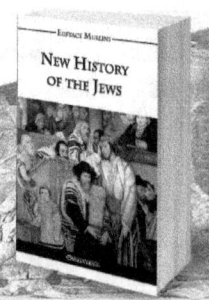

OMNIA VERITAS

Omnia Veritas Ltd presents:

NEW HISTORY OF THE JEWS
by
EUSTACE MULLINS

Throughout the history of civilization, one particular problem of mankind has remained constant.

Only one people has irritated its host nations in every part of the civilized world

OMNIA VERITAS

Omnia Veritas Ltd presents:

COLLECTED ESSAYS
EUSTACE MULLINS

I wish to tell of the things which have happened to me in my struggle against the forces of darkness.

It is my hope that others will be forewarned of what to expect in this fight

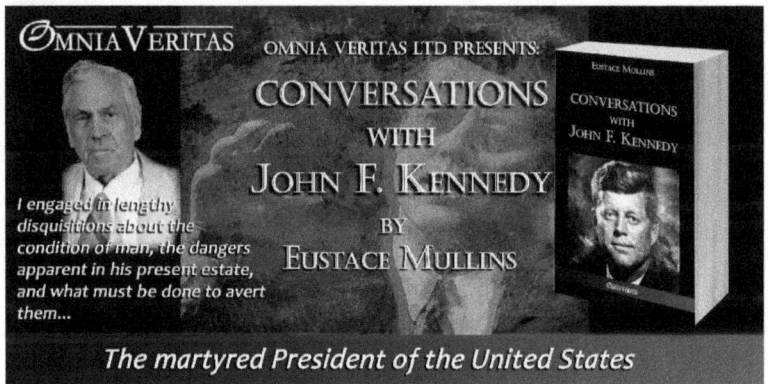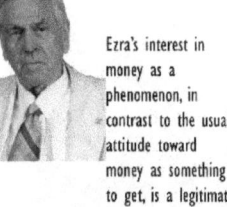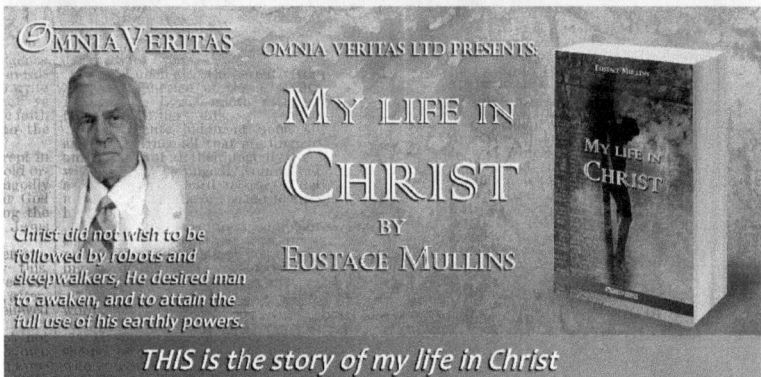

www.ingramcontent.com/pod-product-compliance
Lightning Source LLC
Chambersburg PA
CBHW071315150426
43191CB00007B/631